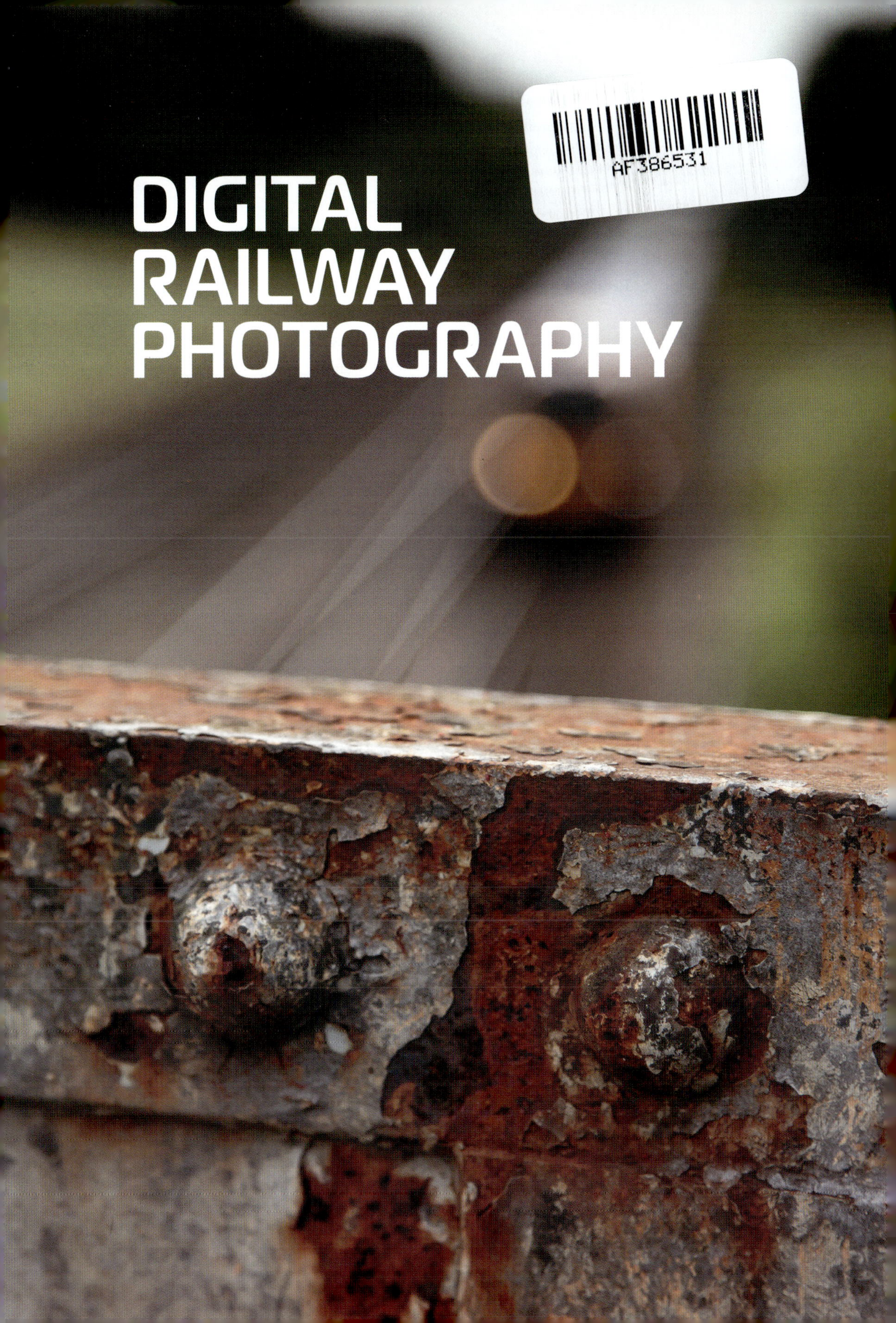
DIGITAL
RAILWAY
PHOTOGRAPHY

Fonthill Media Language Policy
Fonthill Media publishes in the international English language market. One language
edition is published worldwide. As there are minor differences in spelling and presentation,
especially with regard to American English and British English, a policy is necessary to
define which form of English to use. The Fonthill Policy is to use the form of English native
to the author. Jeremy de Souza was born and educated in London and now lives in Alton,
Hampshire, therefore British English has been adopted in this publication.

Fonthill Media Limited
Fonthill Media LLC
www.fonthillmedia.com
office@fonthillmedia.com

First published in the United Kingdom
and the United States of America 2015

British Library Cataloguing in Publication Data:
A catalogue record for this book is available from the British Library

ISBN 978-1-78155-426-5

Typeset in Myriad Pro 10pt on 14pt
Printed and bound in England

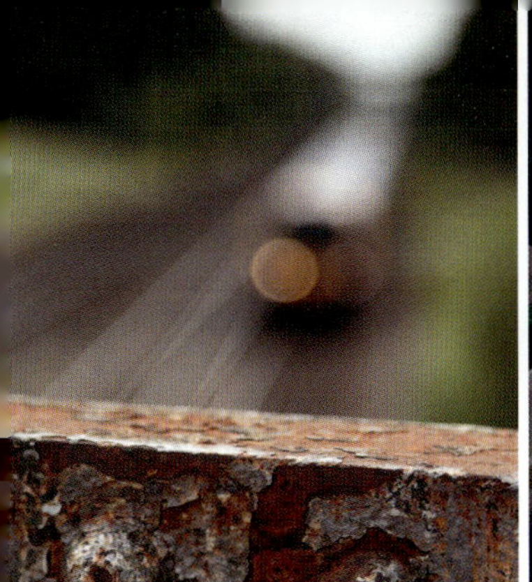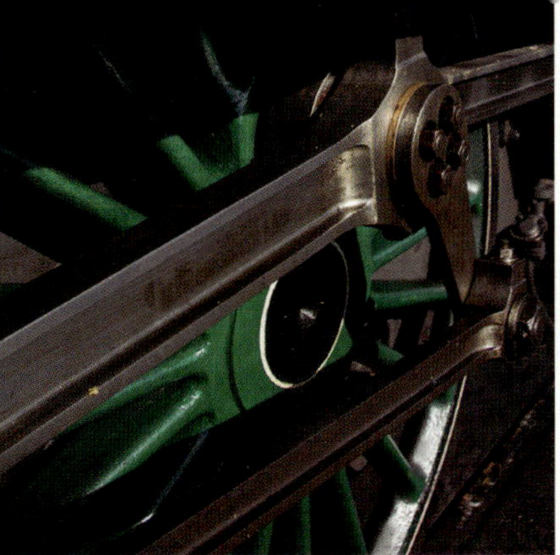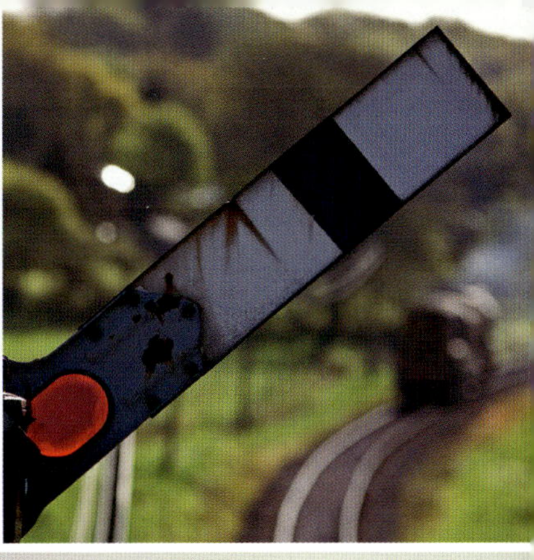

DIGITAL RAILWAY PHOTOGRAPHY
A PRACTICAL GUIDE

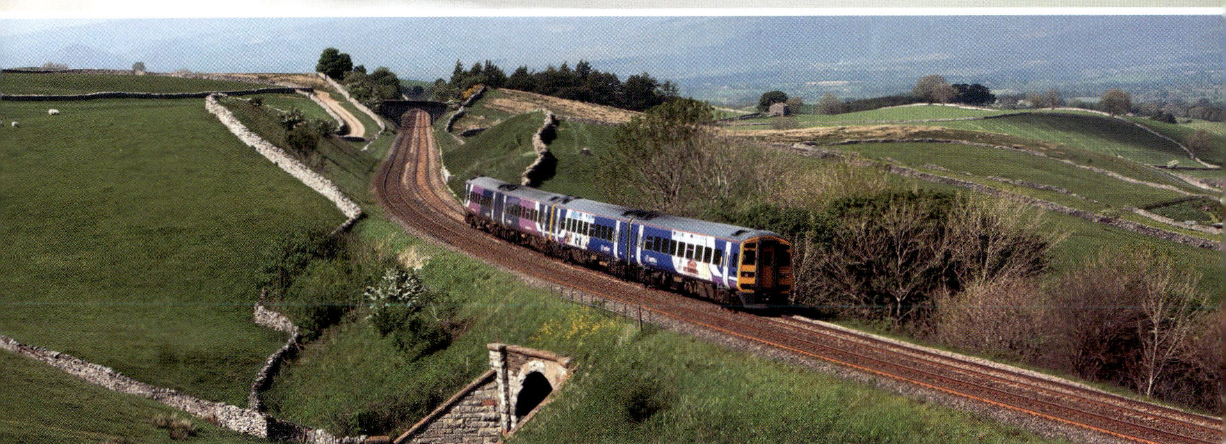

Jeremy de Souza

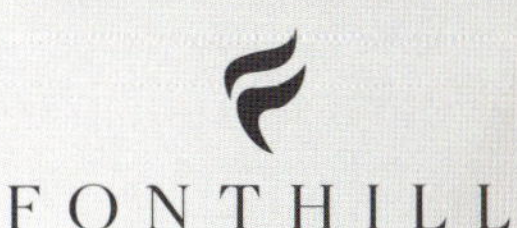
FONTHILL

Contents

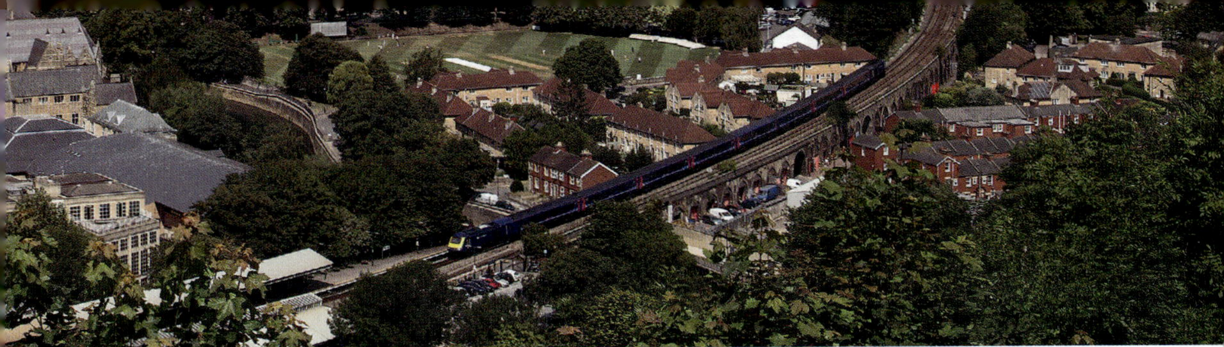

Preface

If you like taking photographs of trains, this book is for you. It's intended to be a guide that will help you capture the passion of your hobby, and express the pictures that you take in a creative way, that will help you enjoy your hobby more. It's not intended to be the definitive guide to all of the technical tips and tricks of photography, whether out in the field or back at home at your computer—there are other books and magazines that look at this area in a better way than I ever could. Perhaps after reading this book, your photographic curiosity will be heightened, and you'll be interested in trying new techniques and processes.

I've always been interested in railways, from a young age when I was given a push-along train on a red plastic track. Moving to west London in the early 1970s, I used to cycle down to Ealing Broadway station, to watch the expresses and freights thunder past. The ubiquitous 'spotting books' helped me learn which trains were which, although I could never quite see the excitement in just collecting numbers. A Kodak Instamatic provided my first images.

Looking back, the results were mediocre at best. I would click away taking loads of pictures, usually on grey and overcast days, but as my interest grew, I graduated into 35mm and later, rollfilm photography, and the eventual realisation that quality was better than quantity.

Like many others, I was a little cynical of the advent of digital photography. The first digital cameras were pretty basic affairs, and not really much use for quality photography. My first was a small Konica compact, which just didn't measure up to my 35mm and rollfilm equipment at the time. The Konica soon gave way to a Canon S40 compact (which I still own) with the ability to apply shutter speed and aperture variation to get the creative edge. The arrival of the Canon EOS 10D was a revelation, as I was able to use my old SLR lenses on a decent quality digital body, without breaking the bank.

I've now graduated to a Canon EOS 5D Mark 3, an excellent camera that delivers professional standard results. My lenses are all Canons: a 17-40mm, 24-105mm, 50mm f1.4, 70-200mm and a 300mm f4 IS, which cover every eventuality that I need.

Some consider that the evolution of the railway network in the twenty-first century is driving a reduction in its interest. It's true that there are considerably fewer locomotives and quirky differences in the system than there were ten or twenty years ago, resulting in greater uniformity. Although times have changed and there are fewer differences to observe, there is still plenty of history to be recorded, innovation to experience, and disappearing trains and places to record. Photograph what interests you now, as you can be certain that it won't be around forever.

Enjoy your railway photography.

Jeremy de Souza
Alton • Hampshire • UK

Introduction

WHY DO WE DO IT?

Is there a perfect railway photograph? Probably… I think I can tell as soon as I press the shutter whether the result is going to be good or bad. Many people think it's just a matter of taking the picture, and that's it. To a certain extent, if you are happy with the results you are getting, that's fine. This book is intended for those, like me, who are still striving for the perfect shot. It could be claimed that we are simply perfectionists, and that it's an impossible search. I don't consider any of my photos to be perfect. There are several that I am very happy with. Have I taken the perfect shot yet?—no, but I always keep trying.

SAFE AND SECURE

Railway photography is a hobby. Some take it more seriously than others. It's a good way of getting out and about, and learning about our rich industrial heritage, with some good elements of design, architecture, and engineering thrown in.

Please don't take it too far. You have a duty to yourself, your friends and family, and your community as a whole to keep yourself safe and secure, and not put yourself or others in harm's way. Never put yourself in a dangerous position and be aware of your surroundings.

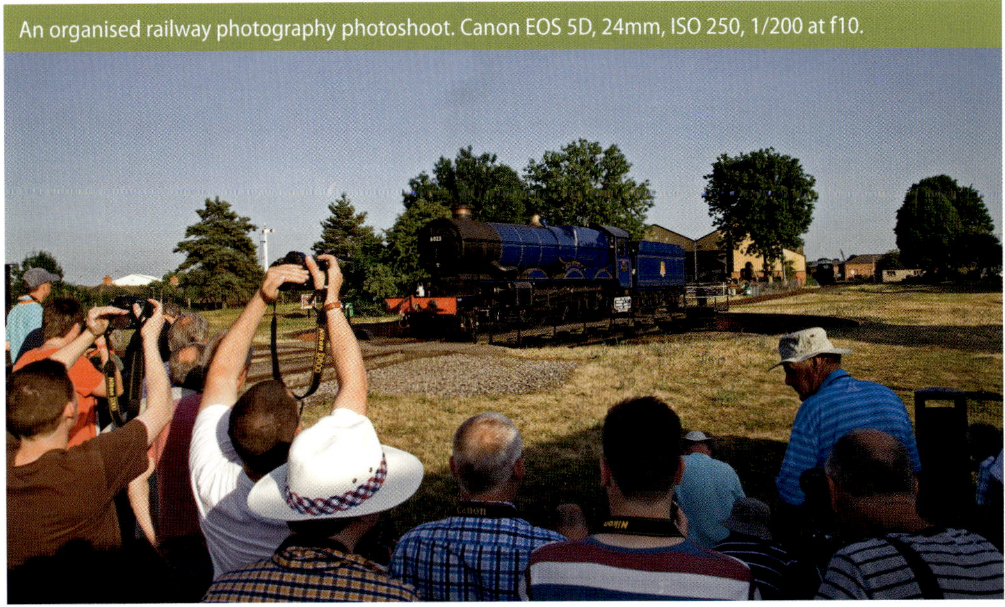

An organised railway photography photoshoot. Canon EOS 5D, 24mm, ISO 250, 1/200 at f10.

Part of the attraction of railway photography is the opportunity to get out and about to follow our hobby. You can learn a lot about the countryside and natural environment, and how to access the 'great outdoors'. It's a good idea to learn to read an Ordinance Survey map, either in hard copy form, or on your mobile device. You will be able to identify footpaths, tracks, and useful vantage points such as bridges. However, observe the Country Code. You do not have an automatic right to enter private land or stray off marked footpaths, and damage to crops or livestock may not only land you in trouble with the owner, but will also bring the hobby into disrepute and jeopardize access for others in the future.

Railway photography is not a crime, nor is it forbidden because of 'security'. You <u>are</u> allowed to take photos of trains—certainly in the UK. Common sense should prevail. If you look and act in a suspicious manner, you should not be surprised if someone asks you what you are doing. Taking photos of security equipment such as CCTV is likely to cause trouble, so don't do it! At stations, as a courtesy, you should identify yourself to a railway official and advise them what you are doing. In the majority of cases, they will appreciate you doing this, and will simply want to be reassured that you are a sensible person, and are not going to position yourself in a dangerous place.

If the official has a reason to decline your request, don't get upset. There may be a good reason why; at that particular moment in time, it may be inconvenient or cause an issue. Quite often, a polite discussion will result in a compromise which keeps everyone happy. Sadly, there are a few officials who find it easier to say 'no' to railway photography, for no apparent reason. You can remind them of Network Rail's guidelines, which welcome the presence of enthusiast photographers, but do not escalate a confrontation. It might help to print them off and carry with you, to show to the official in question.

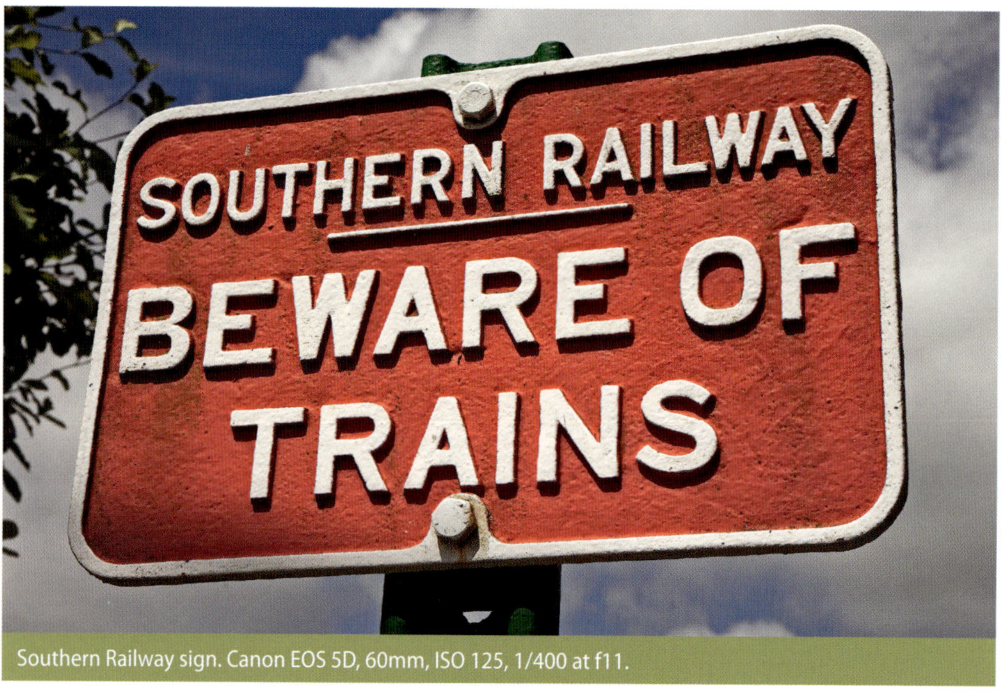

Southern Railway sign. Canon EOS 5D, 60mm, ISO 125, 1/400 at f11.

Railways and Photography

Digital photography is a fascinating medium. It allows you to merge technology with art in a wholly personal way. You can express your interest in so many ways, and railway photography allows you to pursue your interest in trains and travel together. You can record where you go and what you see, and save your interest as a photograph for posterity. There is no real right or wrong railway photograph. If it gives you the result you desire, you have succeeded.

You may want to save a memory your journey. You may want a photo of every particular locomotive in a certain class, or belonging to a particular operator. You may prefer steam, diesel, electric, metro, miniature…. You may wish to catalogue styles of signalling, wagon types, station architecture, or even the staff who run the railway.

Depending on your time and inclination, the mix of travel, engineering, photography and technology may even stimulate completely new activities. It's a hobby that does not demand an 'all or nothing' approach—take your time and see where the interest takes you.

DEVELOPING YOUR TECHNIQUE

After researching a photographic location, many photographers go there with the intention of recreating the image that inspired them in the first place, but to do this at the exclusion of everything else is a wasted opportunity. Look for new angles, try different lenses, and move around—you might just find a viewpoint that others haven't. Another option is to set yourself challenges—only use one particular type of lens for a visit, or challenge yourself to follow a theme—people, detail, or a creative approach. It's fun and will get you thinking more about your photography.

You're never too old (or wise) to learn, especially in digital photography with its rapid development, and it's highly recommended to keep pace with new technology, ideas, and techniques. Despite the popularity of cameras among enthusiasts, railway magazines only offer limited space to the art of railway photography, but there are plenty of digital camera magazines that will not just test new equipment, but showcase portfolios and display 'how to do it' articles.

PERSONAL STYLE

In time, you might develop your own style as a railway photographer. You may prefer to record images in a certain creative way, or look for details or angles that others miss completely. Studying photographic magazines will open your eyes to differing perspectives or methods that you had not previously contemplated. Don't be afraid to experiment. You may surprise yourself!

Getting Started

Whether you are just starting out and looking for help in choosing the right camera, have a basic camera and are looking to upgrade, or are well advanced and looking for more creative techniques, the choice is bewildering and can be confusing to the novice and expert alike.

Although there are many types and styles of digital camera, they broadly fall into four main groups:

| Compacts | Bridge | CSC | Digital SLR |

COMPACTS

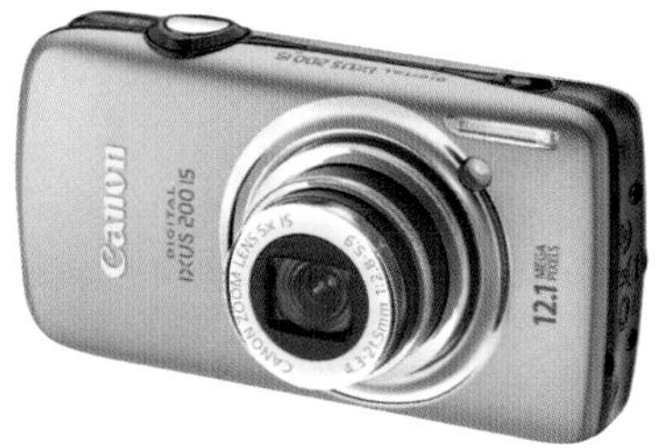

Usually small cameras that can be easily carried, perhaps in a bag or in a jacket pocket. They vary in scope and complexity, but don't underestimate their usefulness. They are ideal if you don't want to carry a larger digital SLR, or you just want the convenience of something unobtrusive that you can use to shoot quickly and easily. Many photographers have a compact in their pocket for 'grab' shots.

Compact: Canon Digital IXUS 200 IS. (*Courtesy Canon UK*)

ADVANCED COMPACTS

Advanced compact cameras are very capable indeed, and produce excellent results. They have the point and shoot ability of the basic compact, but have the option of full shutter, aperture, and image quality control that is often found on full-size digital SLRs.

Advanced compact. Canon G16. (*Courtesy Canon UK*)

BRIDGE CAMERAS

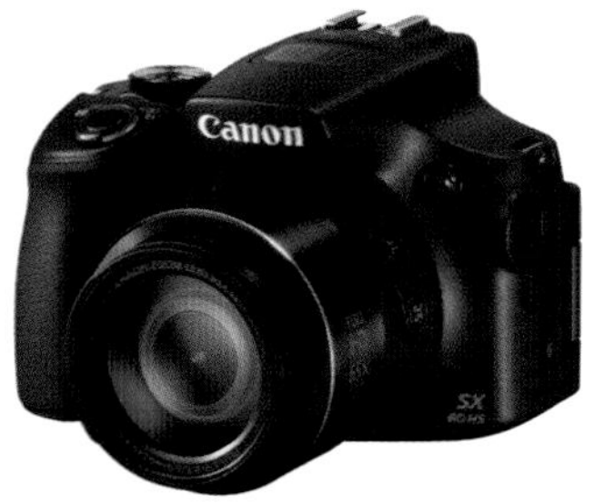

For those looking for an all-in-one unit that offers the look and feel of a digital SLR, without the weight and size, a bridge camera is a good option. These cameras look like mini-SLRs, and the lens, covering a wide range between wide angle and telephoto is permanently fitted to the camera.

Bridge camera. Canon PowerShot SX60 HS. (*Courtesy Canon UK*)

CSCs

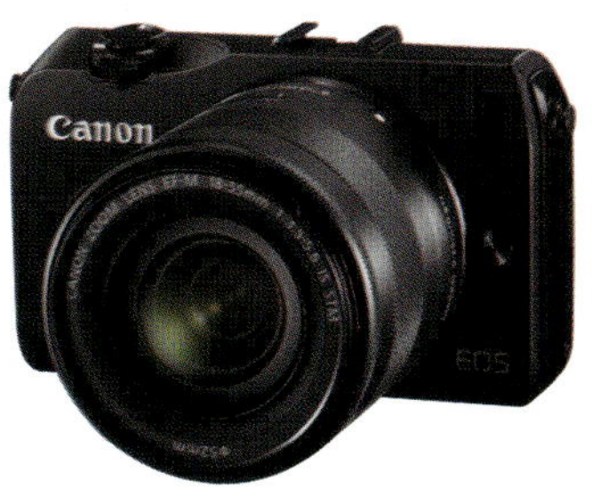

CSC camera. Canon EOS M Black.
(*Courtesy Canon UK*)

CSC stands for Compact System Cameras. Rapidly gaining popularity, these are every bit as powerful as a digital SLR and pack a lot of features. As their name suggests, they are, like bridge cameras, considerably smaller than their full size cousins and therefore a lot lighter and easier to carry around. Lenses can be swapped to give some creativity in your photography, and with mirror-free shutter release, they can be very discreet in their operation and yet yield high quality results. Definitely worth thinking about if you are mobile, and don't want a lot of weight to carry around. If you own a system camera already, you may be able to purchase adaptors to use your lenses with your CSC body.

DIGITAL SLRS

Digital SLR. Canon EOS 5D Mark III with EF 24-105mm lens. (*Courtesy Canon UK*)

Probably the most popular type of camera is the digital SLR and count for the largest sector of camera users by a considerable margin. These are similar in size, shape and operation to earlier 35mm film cameras. You will have full control of every aspect of your photography. Lenses from the major manufacturers that worked on your older 35mm film body may still work on your digital SLR – but check the compatibility!

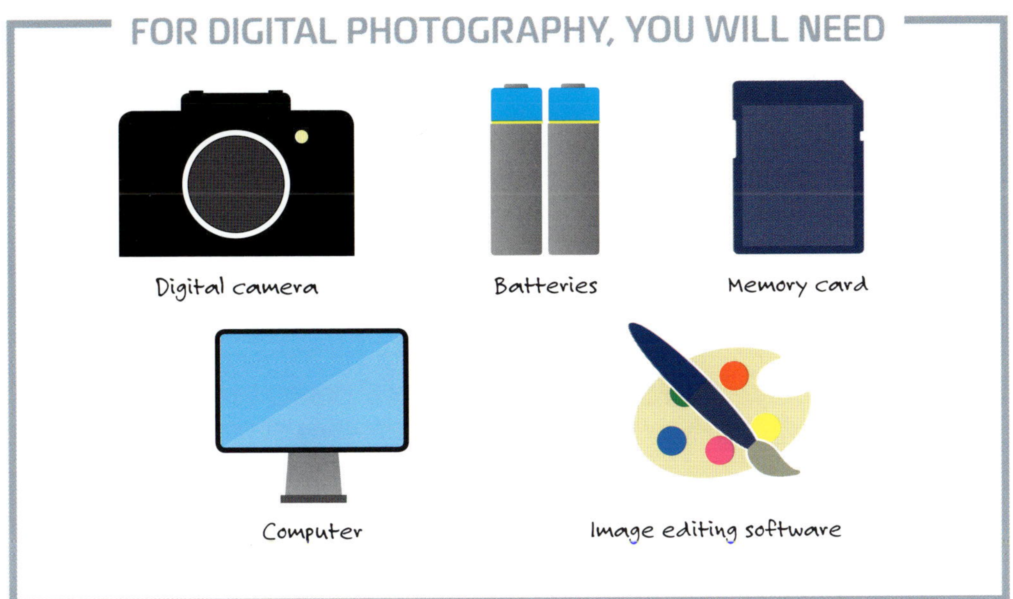

If you purchase your camera new, you should get basic processing software with it in the box. You can always invest in all the extras later, but with these basics, you'll be ready to shoot.

The choice of camera will depend on your individual circumstances, as well as the type of photography you think you might be doing. A smaller, lighter body might be preferable if you are travelling a lot and don't want a lot of weight. A heavier and more solid body might give you the rugged dependability perhaps if you are able to take a wider selection of equipment on a shoot.

Either way, and just like their compact cousins, a digital SLR of either type will deliver good results, as long as you know and understand their limitations.

Resolution is always a talking point among photographers. Resolution is usually expressed in the number of pixels in which the camera is capable of recording an image. There are some people who think that the race to own a camera with the largest number of pixels is one worth winning, and will invest in a new body every time a bigger, better model comes along.

It's a matter of taste, but unless you are a professional shooting top quality images for reproduction, any camera within the range of 10–20 megapixels will deliver good quality results that can be enlarged and printed to A4 or A3 size with no real loss of quality. Some of the top end recent cameras, like the Canon 5D Mark III or Nikon D800, will deliver huge images (in terms of file size) that will be among the best quality that you can get, but processing them on your computer may stretch the boundaries of its memory capabilities.

SENSORS

Surely one of the most confusing areas of digital camera ownership is the debate over camera sensors. Depending on your camera choice, the most popular sensor sizes are either full frame (equivalent to a 35mm image), or the smaller APS-C. The sensors are, as you might expect, the light sensitive areas at the heart of the camera that record the image you're photographing (just like film). Logically, the larger the sensor, the more light falling onto it and therefore the more information gained, and hence the better the image recorded.

It's not that easy, however. A larger sensor is larger in size, and needs a larger lens to capture the information it requires. This will explain why the compact end of the market uses APS-C (or smaller) sensors as they are better suited to pocket-sized cameras, while high-end equipment, where the quality of the result is paramount, can 'go large' in order to deliver an image that offers less noise, a higher dynamic range and usually much better low light performance.

This difference will affect your lens choice, as a lens designed for a full-frame camera will have a different effective focal length when used with a APS-C camera. The smaller sensor 'sees' less of the image, cutting off the edges, and recording only what is in the centre. This crop factor is usually around 1.5x, so a 50mm lens will have an effective focal length of 75mm. As cameras with APS-C sensors are very popular, some manufacturers have developed lenses especially for them. These lenses are built to work with the smaller image size, so may not be compatible should you trade up to a full-frame camera at a later date. Check with your retailer for compatibility before buying.

  Getting Started

An APS-C sensor (top), as used in a Canon 7D camera. A full-frame sensor (bottom), as used in a Canon 5D Mark III. (*Courtesy Canon UK*)

Your lens will be the most important piece of equipment you can buy for your camera. It will help you express your creativity through the mood, style, and impact of the image you are wishing to record. The choice available is wider than the camera itself, as not only can you use those made by your selected camera manufacturer, but also choose from a number of very good independents.

You should firstly understand a little about your lens, as some of its attributes will affect your purchase decision. Some lenses are highly technical pieces of equipment in their own right, which is usually reflected in the cost.

The important items to consider are:

The mount—if you have a system camera, you will need to make sure that the lens you purchase fits your camera. Perhaps obvious, but a Canon lens will not fit straight onto a Nikon camera body, and vice versa. You can purchase high quality lenses from independent manufacturers, e.g. Sigma, Tamron, etc., but you will need to specify the mount to ensure compatibility. Look also at the quality of the mount. Early Canon prime lenses featured metal mounts. Later versions of the same lenses had plastic. The earlier models are considered to be more robust and command high second-hand prices.

Vibration reduction (also known as image stabilisation)—this refers to optical image stabilisation technology built into the lens itself (achieved through sensors and gyros) that counteracts the effect of camera shake, and enables users to use their camera hand-held in lower light situations than might normally be achievable.

Lens choice—not so long ago, a new camera came with a 50mm 'standard' lens. It was called standard as it gave the closest approximation to the 'normal' field of view that you would see with your own eyes.

More recently, DSLR bodies are available either body only—allowing you to use the lenses you might already own—or with a mid-range zoom. This can vary in focal length, but typically offers a zoom range between 28 or 35mm and 70 or 80mm. This is not a huge range at all, but it will allow for basic photography. If your style of photography is record keeping of locos, carriages, wagons, or buildings, and you just want an un-distorted view, then you may not need more. If you want to stretch yourself a little bit more, you may wish to consider a slightly broader range.

Choosing a lens

The focal length of the lens affects the angle of view through the viewfinder. The following images were taken from the same vantage point to demonstrate the variance in perspective from different lenses.

Wide angle

A wide view can create a stunning shot. Keep an eye on your 'horizon'. It can be very easy to take the photo on a slant, either left or right, and this will look very strange unless you adjust it on your computer afterwards. With railway photography, a wide angle can be used, if taken from a low or high position, to emphasize the power and imposing nature of the locomotive, for example. You will need to get closer to the subject than with a standard lens, but this may be helpful if you cannot get any further back, e.g. at the end of a platform.

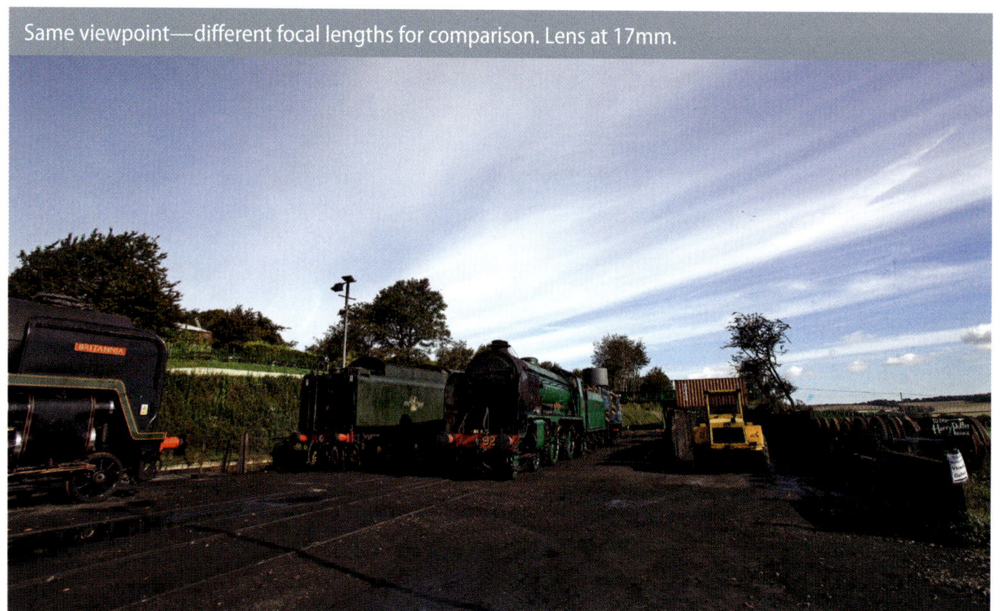

Standard or 'portrait'

The standard lens is considered to be the closest approximation to the viewpoint of the human eye. Once common with any new camera, they are far less prevalent now, although the quality from a fixed prime lens is often higher than a zoom lens. You may want to set yourself a challenge to use only a standard lens for you next expedition…. It's worth trying and you will have a closer replication of your memories.

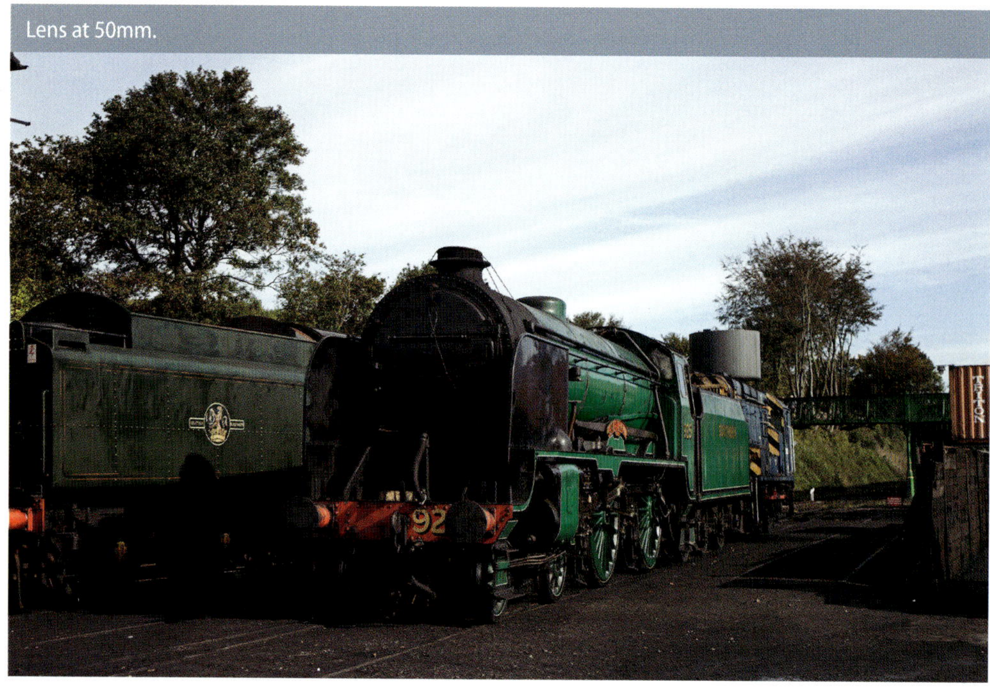

Getting Started

Telephoto

This is a very popular area, and like the wide angle, a crisp telephoto shot of a train at speed is one of the most powerful images possible. The narrow field of view compresses the perspective (called foreshortening) and can create some interesting effects. As a style it's not to everyone's taste, and often overdone, but the concentration of the eye on the subject can really help to make the loco, for example, really stand out from the background.

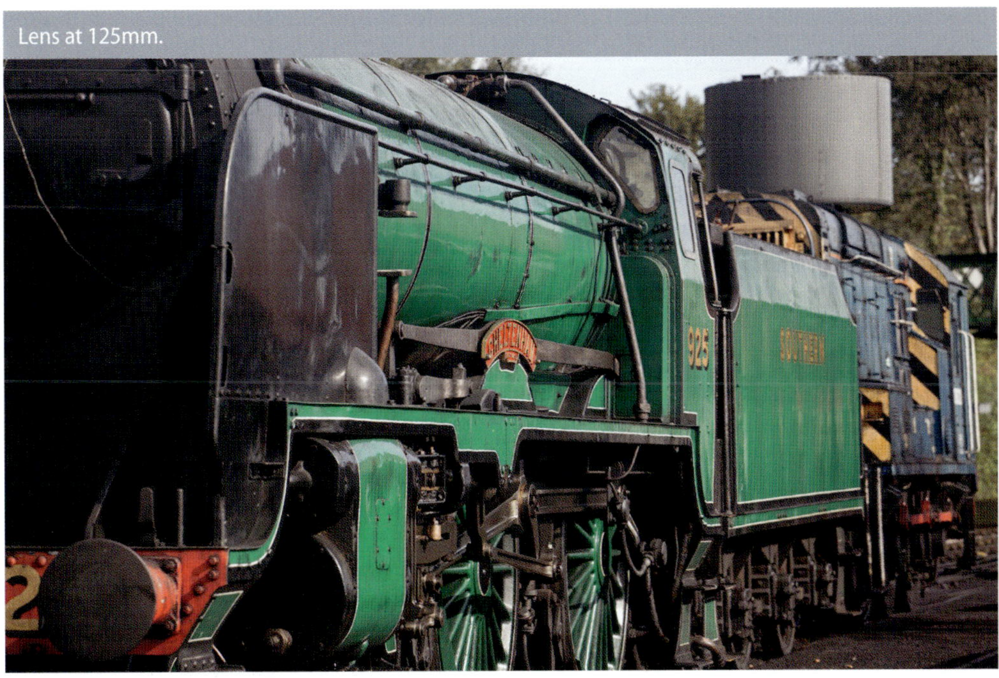

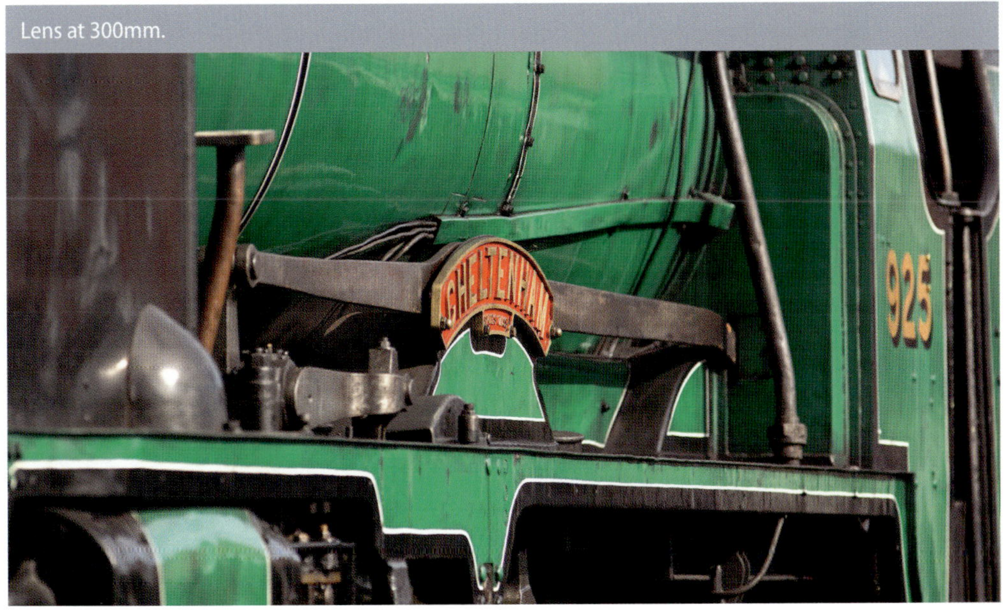

It's important to note that the higher the focal length of the lens, the greater the likelihood that camera shake will affect you photo, creating blurry results. This is why you often see sports photographers, with their extreme lenses at 400mm or higher, using monopods or tripods for stability. A good rule of thumb is to always use a shutter speed for your camera higher than the focal length of the lens being used.

Macro lenses

If you want to take close-up photographs, you might want to consider a lens with macro capability. This means that it will be able to focus on a subject far closer than may be possible with your regular lens. If you have a collection of tickets, for example, a macro lens may be a worthwhile investment.

Lens resolution

This refers to the lens's ability to see, or distinguish, fine detail. Without getting into the complex mathematical formulae, for the average railway photographer, it comes down to a matter of price, with the more expensive lenses having a greater ability to determine, or resolve, detail than the cheap ones.

Buy the best lenses that you can afford, as you should want to match the increasing megapixel capability of your camera with the highest optical performance. It is pointless having a top-of-the-range camera body with a poor quality lens on the front—you will never obtain the results you expect in this way.

A basic lens won't prevent you taking a good picture—but a higher quality lens will deliver a superior result.

Filters

A common debate among photographers is whether to put a skylight or UV filter on every lens as a permanent fixture. If you take a stumble and your lens takes an impact, it might just be the filter that gets damaged, instead of the end of your expensive lens. In addition, dust, grit, and water flying about can be easily removed from the filter, without damaging the surface of your expensive lens.

However, if you're feeling creative, there are others you might like to try out. On a sunny day, and particularly if your composition involves a large reflective surface like water in the foreground, try a polarising filter. Some photographers regard it as one of the most useful filters they own, and for the railway photographer, it can help to reduce glare, boost colour saturation and dramatically reduce reflections such as cab windows. On a sunny day, with a few white clouds, it will help to give the sky a rich and deep blue colour against which the clouds really stand out.

With the polarising filter in place, after composing your photograph, slowly turn the front part of the filter. You will see the effect vary, with the sky darkening. Keep turning until you reach the desired effect. Your camera will choose the exposure values as normal as it meters through the lens, but be aware that the filter will reduce the exposure, so you may need a higher shutter speed to avoid camera shake. Remember to purchase a circular polariser to avoid interference with your camera's autofocus system.

Another creative filter to try is a Neutral Density (ND) graduated filter. Often seen on TV features, they help create a dramatic sky, and on a flat and overcast day, can add real impact to a photo.

ND graduated filters are usually half grey and half clear. The majority are available in the square glass format, which requires a special filter holder screwed onto your lens. Take your exposure reading before you slide the ND grad in, and then carefully align it with your subject.

Some digital compacts have a built-in ND filter for coping with bright situations. This is can be easily switched on and off from the main camera menu.

Hoods

When you buy a lens, you should receive a basic lens hood in the box with the lens itself. It's a valuable accessory and will help to keep flare from the sun or bright light sources from getting into your picture and affecting the exposure.

MEMORY CARDS

Memory cards are the film of a digital camera, and the images are saved onto them. You can either connect the camera to your computer to transfer the shots, or take the card out of the camera and use a bespoke reader. Although there are several different types available, Secure Digital (SD) and Compact Flash (CF) are the most common.

All cards are available in different capacities and transfer speeds, but unless you are looking for professional standard image download capabilities or huge memory size, cards of between 8–32 Gb can be easily obtained for under £20 each. It's well worth having spares in your camera back. Specialist online retailers offer highly competitive rates for memory cards—avoid purchasing from supermarkets or high street stores unless you have no other option, or need a replacement card in a hurry.

The Canon 5D Mark III has dual slots for both SD and CF memory cards. (*Courtesy Canon UK*)

IMAGE FORMATS

In the world of image processing and computer graphics, there are a lot of different ways of storing files, and in particular, graphical designs or photographs. To the novice, the choice can be positively bewildering, with 'TIFFs', 'eps', and 'bitmaps', but unless you are planning to have your image blown up to the size of a roadside poster, or for a high quality art installation, you can concentrate on just two main image format types.

Every digital camera available today will produce its image output as a jpeg file. Jpeg stands for 'Joint Photographic Experts Group'. Your camera may give you the option of choosing the level of quality for your jpeg file. It is recommended to always shoot to the highest quality level possible.

You can always reduce the file size later (for emailing it perhaps) but it's always easier to degrade an image—trying to upgrade later simply won't work. When you press your camera shutter to create a jpeg file, your camera processes the image, so that the image recorded has already been manipulated slightly. Some cameras will allow you to control the amount of in-camera processing carried out. Jpegs offer a good compromise between quality and economical use of file storage space, but remember that some detail, especially in highlight and shadow areas, is lost in-camera.

The alternative to jpeg is to shoot in RAW. As its name implies, it is the closest thing to a digital 'negative' and takes every ounce of image information that is captured by your camera's image sensor. This means that it needs to be processed and converted into another format (typically jpeg) on your computer, but for the discerning railway photographer, it offers the highest level of control over image quality and post processing, i.e. lightening, darkening, sharpening, and any other desired alterations. Most cameras will record images in RAW, and some can be set to save an image in RAW and jpeg at the same time. Note, however, that this duplication of files will reduce the number of photos you can save on a given memory card.

RAW offers the highest quality output for your images, and as long as you are comfortable in making adjustments on your computer, it should be your preferred file medium. Once you get more into photography, you may start to deal with other image formats, such as PSD (Photoshop Document) or TIFF (Tagged Image File Format) files, which offer lossless compression, and therefore maintain the full quality in your photograph. The file sizes will be large as a result, and you may find that you cannot upload them to a website without converting back to a jpeg.

ESSENTIAL ACCESSORIES

Tripods, bags and batteries

Now you've got your hardware, you should consider how you are going to carry your equipment around. For most trips, a rucksack-style backpack is the recommended choice. A camera, and a selection of lenses, batteries, and personal items such as a jacket or provisions, soon start to add up, both in bulk and weight. If you are going to be walking to a location, or just want your hands free, this style of bag will be the easiest to carry and will reduce fatigue. Lowepro, Manfrotto, and Tenba have a wide range of sizes and colours that will suit most pockets and camera collections.

For more general use, the messenger-style shoulder bags are discreet but large enough to carry a full-frame DSLR body and a couple of lenses, as well as a few accessories and documents.

Try to avoid gaudy 'designer' style camera bags. Despite their high quality, they do seem to scream 'I am a camera bag'—an open invitation to theft.

For a tripod, look for a balance between sturdiness and weight. Those with braced legs are preferable, as they will provide a more solid platform for your camera. For travelling, mini versions are available.

Batteries can lose their ability to retain charge over time, and can also be affected by cold. It makes sense to keep a few spare (and charged) batteries with you on your travels. Rotate your stock of batteries through the camera from time to time, so that they are all used in the camera moderately frequently.

This Manfrotto Advanced Active Backpack 1 has a handy camera section that folds out for easy access, and has room internally for a small laptop or tablet computer and other personal items.

Set the ISO speed

This will control how sensitive your camera is to the prevailing lighting conditions. On some cameras this may be handled automatically, but if you want full control, set this manually. The higher the ISO rating, the more sensitive to light your camera will be, but also, the more 'noise', or grain, your pictures may display, so aim for a lower number of you can.

Image size

Your camera will give you the choice of saving your pictures at different sizes. The larger the file, the higher the final image resolution so the better the sharpness and the quality obtained. Larger files mean fewer pictures on your memory card, so remember keep an eye on how many frames you have available for your shoot.

Image quality

Every digital camera will save your image as a jpeg file. If given the choice, save at the highest quality jpeg setting you can. Once you become more experienced, you can experiment with RAW (which is the closest digital equivalent to a film 'negative') but if you are new to digital cameras, stick to jpeg. Some cameras will give you the option of recording both types at the same time. This is very useful, but will place even greater demands on your memory card and the number of files you can save on it.

Image review

One of the most useful features of a digital camera is the ability to see your photograph results as soon as you have taken them. Make sure that your camera is set to display the photo for at least a few seconds after each frame is recorded. There will also be a 'review' control that will allow you to check all your shots in the order that they were taken. You may also be able to view more detailed information, such as the exposure details and the histogram.

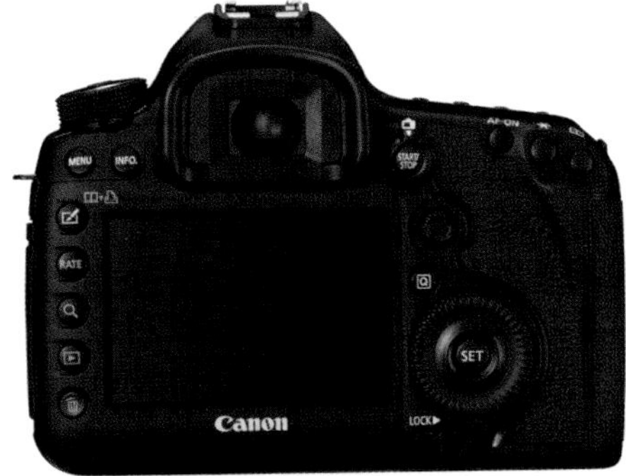

As well as allowing you to check each photo immediately, a digital camera's rear screen will provide a wealth of technical information about each image. (*Courtesy Canon UK*)

Use the mode dial

This is the key control for your camera. There will be variations among the different manufacturers, but the main settings are:

Auto—This is literally the 'point and shoot' setting. The camera will make all the decisions for you, which is fine if you just want a 'snap'. For serious railway photography, it's best to avoid this setting, as with it enabled, you will have no control over the exposure.

Program mode (P)—Although similar to Auto, you will have some control over how the photo will turn out. The camera will still choose the shutter speed and aperture, but you will be able to adjust some settings to compensate for different conditions.

Shutter priority (T or Tv)—as railway photography is predominantly about catching the movement of moving trains, you may wish to keep your camera set to Tv (which stands for Time Value).

You set the shutter speed, and the camera will select the aperture value depending on the conditions. The higher the shutter speed, the faster the train's movement that you will be able to freeze, or conversely, the greater the blur. A fast shutter speed will also help you avoid camera shake.

Aperture priority (A or Av)—in a similar way to the Tv setting, you select the aperture setting and the camera will determine the shutter speed to suit. It's good for use if there is a specific effect you want to achieve—i.e. a subject sharp in the foreground but blurred in the background.

Manual mode (M)—as you might expect, you set both the shutter and aperture values. The camera will just handle the autofocus. Good setting for specialist photography such as time exposures, but for the novice, best left alone until you are more experienced.

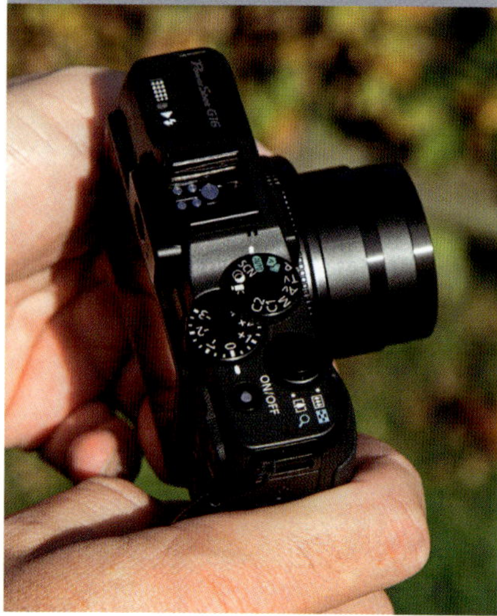

Scene mode—some cameras, especially compacts, have a variety of special modes that can be engaged. These can include: sport, landscapes, night scene, macro, and many more. The camera will adjust all sorts of values such as shutter or aperture prioritization, colour saturation, etc., but unless there is a specific effect you require, they are best left unused for railway photography.

What sort of metering?

In the more advanced compacts and majority of DSLRs, you will also be able to control the way in which your camera takes a meter reading on the prevailing light. As this will dictate what settings the camera chooses in the split second between you pressing the shutter button and the photo being recorded, it's pretty important stuff. The metering processes are ever-more complex and intelligent, and even if you make a mistake, software will help you rescue the shot afterwards, but it's worth understanding how your metering works to save wasted shots and raise the chances of getting a quality image first time, even in tricky conditions.

Matrix or multi segment

With the user worrying about the complex development and the technology behind the scenes, this mode is usually the default setting when you turn your camera on. The camera will take a light reading from a variety of points around the frame, and then analyse them to determine an average final exposure setting. If there is a lot of bright light in the scene, it may compensate to make the photo darker. If there are dark areas, it may compensate by brightening them up.

Centre weighted

As the name might suggest, this mode also assesses the conditions across the frame, but applies a bias toward the centre of the picture, as this is likely to be where your subject would normally be. It's a good fail-safe setting for general photography and will give consistent results in most conditions.

Spot or partial metering

Depending on your camera, spot or partial metering modes will make a reading from a very small section of the frame, anywhere between 1–15 per cent. They are particularly useful if there is an overwhelming dominance of light or dark areas in the view you are trying to record, which might otherwise confuse the camera. For the best results, try to pick a point for the spot metering that has an average (or mid-tone) light value. Although spot metering use takes practice and experience, it will help achieve the most accurate results.

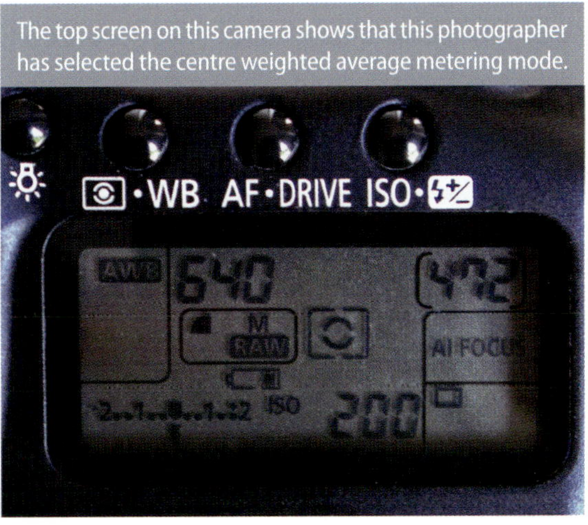

The top screen on this camera shows that this photographer has selected the centre weighted average metering mode.

READING THE HISTOGRAM

Your camera's LCD viewing screen may display a graph alongside the photo you've just taken, as well as the settings used for the shot. Although a little confusing for the novice, the graph, called a histogram, will help you understand the tonal range of the photo, and whether it's over or under exposed. A correctly exposed image histogram will look like a mountain range in the middle of the chart, and should tail off to zero on either side. If the peaks are predominantly over to the left, your image is likely to be under exposed, and probably too dark. Your shutter speed may be too fast, or aperture too small. With the peaks to the right, too much light is reaching the camera's sensor, and the photo will be too bright. Choose a faster shutter speed or higher aperture.

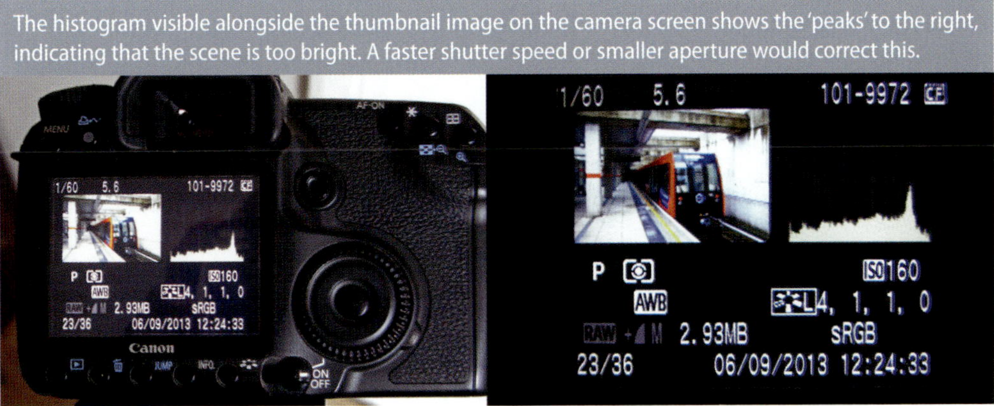

The histogram visible alongside the thumbnail image on the camera screen shows the 'peaks' to the right, indicating that the scene is too bright. A faster shutter speed or smaller aperture would correct this.

Although we don't notice it ourselves as our eyes and brains compensate for us, the light sources all around us emit at different wavelengths, which we see as colours. Artificial lighting can generate a distinctly coloured hue, while even the time of day can affect the natural light cast. These can have a huge effect on railway photography. Your camera should have a light balance control, which will take into account the ambient colour temperature and adjust your photograph accordingly.

Most DSLR's have Auto White Balance (AWB) as their default setting, which will cope with the majority of situations. It's good practice, however, to be aware of time of day or artificial light sources that may affect it. For example, a strong light source falling on a subject of a particular colour may confuse the camera into making a wrong adjustment. Luckily, your camera should have a number of other settings that will allow you to make manual adjustments. These are:

Direct sunlight for harsh and contrasty conditions in bright outdoor situations.

Shade compensates for the slight blue cast that a shady situation creates.

Cloudy for heavily overcast cloudy skies, avoid flat colours by choosing this slightly cooler setting.

Fluorescent most artificial or strip lighting has a definite cast, sometimes blues, oranges, or greens. Use this setting to correct for their effect.

Flash unlikely to be used for railway photography, flash photography warms up the cool effect tended to be produced by flash units.

Remember to reset your camera to AWB when your shoot is complete, so that you have a general setting for your next project.

Railway Photography

HOW TO TAKE A SHARP PHOTO OF A TRAIN AT HIGH SPEED

The shutter speed choice is the paramount decision to be made here. At up to around 100 mph, a shutter speed of 1/1000th second will normally freeze the action. Despite your camera's fast autofocus system, if you want to be 100 per cent certain of the focus at a particular point, pre focus on that location before the train arrives, and use the AF lock option, or set the lens to manual focus. Make sure your camera is on shutter speed priority (Tv) then simply press the shutter when the train passes the desired point. Evaluative metering will give a balanced exposure.

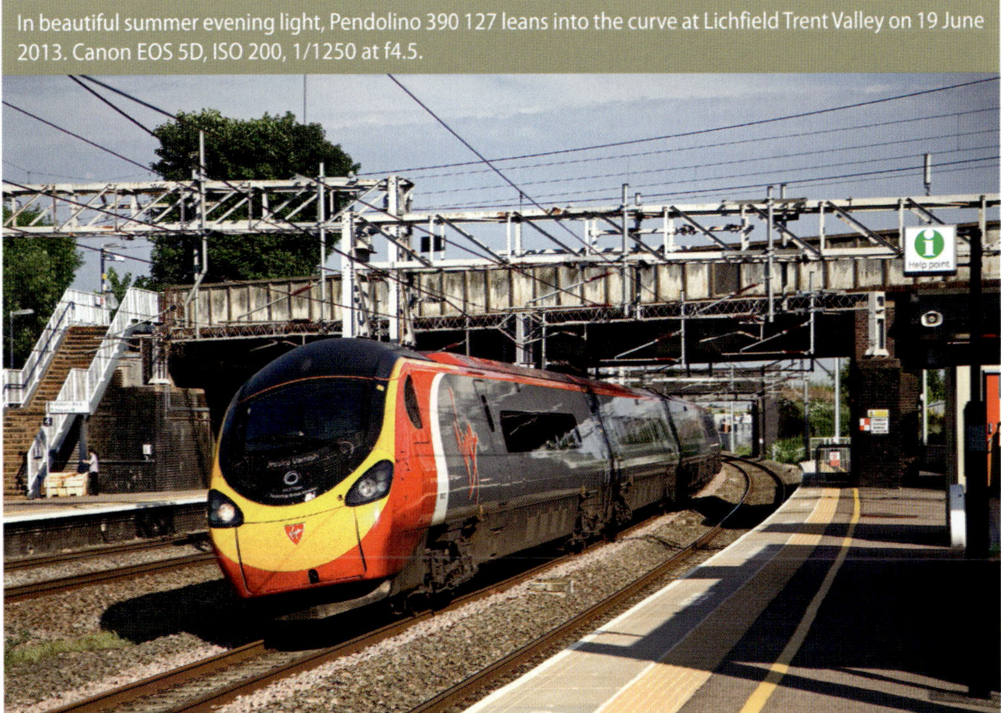

In beautiful summer evening light, Pendolino 390 127 leans into the curve at Lichfield Trent Valley on 19 June 2013. Canon EOS 5D, ISO 200, 1/1250 at f4.5.

HOW TO MAKE SURE THE EXPOSURE IS CORRECT

Be aware of a dominant lighting condition that might affect your photo. Is there a large bright or dark area that might confuse your camera into over or under exposing? Remembering to take into account the shutter speed needed to freeze the train's movement, the simplest way of checking is to take a test photo before the 'main event'. If not satisfactory, adjust the exposure as necessary.

Possibly obvious, but unless you have a specific composition in mind, try to get the whole of the subject in the frame. Some cameras, such as compacts with an optical viewfinder not linked to the lens, will have a very slightly offset viewpoint. For DSLR users, think ahead and pre-focus on the spot in the frame where you know the train will be. Ppress the shutter when the subject reaches hat point. Not usually noticeable in general photography, but where space is limited, perhaps at the end of a platform, use the live view option to make sure you are getting everything in. You can always crop out unwanted details later.

HOW TO TAKE A NIGHT SHOT (TIME EXPOSURE)

Fix your camera to your tripod or solid, flat surface. Footbridges or wooden platforms are notorious for vibrations as people move about behind you. If your camera allows, shoot in RAW, so that your images retain the most information, allowing you to enhance them later on your computer.

Once you have settled on your location, and chosen your subject, compose the shot and focus. Set your camera to M (manual) and aperture of f8–f16. Then, adjust the camera's shutter speed until the exposure level is in line with the middle of the exposure indicator in the viewfinder, or on the camera's top display. This should give a fairly accurate exposure, with a typical exposure value between one and 30 seconds.

A remote release is also recommended for night shots, as even the gentlest touch to press the shutter release can create vibration. If you don't have one, use the camera's self-timer to fire the shutter for you.

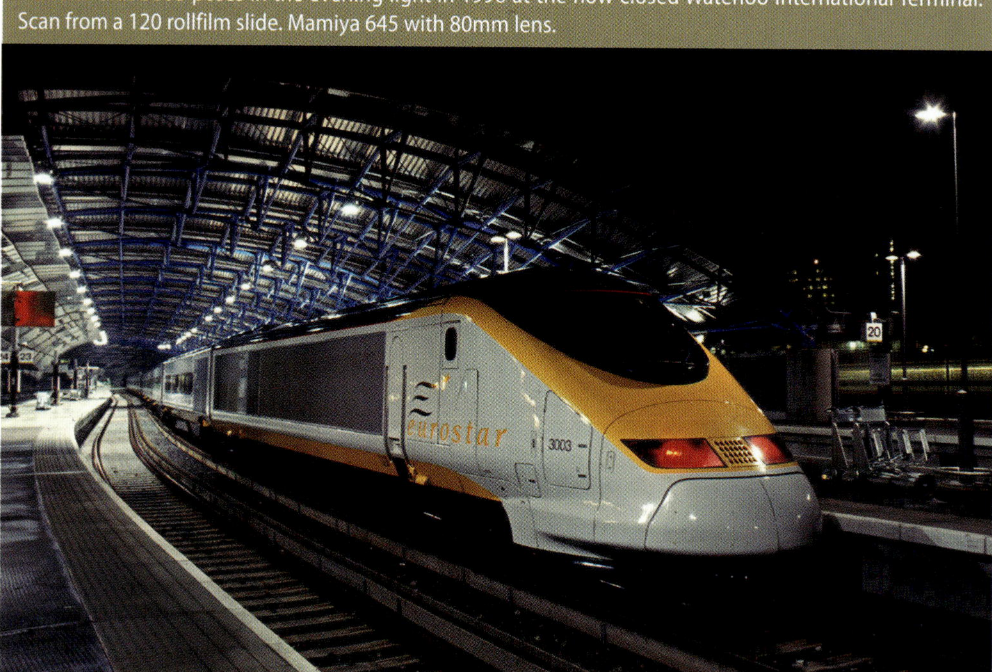

Eurostar unit 3003 poses in the evening light in 1996 at the now closed Waterloo International Terminal. Scan from a 120 rollfilm slide. Mamiya 645 with 80mm lens.

Composition begins to apply a more artistic approach to railway photography. Through notional lines, spirals, or frames, the eye can be drawn to the subject. It's an entirely subjective area, in which the skill of the photographer to interpret the location and surroundings make the transition from a record shot to a more meaningful image. The use of perspective, contrast, even repetition, can all add to a powerful result, but take care to consider every aspect of the scene—it can be very easy in the field to miss a foreground or background detail that can be distracting in the final result.

A London Underground S stock unit approaching Bayswater station. The colour has been removed from the image in Photoshop apart from the nose of the train itself, creating a powerful composition. Canon 5D Mark III. 24-105mm, ISO 1250, 1/500 at f5.6.

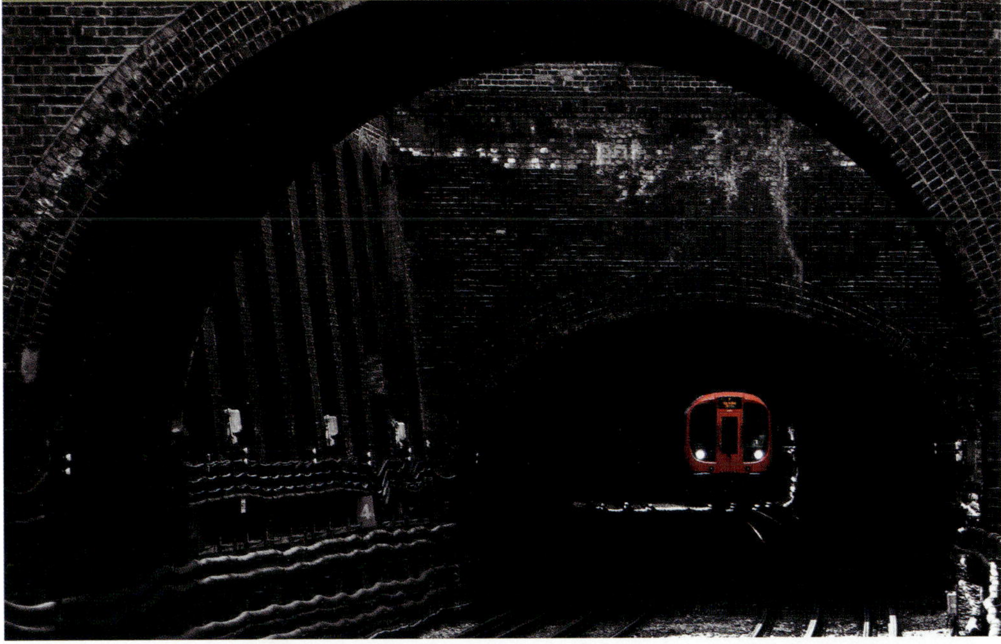

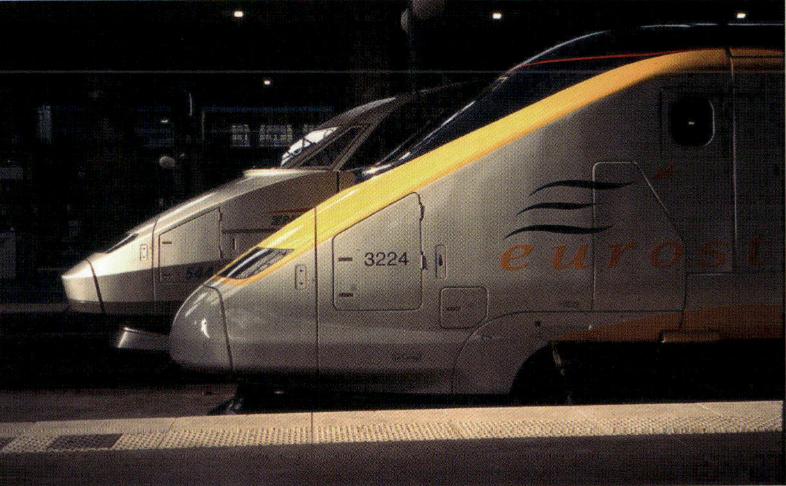

Nose comparison. Eurostar unit 3224 poses alongside a TGV unit at Paris Nord station. The sunlight falling on the trains in the otherwise cavernous station makes the composition stand out from the background. Olympus 35RC compact film camera.

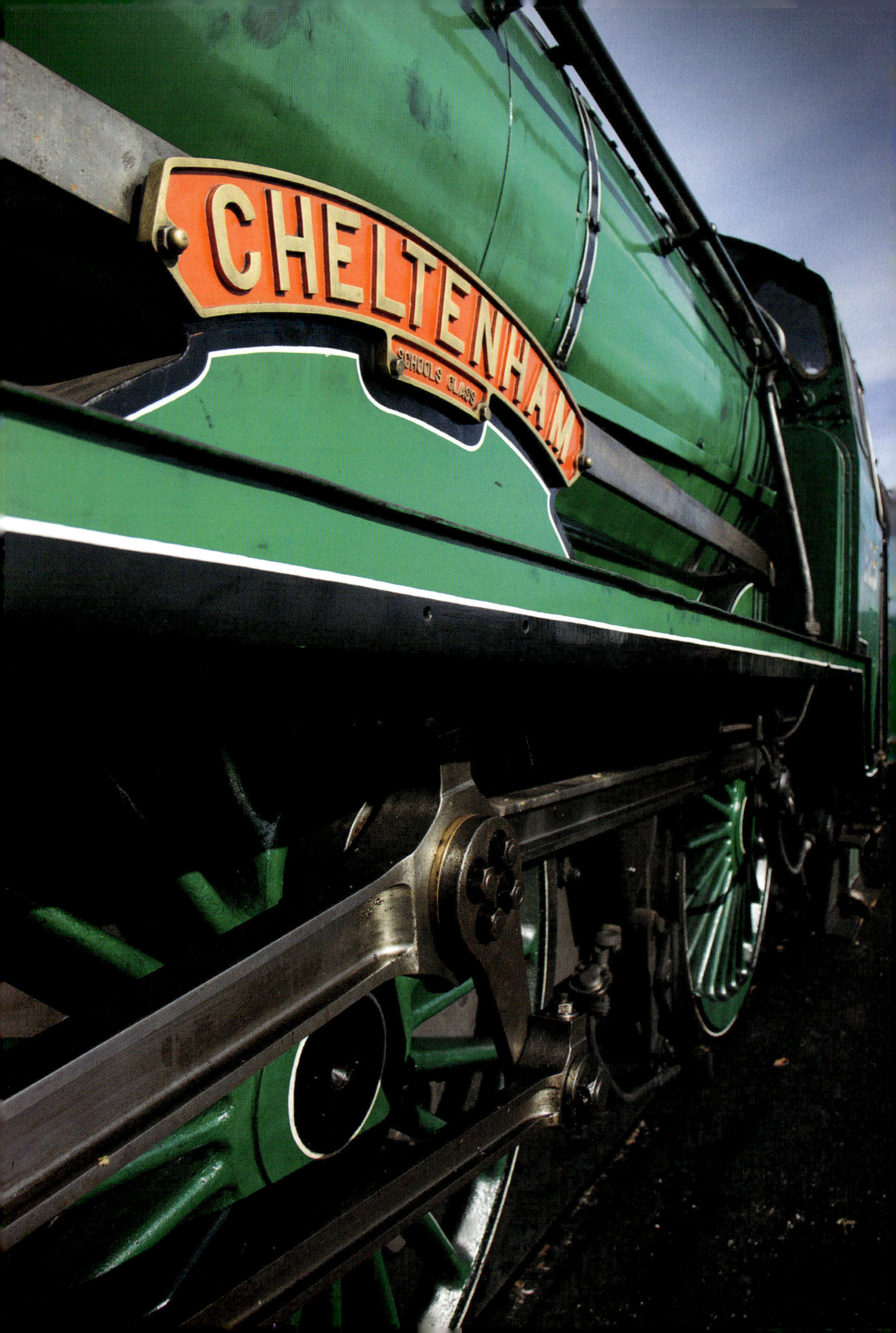

CHELTENHAM
SCHOOLS CLASS

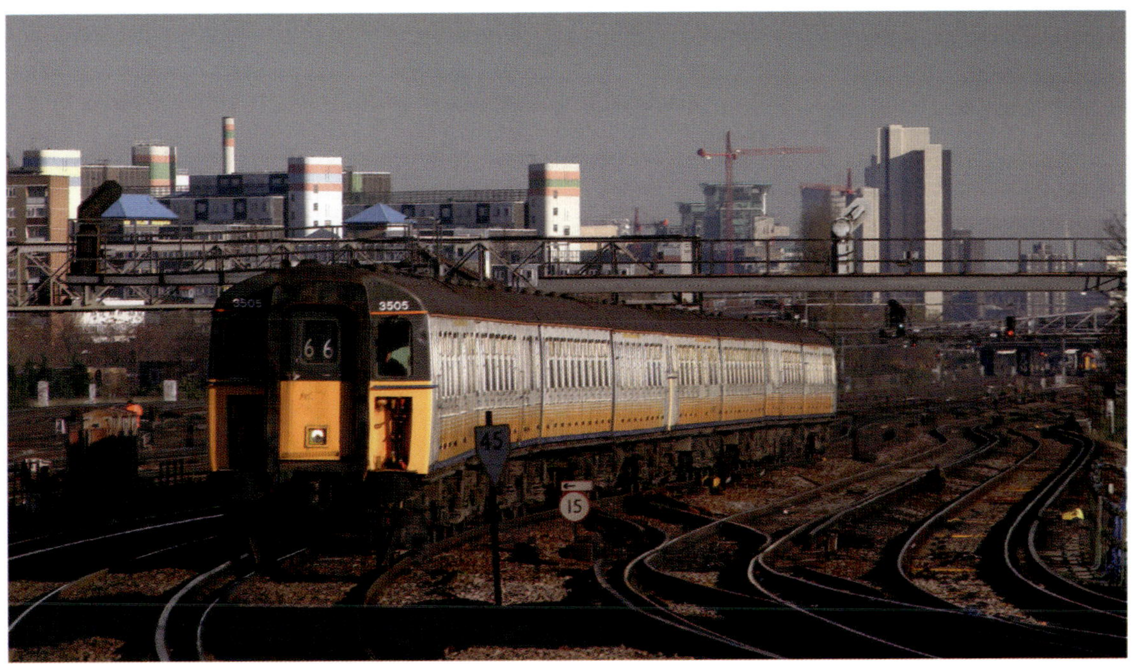

A telephoto lens provides foreshortening of 8 VEP formation led by unit 3505 as they approach Clapham Junction in 2004. Canon 10D, 80-200mm lens, ISO 400, 1/250 at f16.

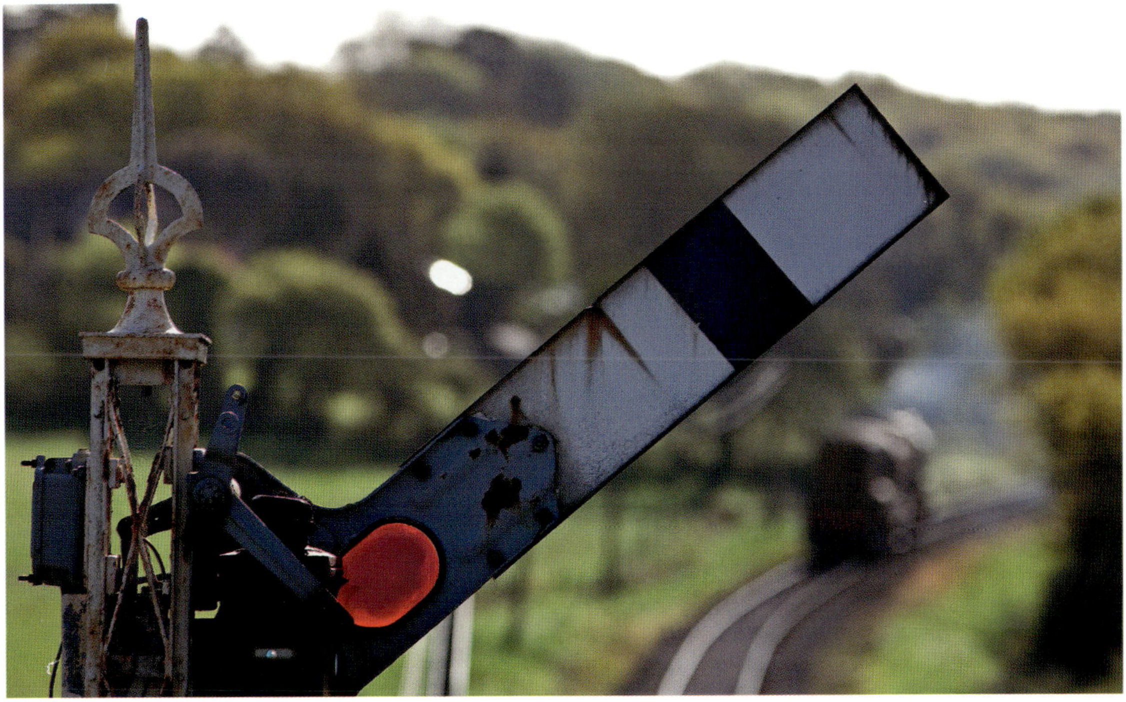

Using selective focusing, attention is fixed on the semaphore signal arm. The train's approach was then allowed to fill the remainder of the frame. Canon 5D, 300mm, ISO 250, 1/640 at f6.3.

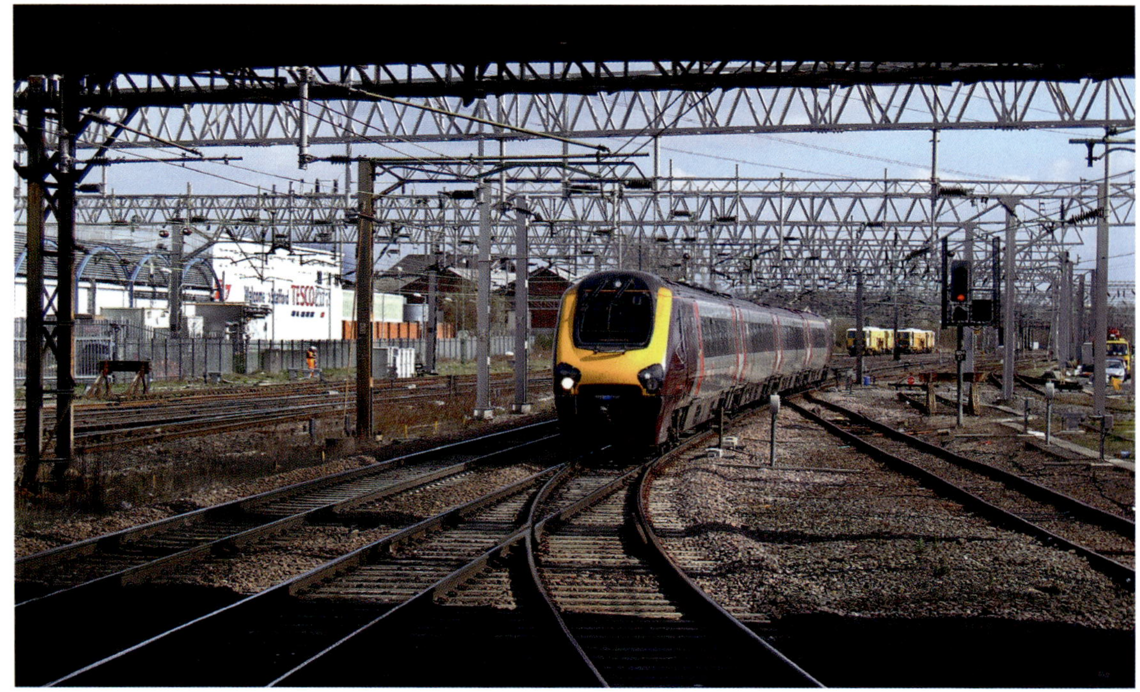

Voyager unit approaching Stafford on 19 April 2013. Although the catenary masts make for a 'busy' photograph, the eye is drawn towards the train by the framing of the road overbridge. Fuji FinePix S3Pro, 28-80mm lens, ISO 200, 1/500 at f5.6.

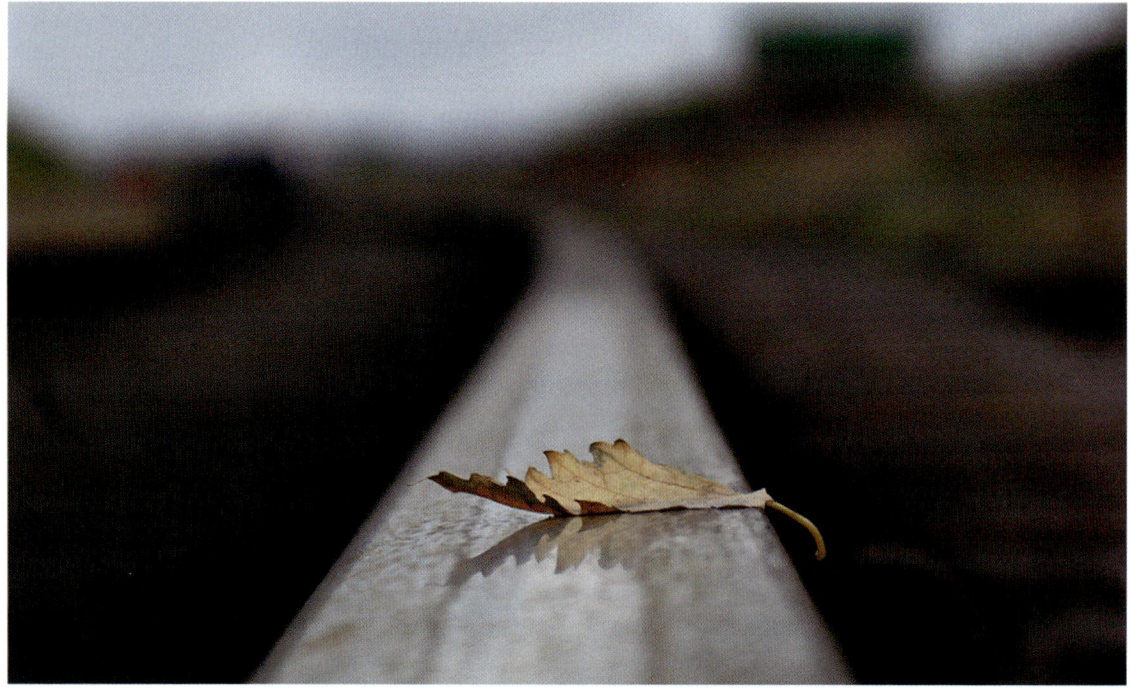

Leaves on the line! Hardly likely to cause a problem, this was a posed image during a 'walk the line' event on a preserved railway. Canon G9 compact in auto mode. ISO 160, 1/320 at f4.8.

► If you go down to the woods today, you're in for a big surprise! An unexpected visitor to the Fleet services on the M3 motorway was 56 098, on its way back from an enthusiasts' weekend in July 2009. The loco on a road trailer in the car park was unusual, but not visually interesting. However, framing by the silver birch trees provided a more picturesque view. Canon 40D, ISO 250, 1/200 at f5.

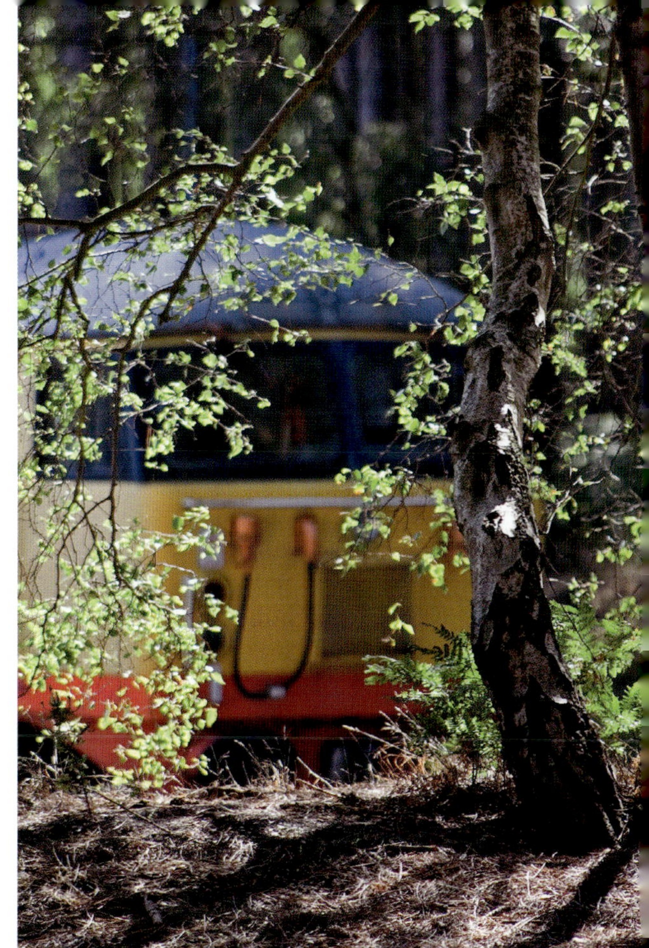

▼ 60 079 speeds down the GW main line at Compton Beauchamp with the Theale to Robeston oil empties on 29 March 2012. A 'traditional' railway photograph, recording the train in a location that will change dramatically in the near future with electrification. Canon 5D, 24-105mm lens, ISO 320, 1/800 at f7.1.

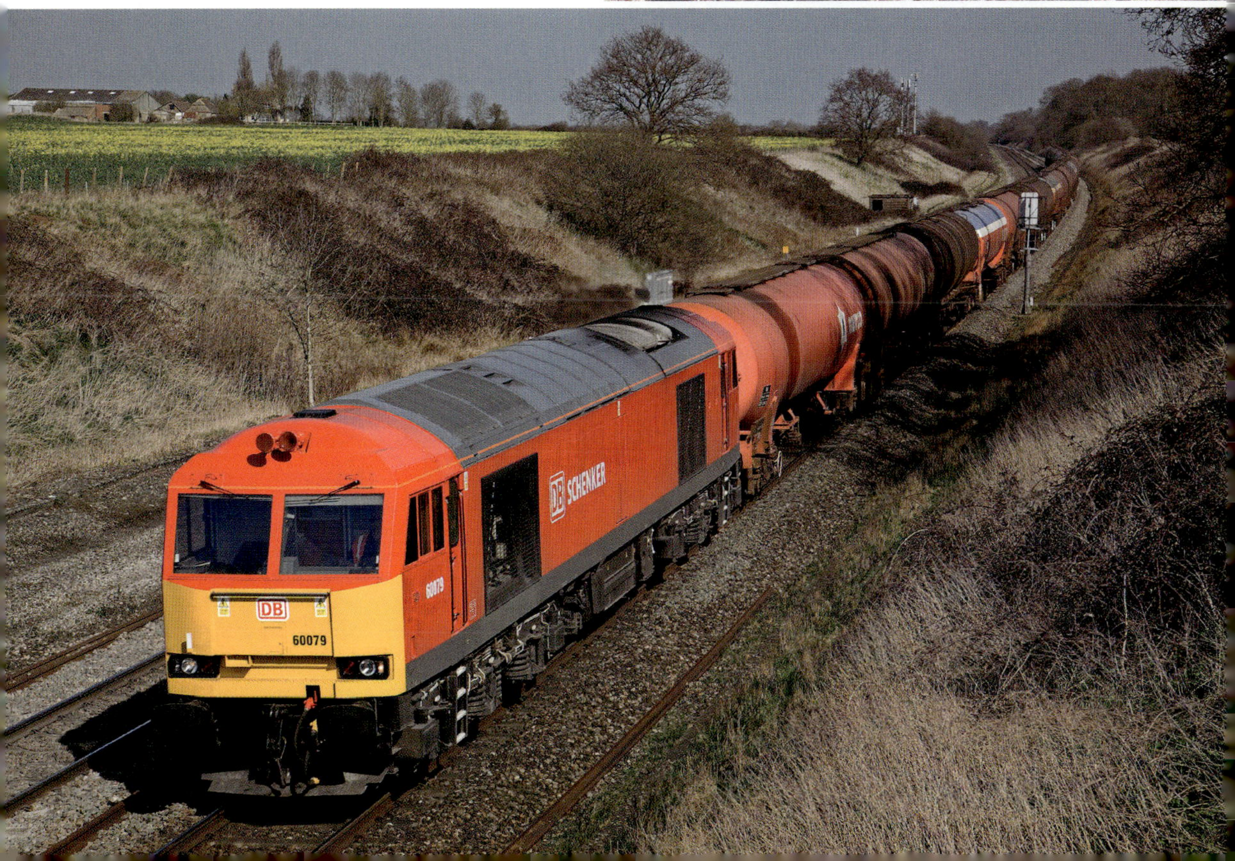

Some photographers religiously adhere to the so-called 'rule of thirds'. This is a notional split of what you see in the view finder of your camera, into nine equal rectangular areas. Try to keep a balance of the subject in the frame based on these rectangles. Some cameras will overlay a grid in the viewfinder to allow you to compose in this way. Back home after a shoot, image processing software will allow you overlay a 'rule of thirds' grid onto a photo you have taken to see how well you did.

If you are out in the field, don't forget to allow for the train to come into your composition. In practice, place the horizon on one of the horizontal lines, with the sky occupying the remaining third of the frame. It will be your choice to decide whether a dramatic sky or an interesting foreground will make for a better photo, but either way, you should achieve a pleasing result.

Of course, some say that rules were meant to be broken. A published or award-winning photo might just as likely be one that breaks with convention. What matters is what you like as a result. If others like it too, that's a bonus. Don't feel the need to copy others religiously. The best photos are the ones that give you the most satisfaction.

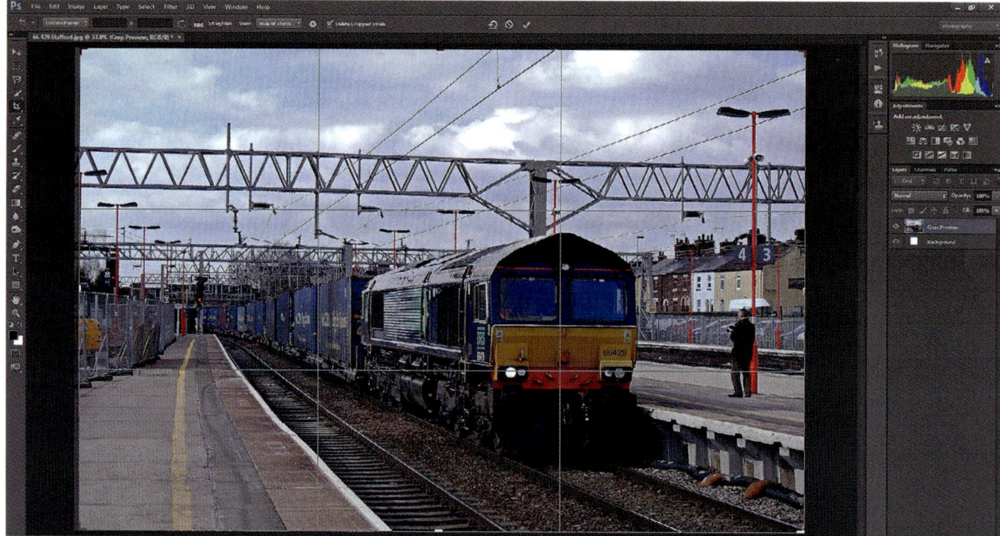

DRS 66 429 passes through Stafford with a southbound freightliner train. The overlaid grid shows the 'rule of thirds' concept as an aid to composition.

▶ The vivid blue sky and bright colours of these Caltrain locomotives in San Francisco dominate the frame, with the rails and platform markings providing perspective that takes the eye towards the station buildings. Canon 5D, 24-105mm, ISO 160, 1/320 at f13.

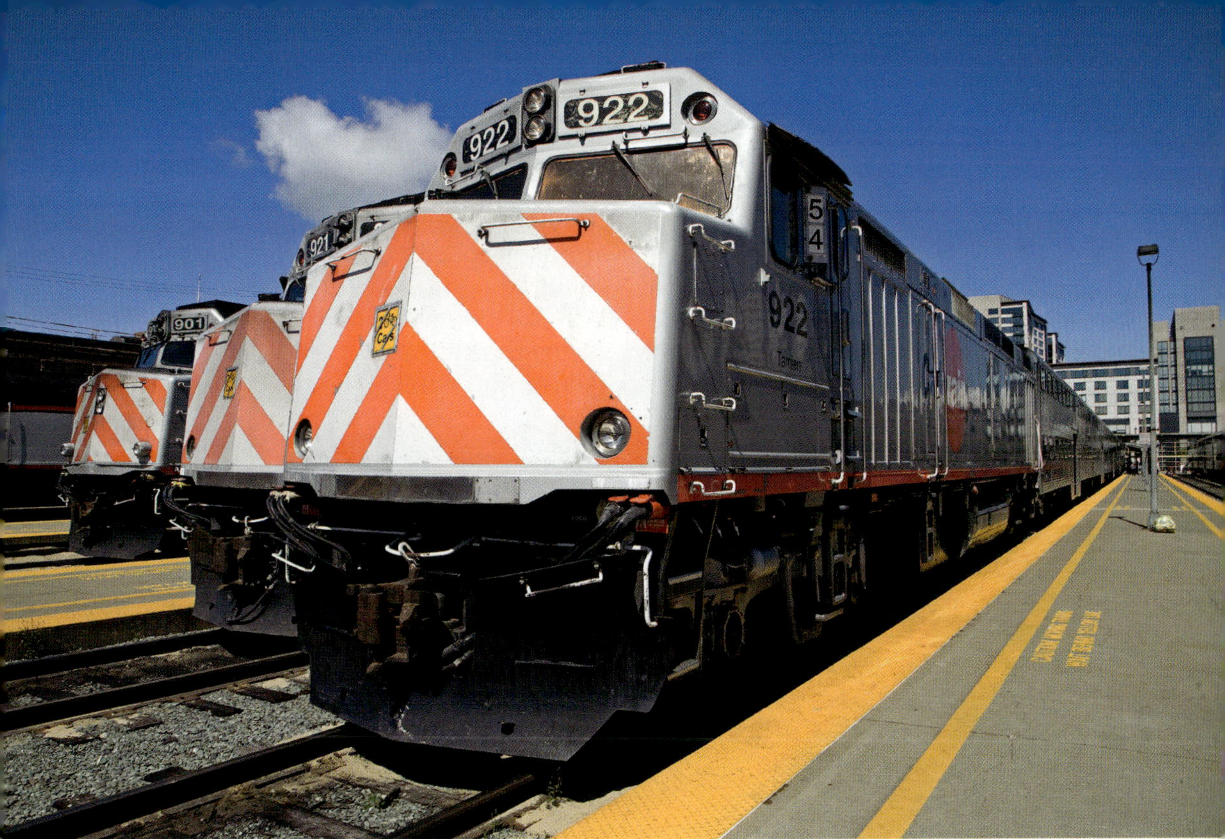

PICTURE STYLES

Here are some common styles will be familiar to railway photographers.

The 'standard' sunny front three quarter. If you just want a record shot, this is the type of image you will normally take. The three-quarter standpoint will allow you to see the front and side of the subject. If detail is important to you, ensure that your depth of field is sufficient to include the whole of the loco body, for example. Your camera will probably sort the focusing for you, but in order to be absolutely sure, set the lens to manual, and focus just behind the cab. This should ensure that as much of the body is sharp as possible, while the front is taken care of by the depth of field.

Telephoto. A photograph of a speeding train taken with a telephoto lens is one of the most powerful images possible. Whether steam or diesel, you will easily be able to create a feeling of speed and power. To ensure a sharp image, set a relatively fast ISO so that a high shutter speed is possible. If possible, try to balance this with a low f-stop value, so that the subject is sharp but the background is out of focus. This will add to the drama of the image. Set your camera to continuous AF, so that the camera will track the movement of the train towards it and adjust accordingly. If your camera doesn't have this feature, set the lens to manual, and pre-focus on the position at which you want the shot. When the train reaches that point, press the button.

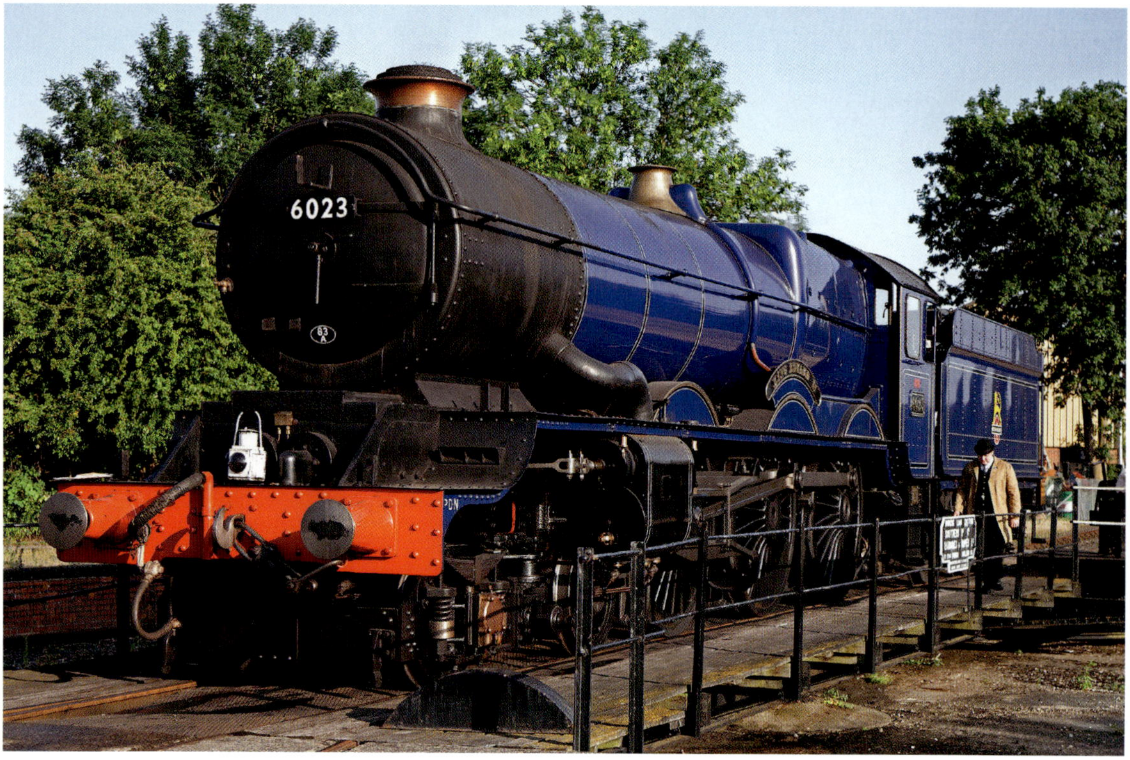

During a photographic charter, King class 6023 poses in the summer sunshine on the Didcot railway centre turntable. Canon 5D, 24-105mm lens, ISO 250, 1/200 at f5.6.

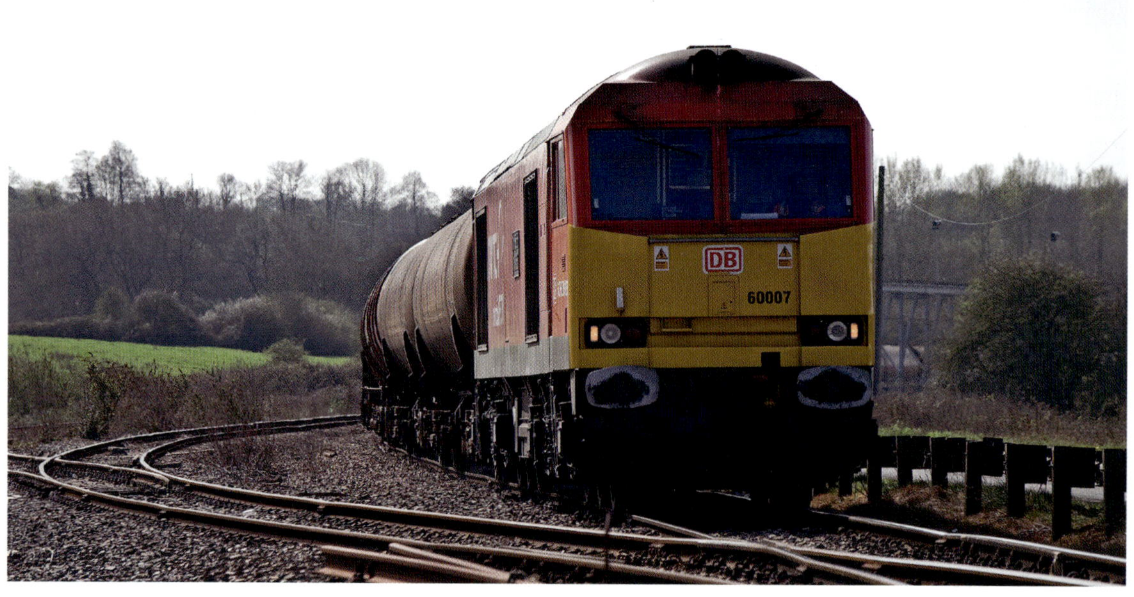

Bright sunshine and strong colours allow for an almost abstract image, as 60 007 shunts its load of oil tankers at Westerleigh oil terminal on 29 March 2012. Canon 5D, 70-200mm lens, ISO 250, 1/640 at f7.1.

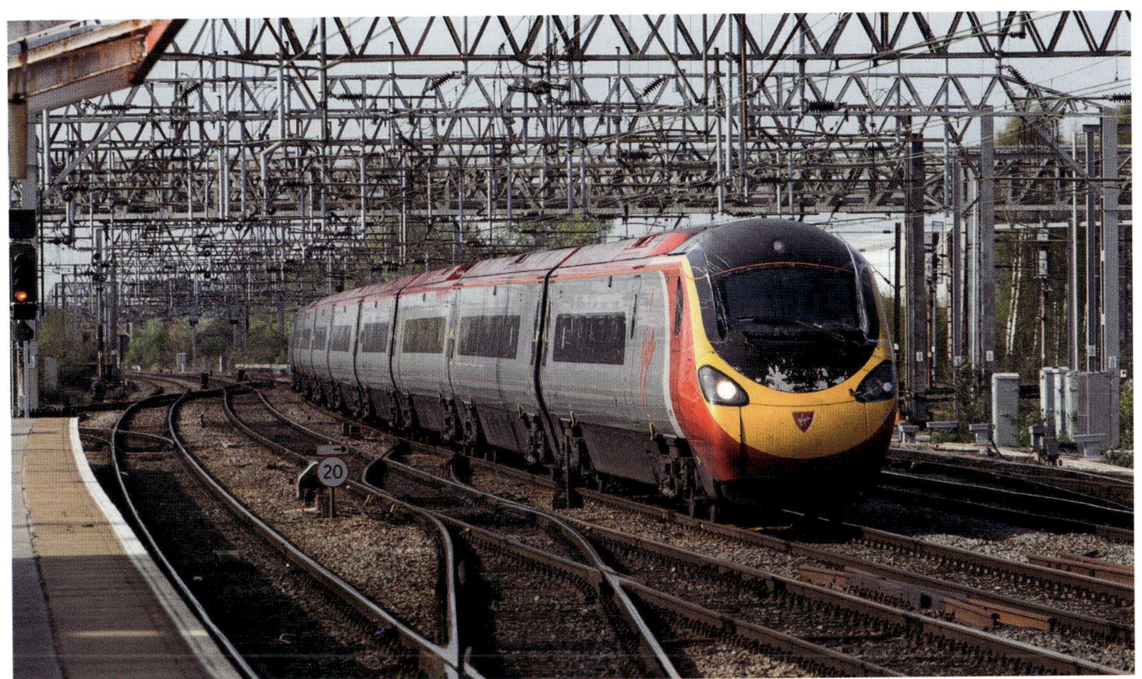

A south-bound Virgin Pendolino unit passing south-bound through Crewe. The telephoto lens compresses the view of the train, and combined with the overhead catenary and points 'leading' the eye towards the train, add to the impression of speed. Canon 5D Mark III. 24-105mm, ISO 320, 1/640 at f8.

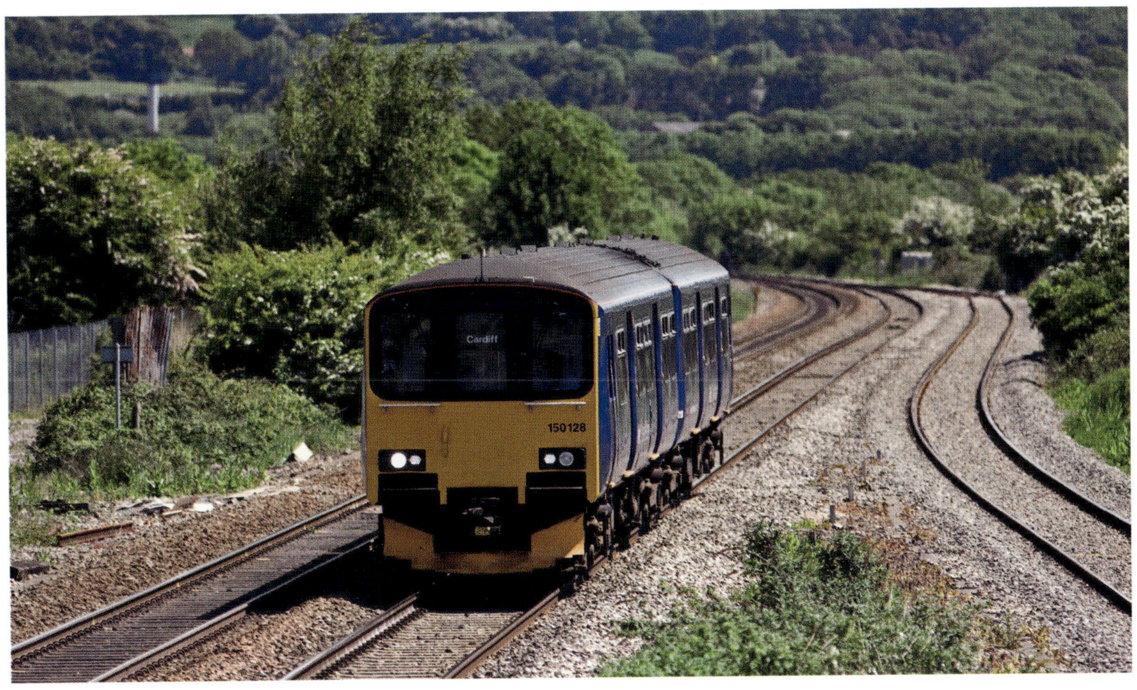

Short formation diesel units can seem even smaller when viewed through a telephoto lens. 150 128 is about to speed through Pilning station *en route* to South Wales in this June 2013 view. Canon 5D, 30mm lens, ISO 250, 1/800 at f5.

Wide angle. A wide view may be forced upon you where an image may not be possible any other way—at the end of a platform perhaps. However, there are also great effects you can achieve with a wide angle lens. A low viewpoint will give a dramatic and powerful view of your subject. The wider your lens, the more pronounced the effect. This look is not for everyone and should not be overdone. Care should also be taken to make sure that your horizon is level. It's easy to take a 'wonky' photo when shooting wide angle, and if you are filling the frame with the subject, you may find it hard to correct afterwards. The wide angle lens may also distort the verticals, so that signals, walls or telegraph poles may seem to be leaning outwards. For some, these effects are the attraction of wide angle photography. For others, they are a heinous crime. Consider the effect is what you desire before you shoot.

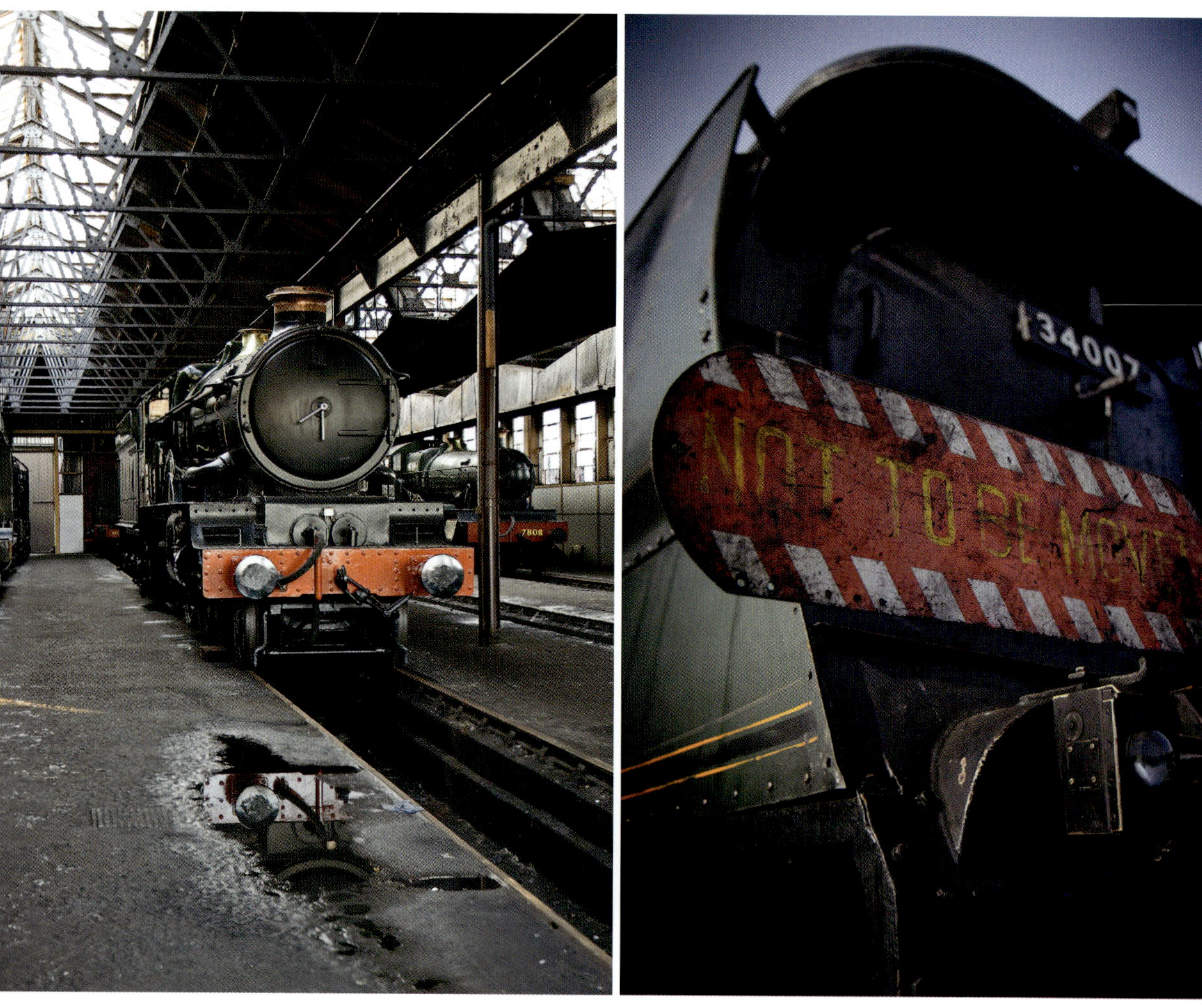

◀ Use of a wide angle can open up the possibility of a reflection in a handy puddle. Photo charter at Didcot railway centre. Canon 5D, 24-105mm lens, ISO 400, 1/15 at f4.

▶ Short depth of field in this wide angle view of 34007 at Ropley concentrates attention on the 'Not to be Moved' sign. Canon 5D Mark 3, 24-105mm lens, ISO 100, 1/250 at f4.

Detail. If ever there was a hobby that cries out for attention to detail, it's railway photography. There are so many fascinating details that can be found if you look hard. Not just the minutiae of the train or station, but a myriad of other items. Tickets, signs, plants, even people—the list is potentially endless. To ensure you get the shot you want, use a lens that has a macro facility, i.e. it can focus really close to your subject. If your subject is very small, or you want to record tiny detail, you may need to purchase special close up lenses or filters.

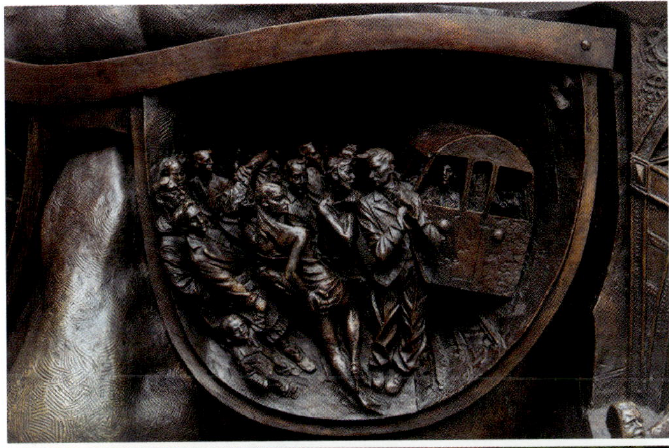

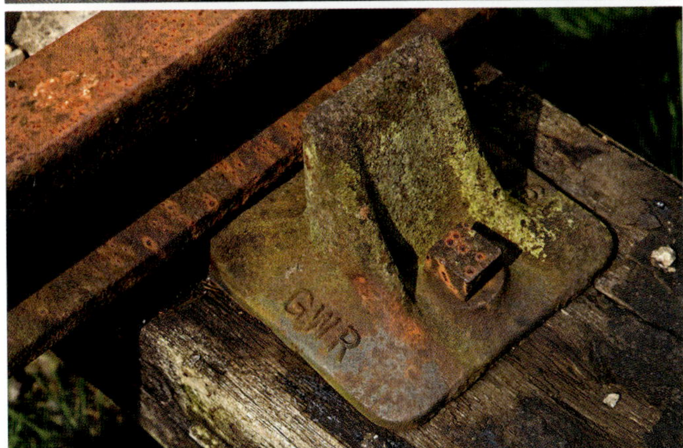

▲ Sculptor Paul Day's statue 'The Meeting Place' dominates the upper concourse at St Pancras International in London. On close inspection, there are many detailed scenes depicting everyday London scenes around its base. Canon 5D, 24-105mm lens, ISO 400, 1/20 at f5.

◄ A sharp eye for detail yields this GWR rail chair at Parkend on the Dean Forest Railway. Canon 5D, 24-105mm lens, ISO 400, 1/400 at f8.

▼ These old railway lamps and late summer sunshine combine to cry out for a photograph. The rust and muted colours make for a timeless scene. Canon 5D, 24-105mm lens, ISO 320, 1/30 at f5.6.

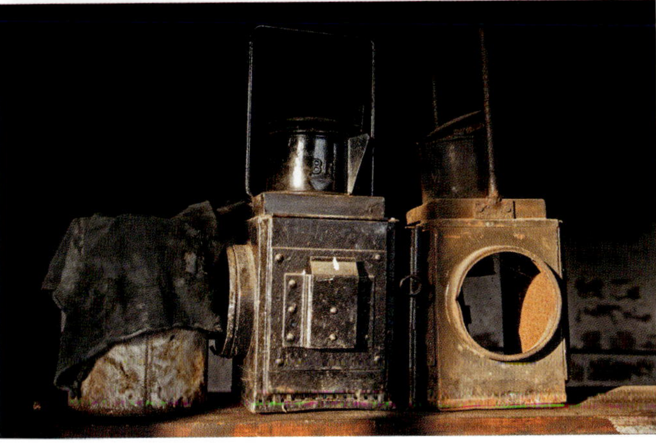

Shadow side. Many photographers will not countenance taking a shot on the shadow side of a train. It's understandable that it may not be quite as colourful as the sunny side, but you may be missing out on a totally different viewpoint to the norm. Bright sunshine will create deep shadows that may seemingly swallow up detail, but don't be afraid of trying the shot and using your processing software at home to bring out the detail. You can help this by setting your camera to underexpose by one or two stops.

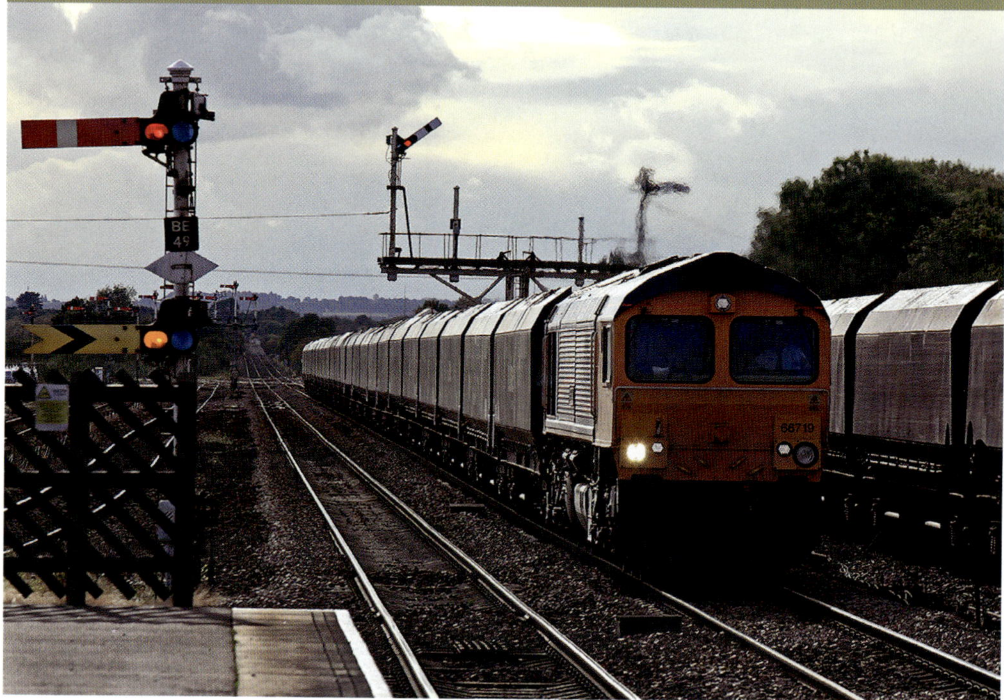
Shooting almost directly into the sun presents similar challenges. 66 719 approaching Barnetby with sunshine behind the train. Canon 5D, 70-200mm lens, ISO 320, 1/800 at f8.

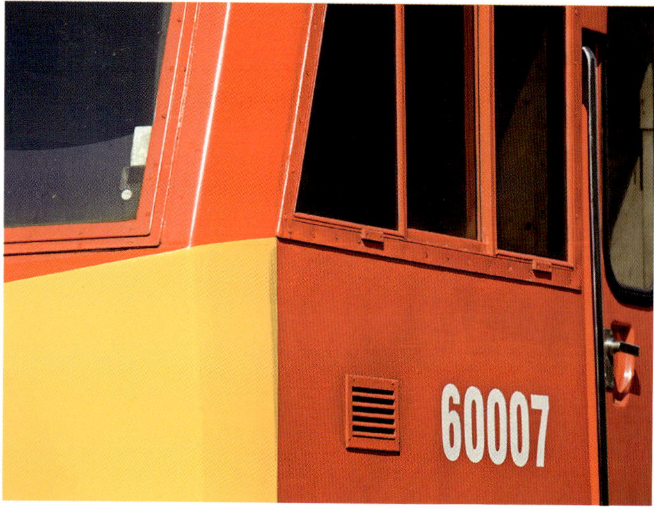

Shooting into shadow always presents difficulties for railway photographers. Choosing an average exposure gives some shadow detail without washing out an over-light background too much. Set your camera to centre-weighted average metering and use the over/under exposure as necessary. Equally, bright colours and deep shadows can also present problems, requiring careful metering. 60 007 at Westerleigh oil terminal in March 2012 (photo taken from public footpath). Canon 5D, 70-200mm lens, ISO 250, 1/640 at f7.1.

An easy way of developing a creative look to your railway photography is to look for frames. Take a step back and see if there is a tree or signal gantry that might help provide a visual focus for your picture. It will add interest to the finished result, and help draw the eye to the subject.

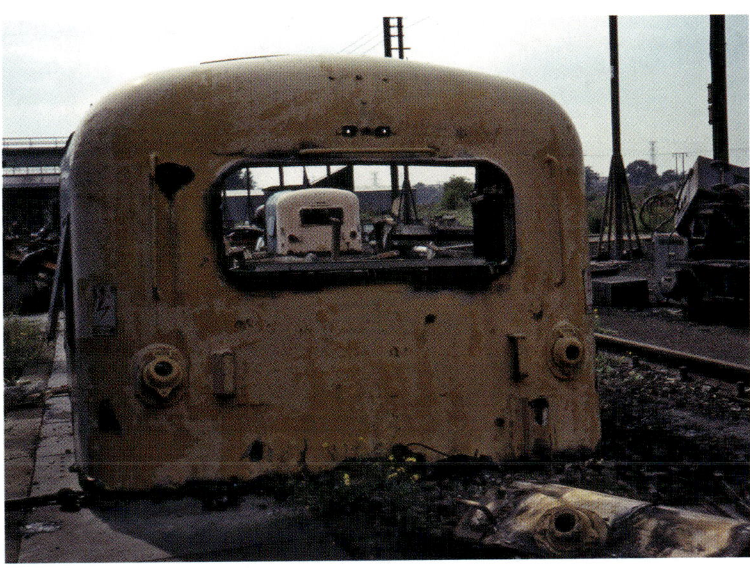

A visit to Doncaster works during the period when the famous Class 55 Deltic locomotives were being scrapped was an opportunity not to be missed. The headcode panels of 55 020 form an interesting perspective of this sad scene. 35mm slide scan.

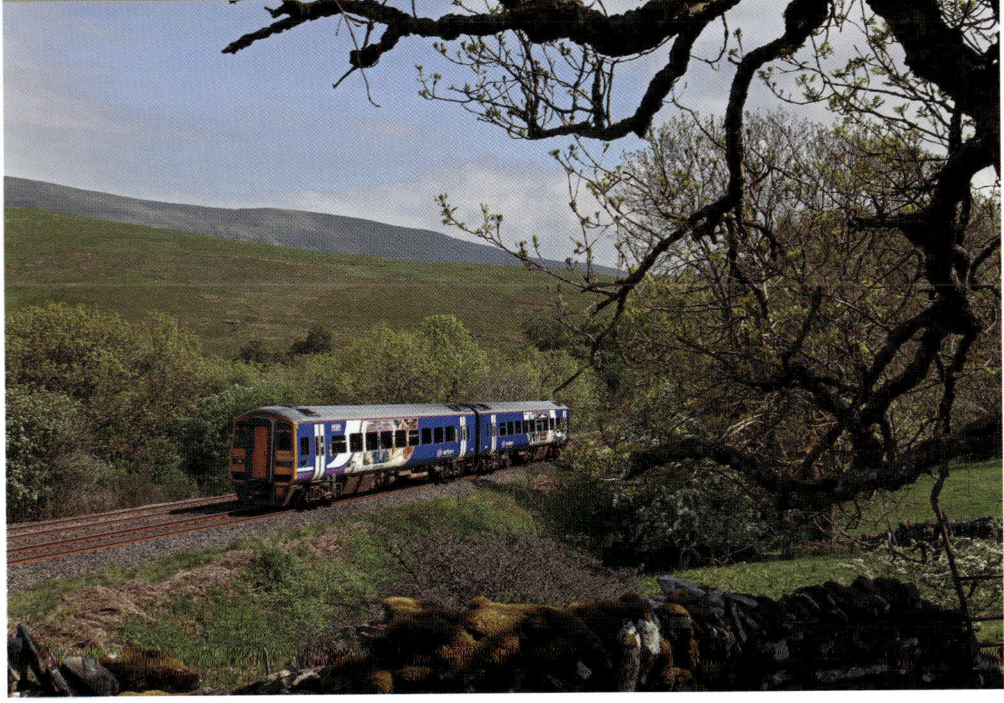

The Settle & Carlisle line is a photographer's dream and very popular as a result, but I've not seen this shot elsewhere yet. Unit 158 796 heading north at Birkett Common, framed by trees and a stone wall. Canon 5D Mark III, 24-105mm lens, ISO 320, 1/640 at f9.

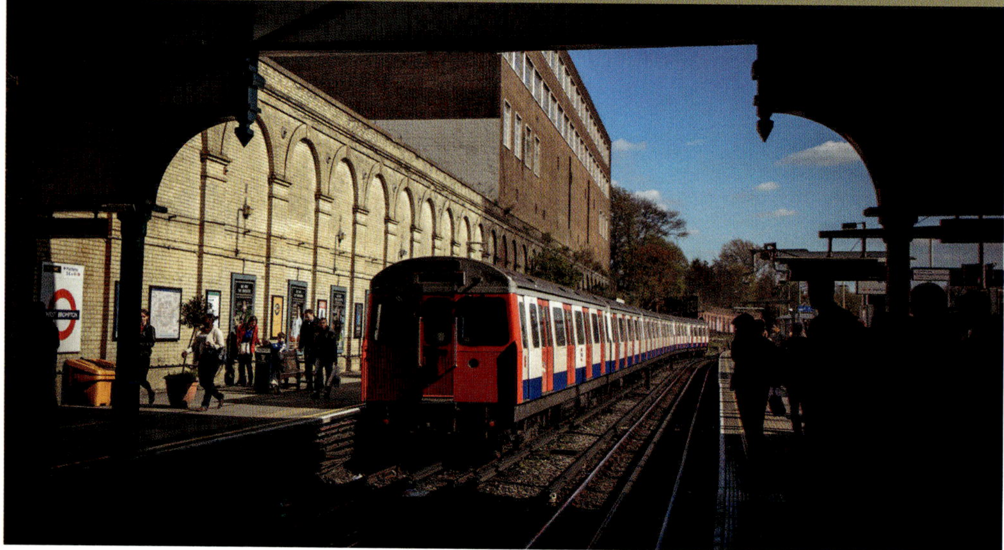

The platform canopy at West Brompton station on the London Underground frames C stock unit 5516 on 9 April 2014. The travellers appear in silhouette, emphasising the crowded nature of the station, but not detracting from the subject. Canon 5D Mark III, 24-105mm lens, ISO 200, 1/400 at f10.

MOVEMENT

Most of the time in railway photography, you will be aiming to arrest movement in your photography. You'll be trying to freeze the motion of a speeding train, capturing as much detail as possible in sharp focus. Shutter speed is king here. You will need to assess the speed of the train passing you, and also take into account the angle at which the subject will be passing across your field of view. As a general rule of thumb for outdoor photography, aim for a shutter speed of 1/1000th second to be sure of freezing the action. Once you get to know your location, and can assess to speed of passing traffic, you can experiment with slower selections. For high speed trains such as Eurostar or a Pendolino, you should select an even faster shutter.

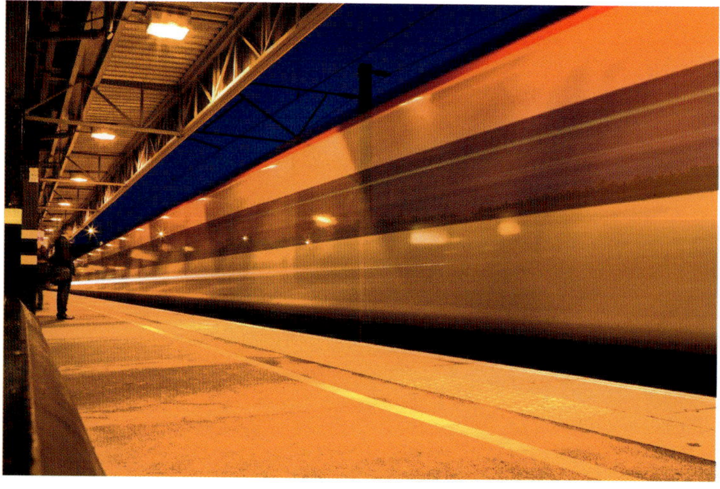

Movement can be recorded in several ways. While waiting for a train at Milton Keynes one evening, I noticed that the passing Pendolinos were well lit as they passed the platform. Although I did not have a tripod with me, a flat guard rail offered a suitable support. Canon 5D, 24-105mm lens, ISO 160, 6 seconds at f16.

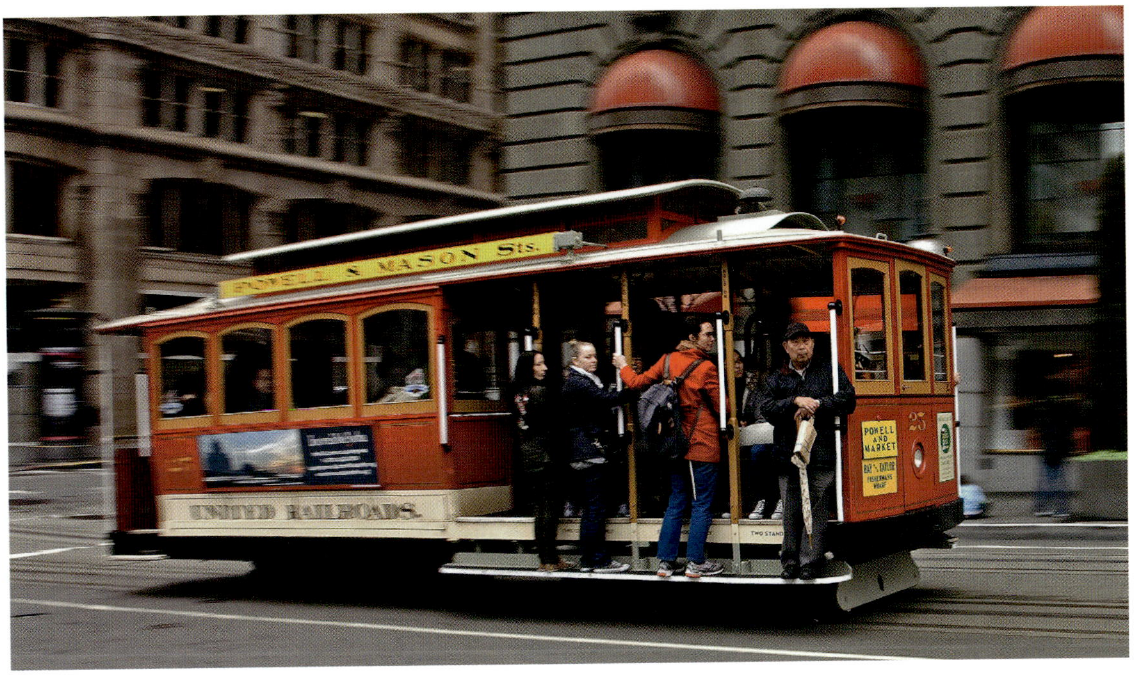

Panning can help make a moving subject stand out from a crowded background, as this image of San Francisco cable car 25 at Hope Square shows. Canon 5D, 24-105mm lens, ISO 125, 1/30 at f8.

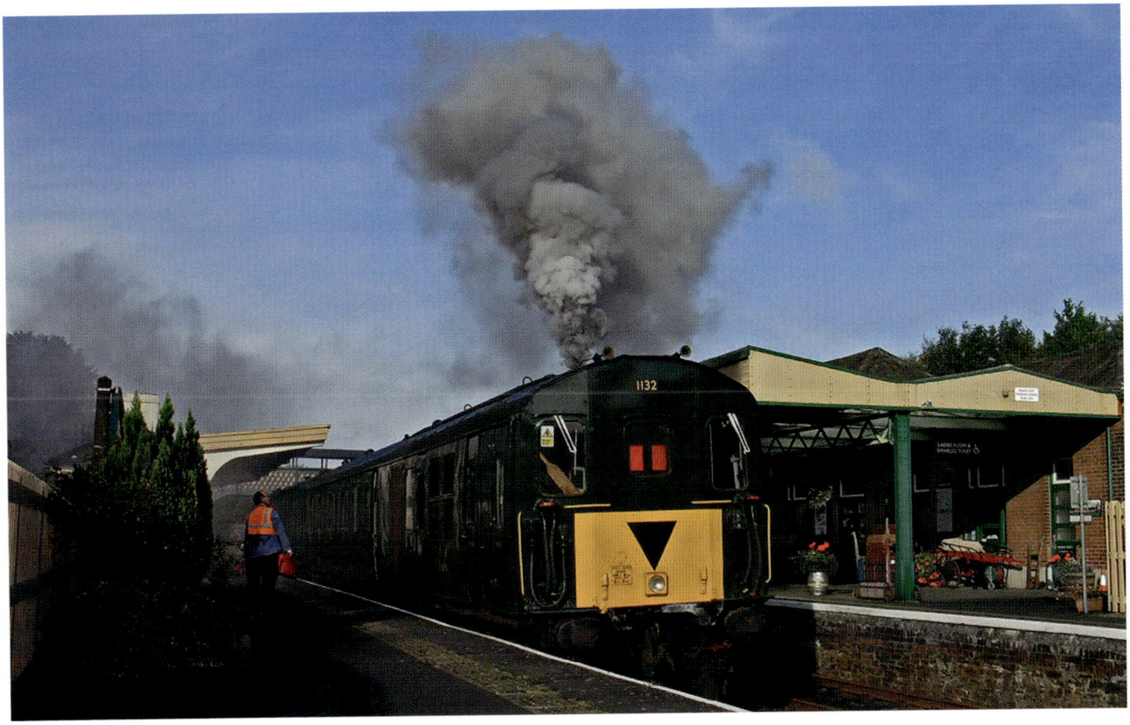

Although stationary, the eruption into life of 1132's engine at Okehampton gave this photo much more impact, complimented by the reaction of the driver on the platform. Canon G9 compact. ISO 400, 1/1250 at f5.

A silhouette, or backlit shot, will deliver a very powerful image, and is relatively easy to achieve. The trick is finding the right location that will allow you to see your subject against a relatively clear background. To create a silhouette, try to expose for the sky, so that everything in the foreground is dark, if even black. If your camera has an exposure lock button, this is a perfect time to use it! Expose for the sky, and lock the settings in for when your train or other subject reaches the desired position. You are looking to get the outline of the train or structure in question, with no other detail. A big challenge may be flare from the sun or bright lights shining right into the lens barrel. Try to position yourself so that the light source is behind the subject. Use a small aperture to keep reflections to a minimum, and of course use a lens hood.

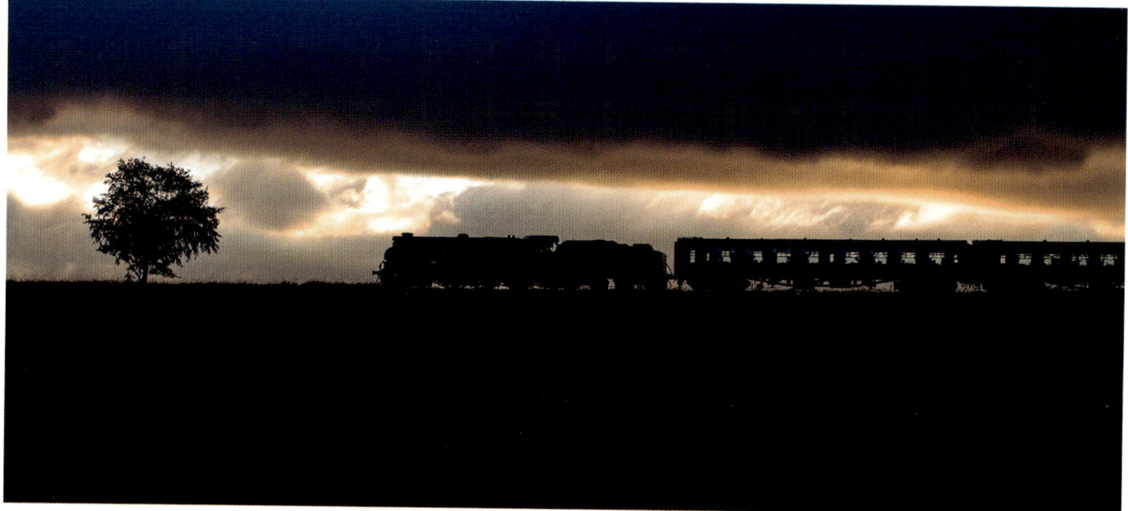

These two images were both taken in the summer of 2014, alongside the A31 in Hampshire where it runs parallel to the Mid Hants Railway. The location was chosen to offer a low viewpoint of the line against the western sky at sunset. Canon 5D Mark III, 70-200mm lens, ISO 320, 1/500 at f4.5.

MOOD

To successfully convey mood in a photograph is a skill. For a railway photograph, it may be a sombre scene that signifies decay. An image of rust, overgrown vegetation, or a scrapyard perhaps. The weather can also play a part—a shadowy train looming out of the fog, or an icicle hanging off a frozen pipe. Keep an eye out for details that may help convert this style—a spider's web or hoar frost. Converting a colour image to black and white can also add mood to an image.

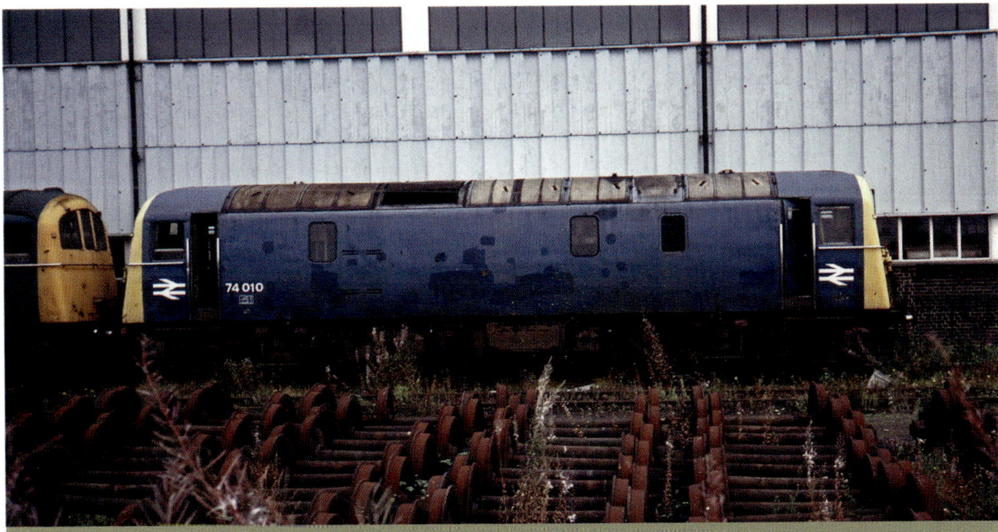

As if the sight of Class 74s for disposal at Doncaster was not sad enough, the sombre mood is heightened by the large number scrapped wagon wheels in the foreground. 35mm slide scan.

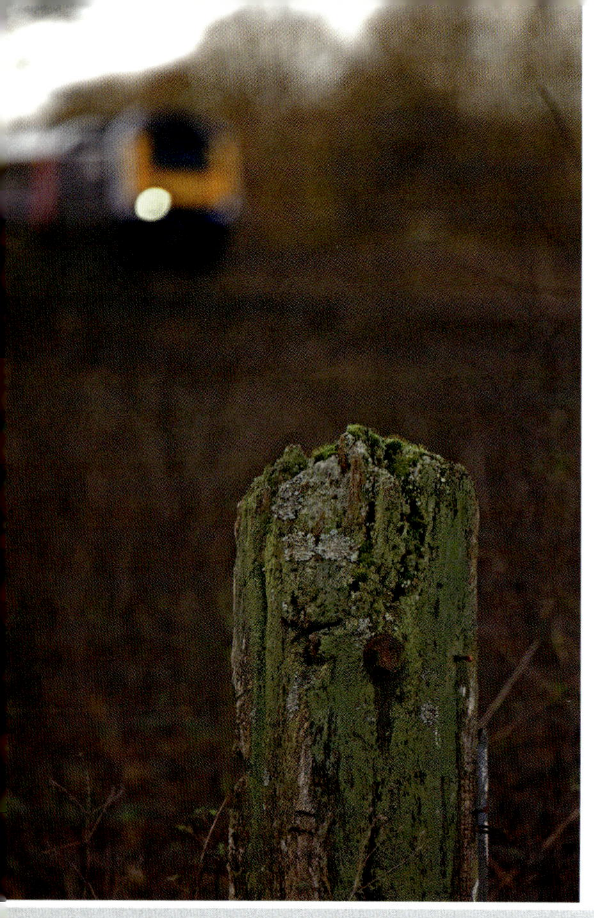

◄ With the wooden post and line in shadow, a conventional railway photo would lack impact and interest. For a different approach therefore, focus was held on the post and the passing HST was allowed to be blurred. Canon 5D, 70-200mm lens, ISO 400, 1/1000 at f4.

▼ 76 043 is unlikely to have its wishes granted in this early 1980s view of Reddish depot near Manchester. Snow on the ground and overcast weather add to the depressing mood. 120 rollfilm negative scan.

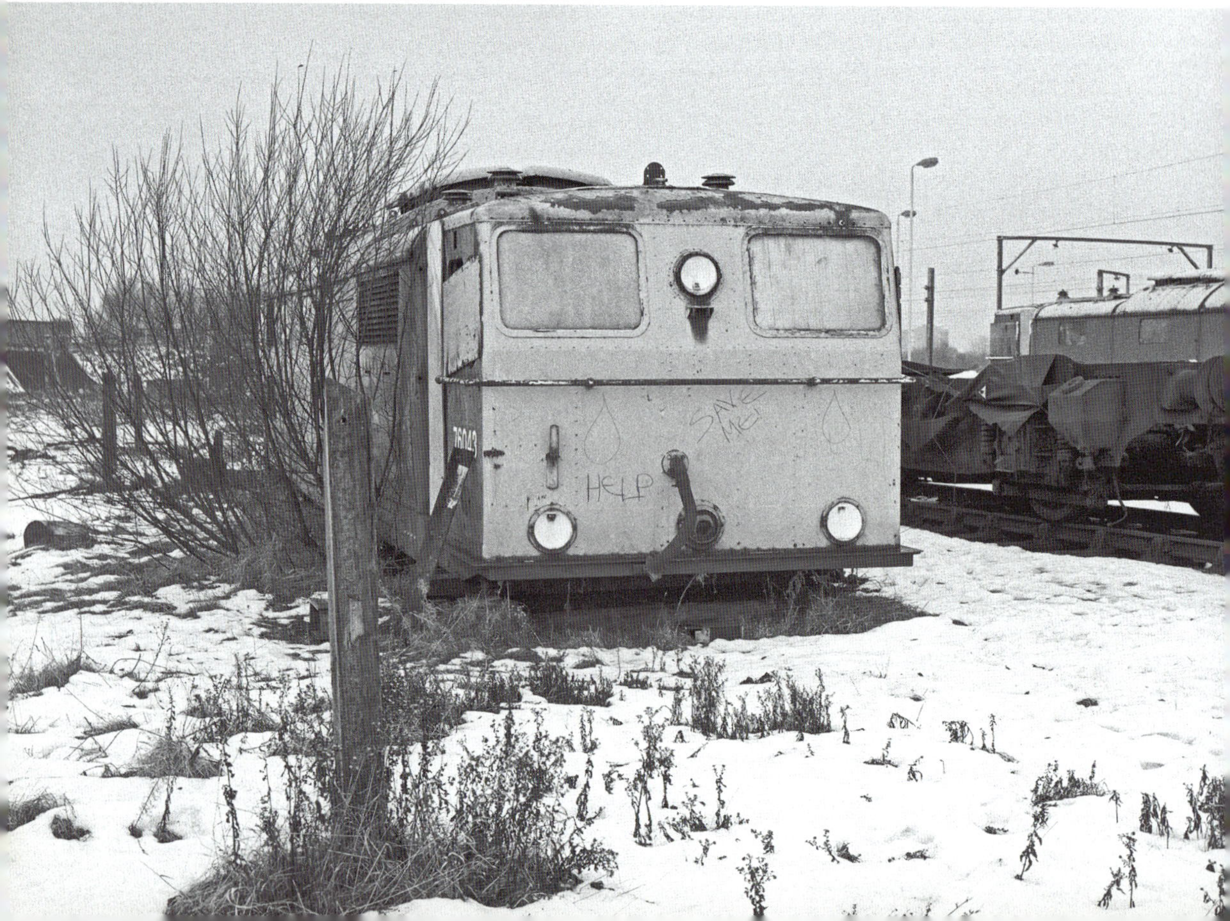

The weather will be a major factor in your decision to head out on a photographic trip. There are photographers that won't get their cameras out unless the sun is shining, but you should not be dissuaded from venturing out, or pack up and go home if cloud, rain, fog, or even snow are forecasted.

Clouds have a dramatic effect on the quality of the light, and add interest and perspective. A fully grey sky is admittedly the hardest for satisfactory railway photography, with muted colours and shadows non-existent. However, the even light will be ideal for capturing details, perhaps at a station or in a depot, where you can take time to use a higher ISO or slower shutter speed.

If rain comes, firstly make sure that both you and your camera are protected from the elements. As long as the rain isn't too heavy, it can provide some added contrast and depth to the image, and wet sleepers can help to reflect light up again onto the train. Take care that the raindrops don't affect the image. If it's really heavy, they will show up as short, blurred lines all over the image.

Stormy weather can provide the most dramatic effects, and some of the most powerful railway photographs depict a train bathed in a shaft of sunlight against a black and threatening sky. It's impossible to plan for such an event, but your experience will hopefully allow you to be in the right place at the right time and capture the magic.

Often, after a storm or heavy shower has passed, a rainbow makes a brief appearance. Hard to plan for, and always fleeting in visibility, but wonderful to see. Keep the sun behind you and try to shoot so that the colours are seen against a dark sky.

Fog seems to flatten the landscape and mute colours, making a distant or mid-range landscape view impossible. Consider a medium telephoto shot so that you are almost shooting in silhouette—the lack of colour and tonal range will help this effect. Post-shoot, you might also consider converting the image into black and white.

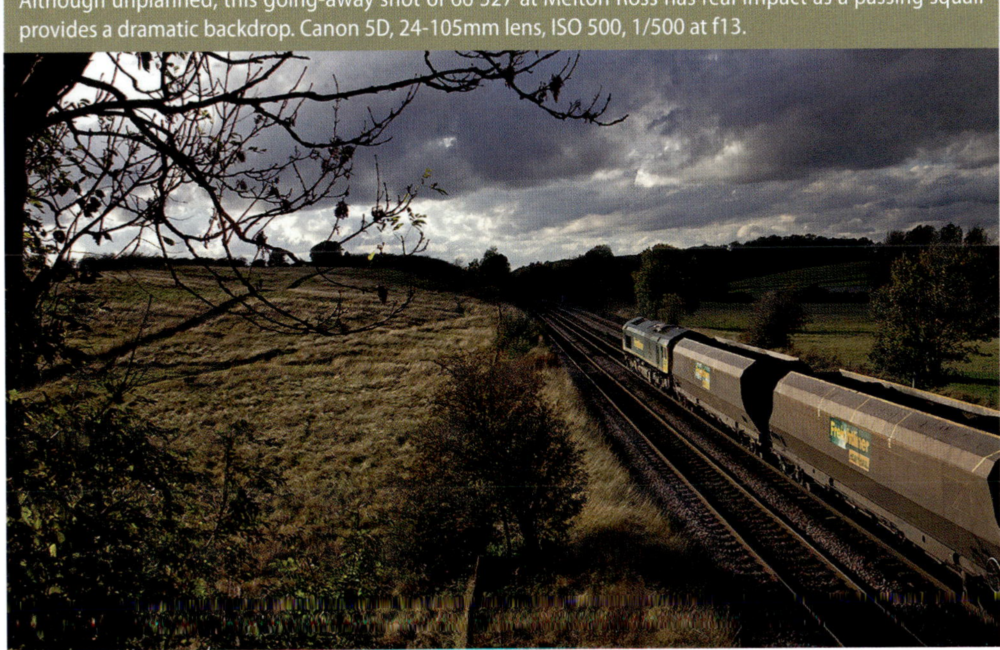

Although unplanned, this going-away shot of 66 527 at Melton Ross has real impact as a passing squall provides a dramatic backdrop. Canon 5D, 24-105mm lens, ISO 500, 1/500 at f13.

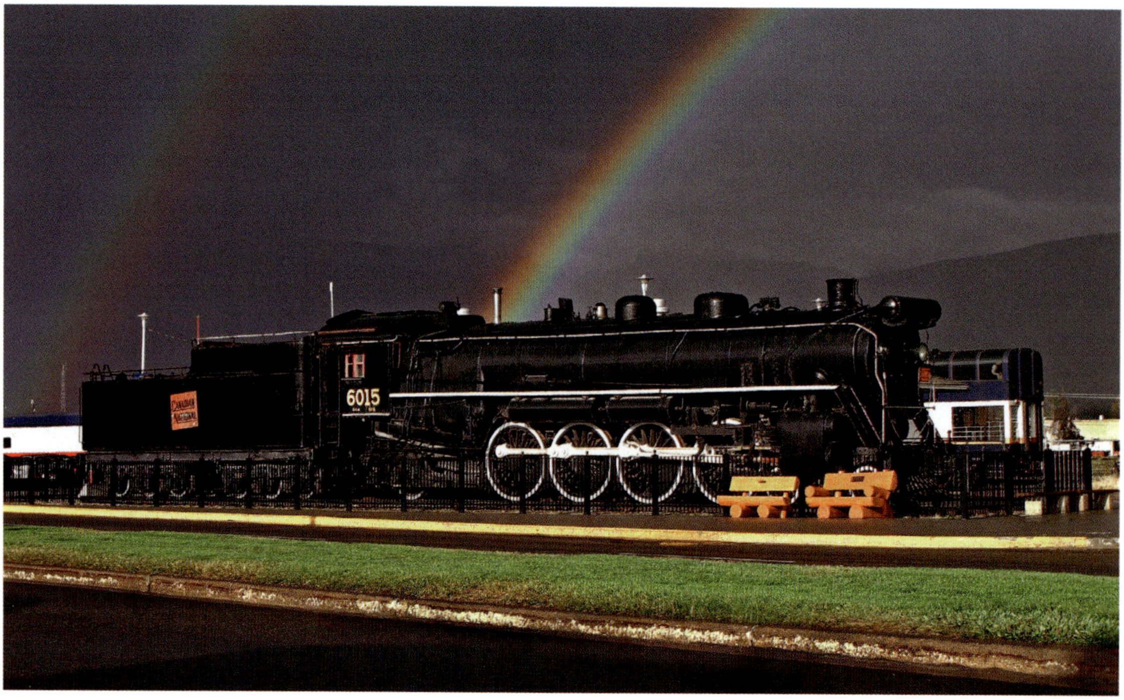

You will need to act fast to get a railway photo with a rainbow. Dark rain clouds make the colours stand out against the background. Canadian National 6015 at Jasper in 2007. Canon 10D, ISO 400, 1/180 at f11.

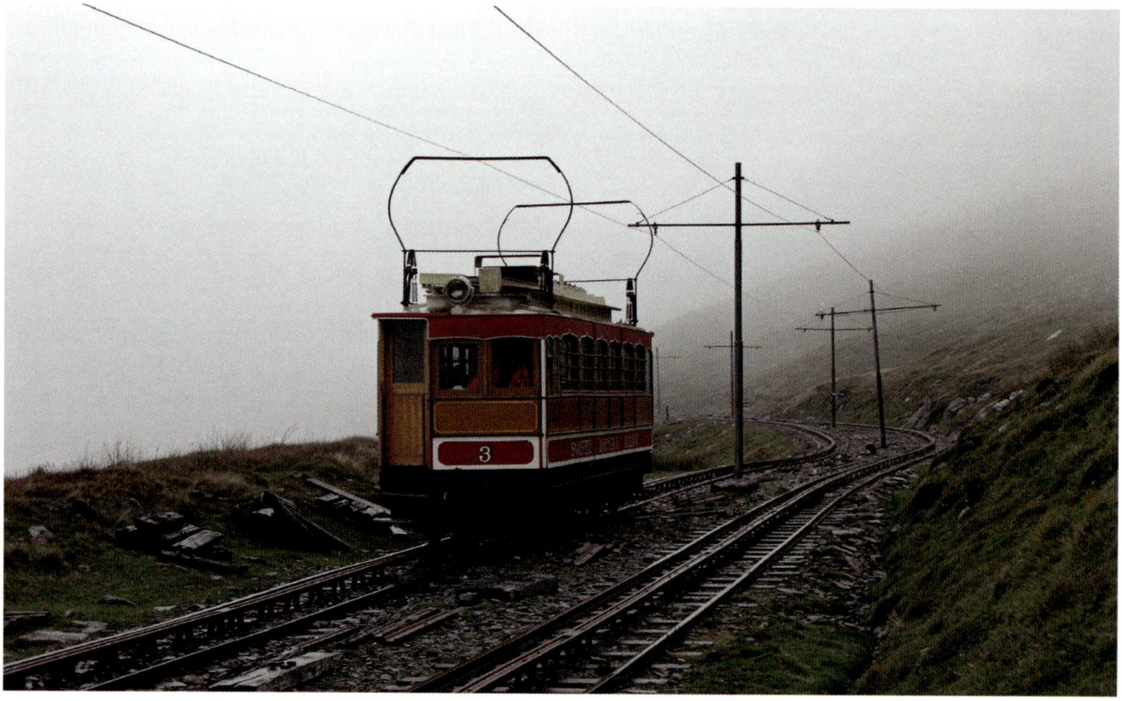

It's said that the views from Snaefell in the Isle of Man are incredible—well not on the day of this visit. Snaefell Mountain Railway car no. 3 descends through the fog in September 2010. Canon G9 compact, ISO 400, 1/800 at f4.

 Railway Photography

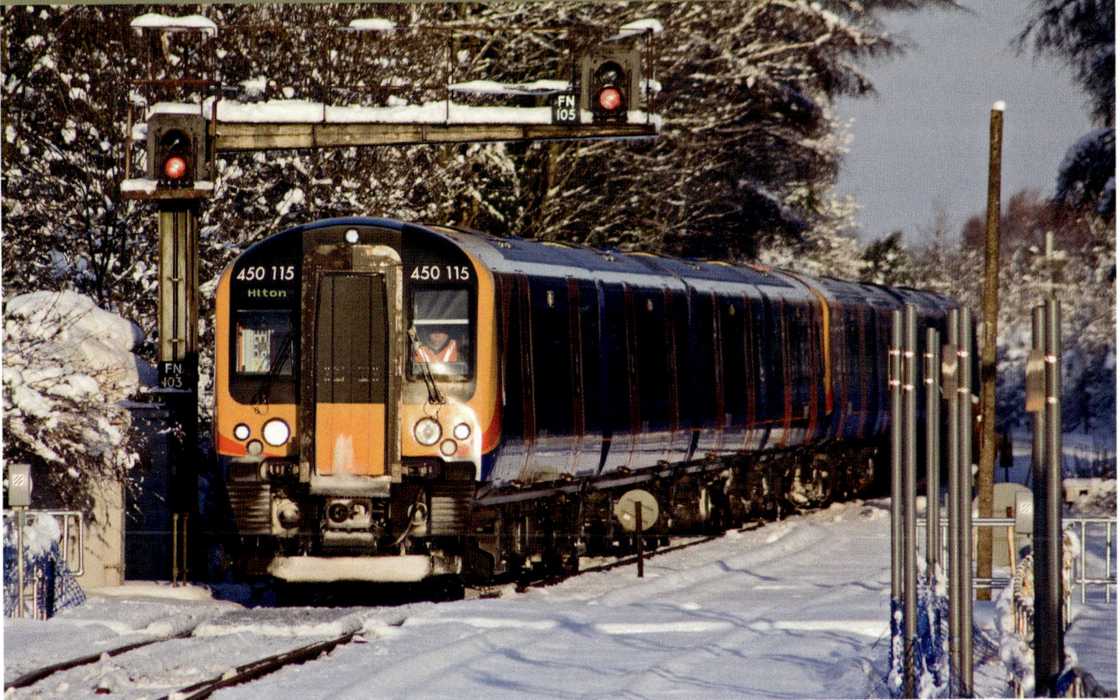

Sunshine after snow presents unique challenges—not least a really bright image, as the strong reflections will definitely affect the camera's light meter. SWT Desiro approaches Alton after a heavy snowfall in January 2010. Canon 40D, 70-300mm lens, ISO 160, 1/400 at f7.1 (NB: reading taken manually.)

Snow is probably the most challenging of conditions. You may experience difficulties in travelling to your chosen location, as well as the train timetable being affected by the weather. If there is snow on the ground but the weather is cloudy, colours will be flat. On the plus side, the snow will provide added reflected light to wheels and lower parts of the train. This brightness, especially if the sun does come out, will affect your camera's metering, so take test shots if you can and underexpose as necessary.

PEOPLE

It's all too easy to concentrate on the hardware in the railway scene and ignore the people, yet it's thanks to their hard work and dedication that the services run every day. Look out for people that can truly add to your photo's composition, or better still, use the character of the person to get greater involvement or tell a story.

In one of the pictures that follow, we can see the concentration on the fireman's face as he tops up the oil in his locomotive's cylinders. Look for expressions of concentration. A knowledge of the activities involved in the railway scene—handing over a signal token or a driver looking for a 'right away' signal—can be helpful.

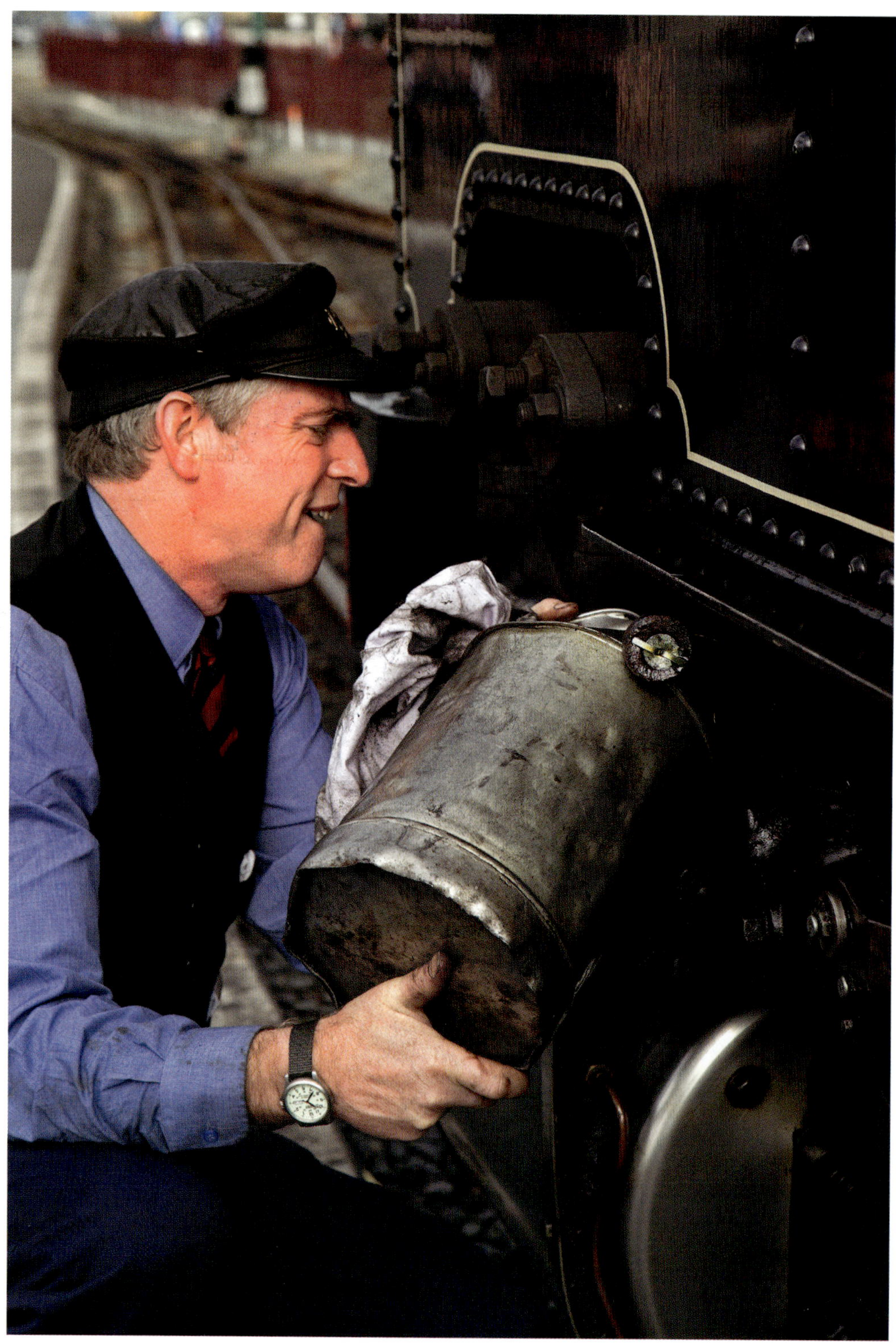

Easy does it. Topping up the lubricating oil ahead of a busy day on the Welsh Highland Railway. Canon 5D Mark III. 24-105mm lens, ISO 200, 1/320 at f7.1.

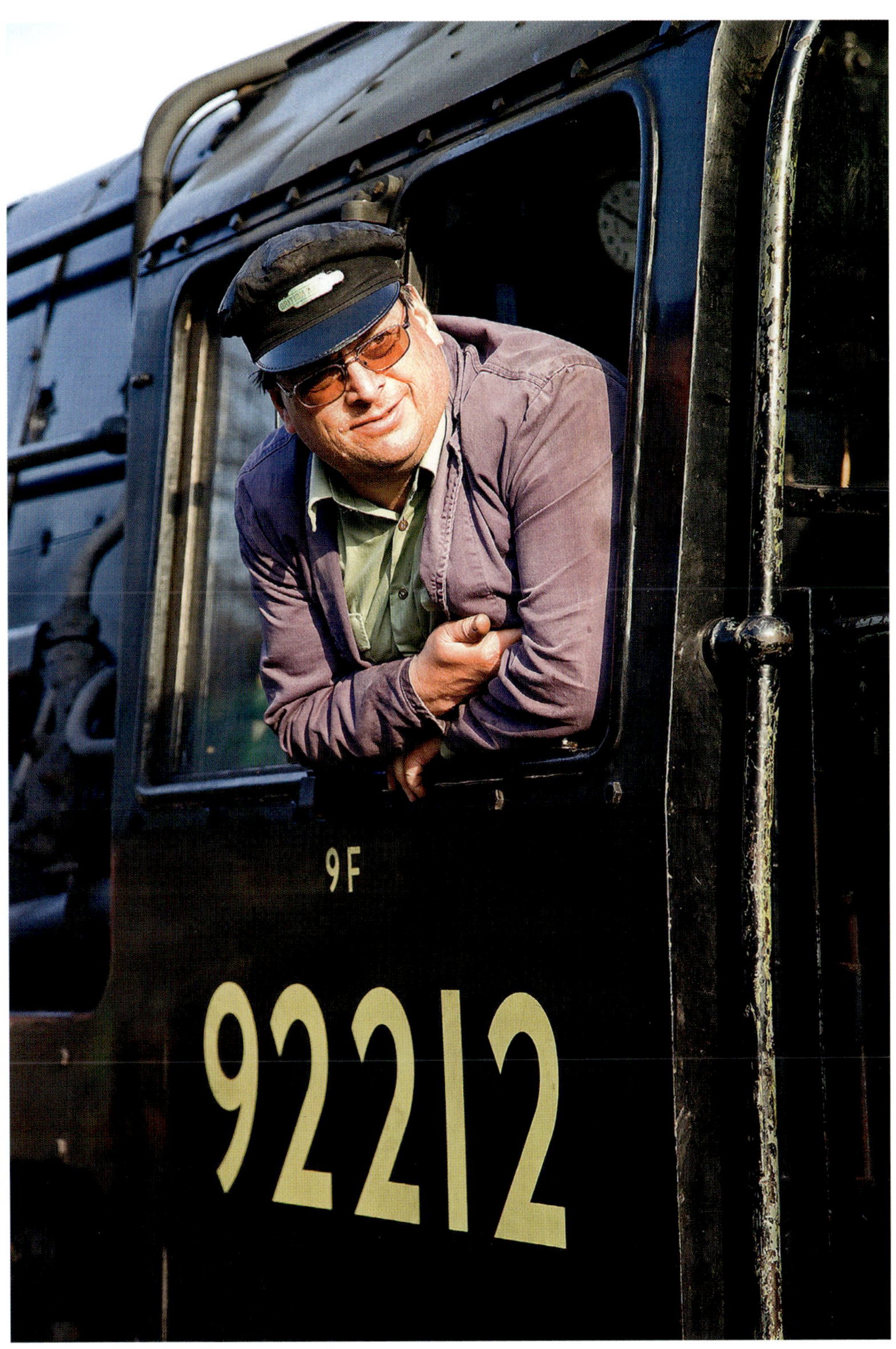

Catching the late afternoon sunshine, the driver of 92212 looks for the 'right away' on Ropley. Canon 5D, 24-105mm lens, ISO 250, 1/160 at f5.

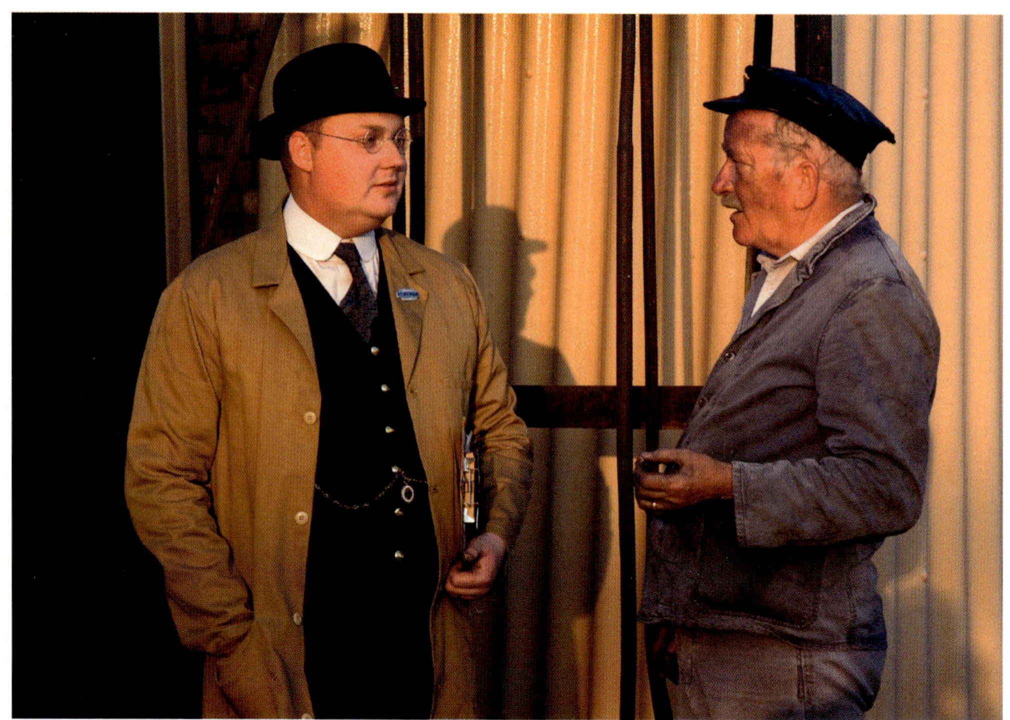

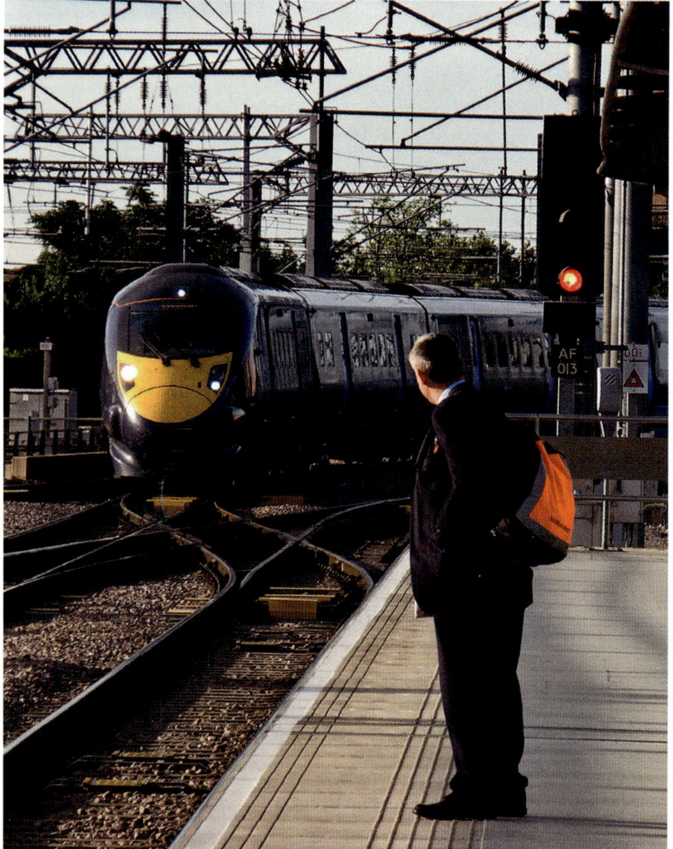

▲ Several photo events now include re-enactors who dress in period costume to add the final touches to a scene. Staged tableaux can really add character to a shoot. In this shot at Didcot railway centre, an 'errant' driver claims innocence from a clearly unimpressed depot foreman. Canon 5D, 24-105mm lens, ISO 400, 1/125 at f10.

◄ Waiting to take over the controls of a SouthEastern Javelin service at St Pancras, the relief driver watches the arrival of his steed at the end of the platform. Canon G9 compact. ISO 100, 1/320 at f4.8.

► A brand new S stock unit arrives at Barbican station in London while a London Underground worker looks on. Canon G9 compact, ISO 200, 1/250 at f8.

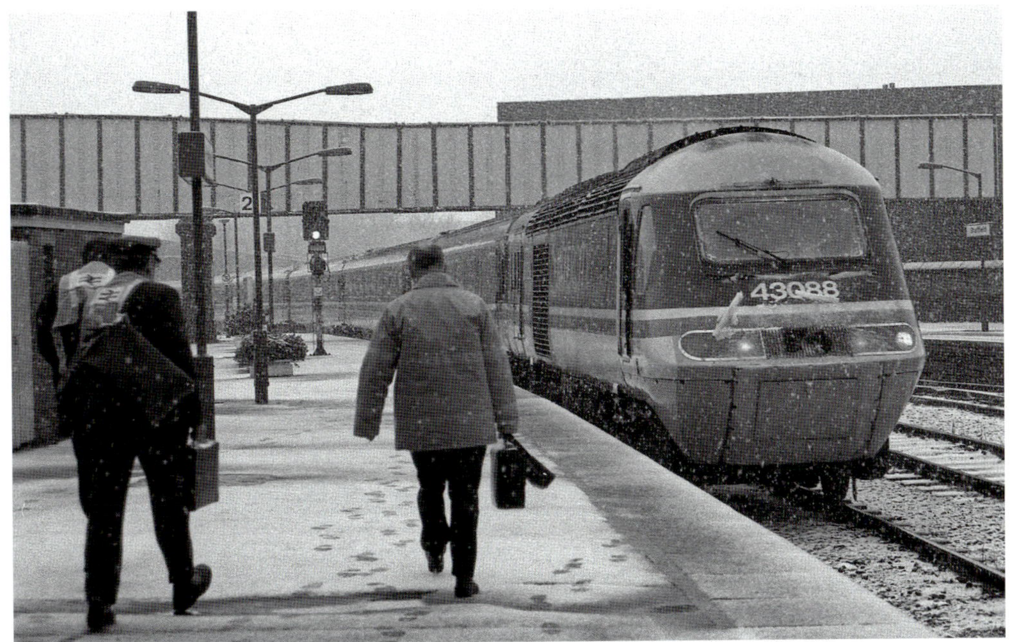

▲   Winter often provides moody scenes of the people who deliver the railway services every day. In this 1980s scan of a black and white negative, a BR crew brave the elements as an HST from London eases into the platform at Sheffield.

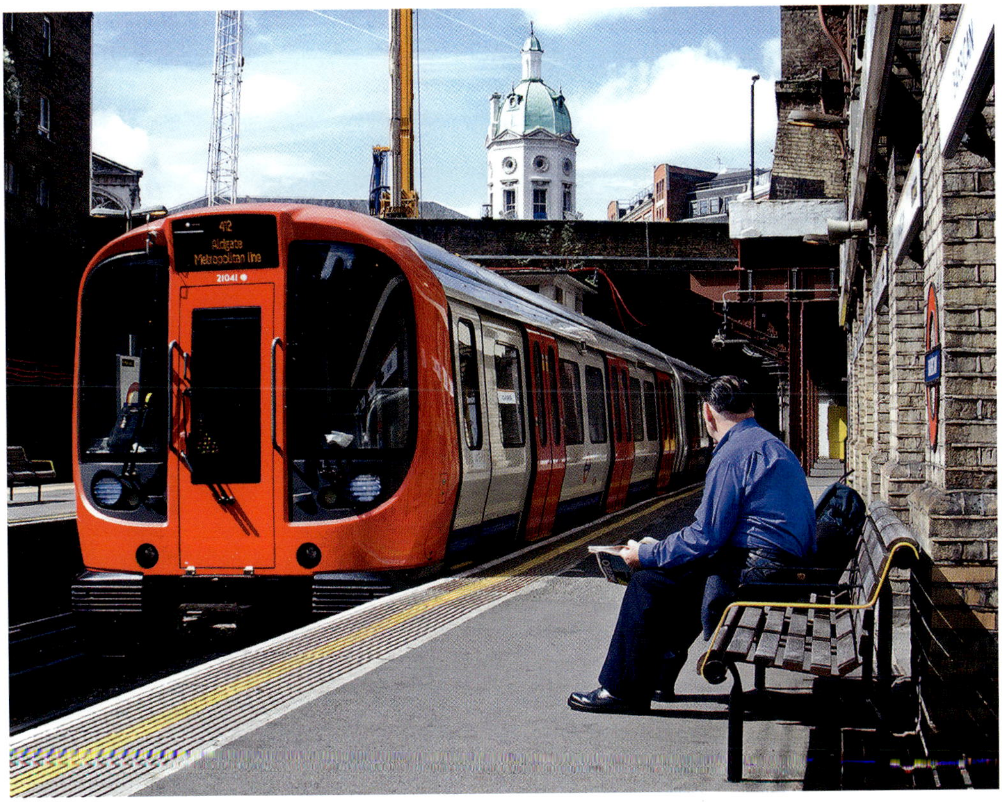

Telling the story

Similarly, the picture can tell a complete story in itself, with the train just being part of the scene. It's sometimes as easy as taking a step back—literally or metaphorically—and looking at your photo subject in a different context. Why is the train in that particular place at that particular time? Can you display the purpose of its journey, or activity, in the image? If your photo can convey that message, it begins to tell a story in itself, and possibly even becomes a valid historical statement.

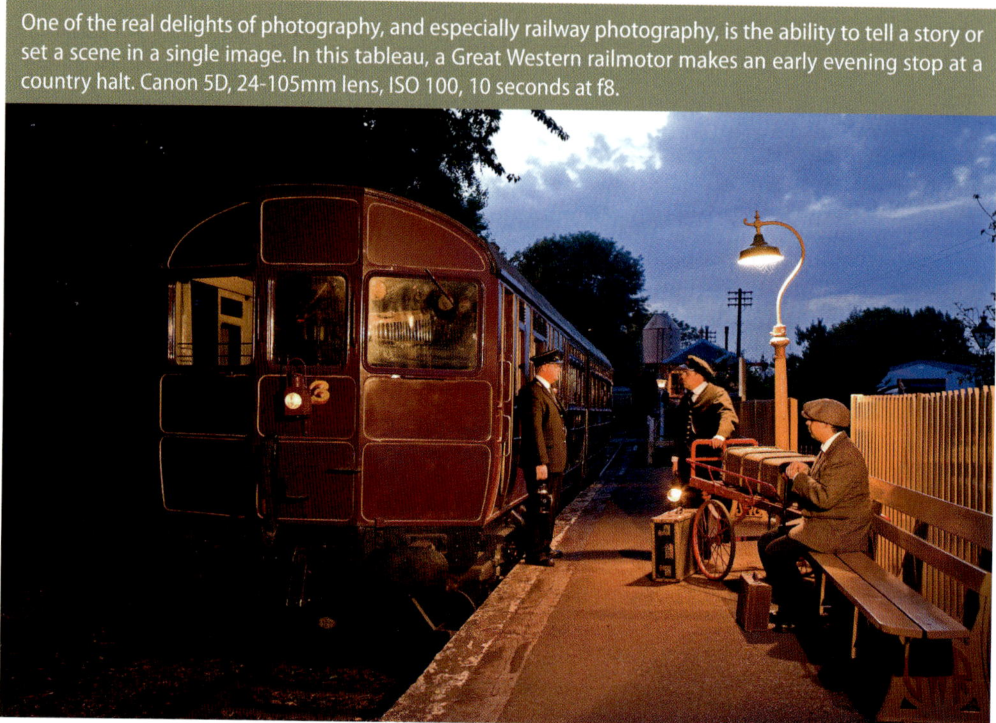

One of the real delights of photography, and especially railway photography, is the ability to tell a story or set a scene in a single image. In this tableau, a Great Western railmotor makes an early evening stop at a country halt. Canon 5D, 24-105mm lens, ISO 100, 10 seconds at f8.

INFRASTRUCTURE AND ENVIRONMENT

Buildings and structures

Quite apart from the trains and other rolling stock, the infrastructure of the railway network is rich in interest and detail, and can yield beautiful results. You may be attracted by the art or symmetry of light and shadow, or by the grand style of buildings old or new. Ultra-modern can, in its own way, be as captivating as historic or derelict. Approach any visit to a location with an open mind, and be on the lookout for hidden gems.

Photography of buildings and other structures can present challenges. To include the whole of the subject in the frame, you may need to either use a wide angle lens, or move your viewpoint backward. A wide angle will cause distortion (the straight vertical lines, will appear to diverge), so be prepared for that.

Floodlighting or neon signs may help transform an otherwise drab structure—look for opportunities to show these. Equally, a low morning or evening sun may create interesting colour patters or silhouettes. Expose for the lightest area in order to create a bold and dramatic image.

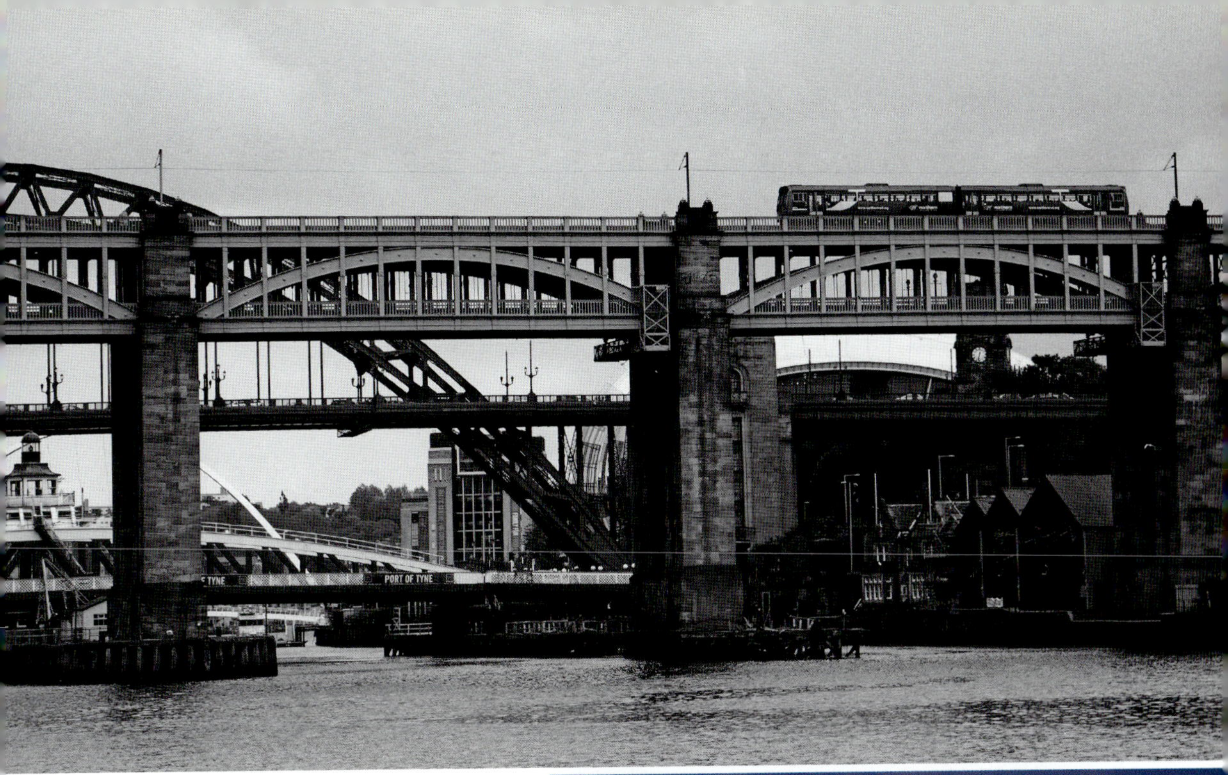

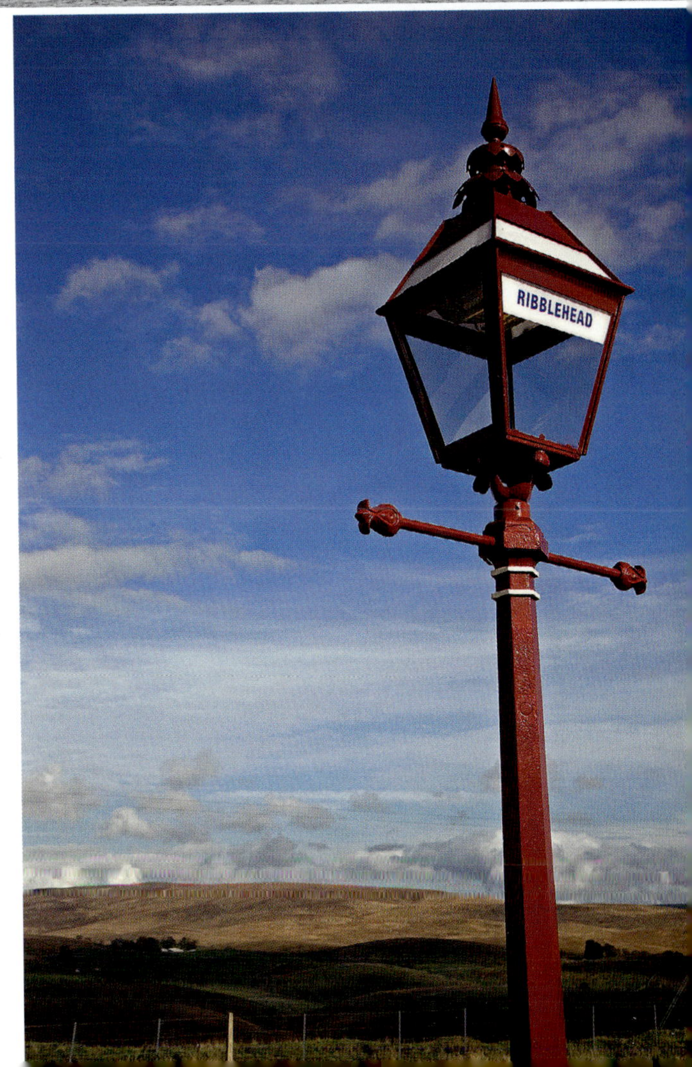

▲ The classic lines of the bridges over the Tyne in central Newcastle are recognisable the world over. The tiny two-car diesel unit slowly traverses on its approach to Newcastle Central station. The hoped-for sunny weather did not materialise for this shoot, so conversion to black and white gave this industrial image a lift. Canon 5D Mark III, ISO 320, 1/400 at f8.

▶ Change at Ribblehead for … well, not very much, unless you like the great outdoors. One of the platform lamps sets the scene of the remote station on the picturesque Settle to Carlisle line. Canon 5D, 24-105mm lens, ISO 200, 1/320 at f10.

Detail

Advance research, such as looking at the work of other photographers, may help you identify fascinating historic details. All over the railway network, there are many clues to the heritage of the system, such as rail chairs, boundary markers, or signs. This is a whole area of interest in itself, and a valuable way of recording the heritage of rail transport. It's also worth recording the detail when you see it—the relentless march of change often sweeps away the little items that make the railway unique.

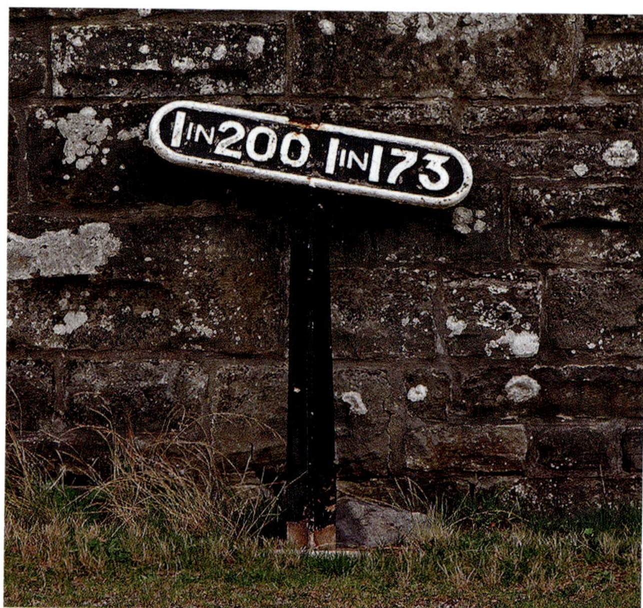

◀ Many preserved railways strive to keep the entire railway environment as genuine and realistic as possible, and that includes small details such as gradient posts. Many are original, although in some locations replicas take their place to deter theft. This gradient post can be seen at Parkend on the Dean Forest Railway. Canon 5D, 24-105mm lens, ISO 200, 1/320 at f10.

▼ Locomotive nameplates are an obvious target for photography. Canon 5D, 24-105mm lens.

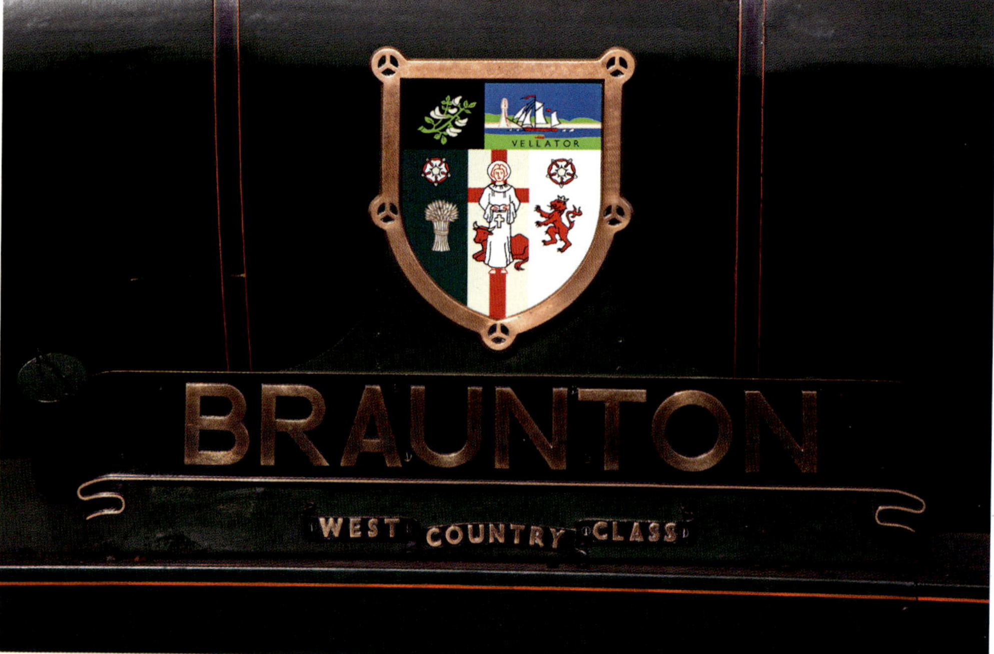

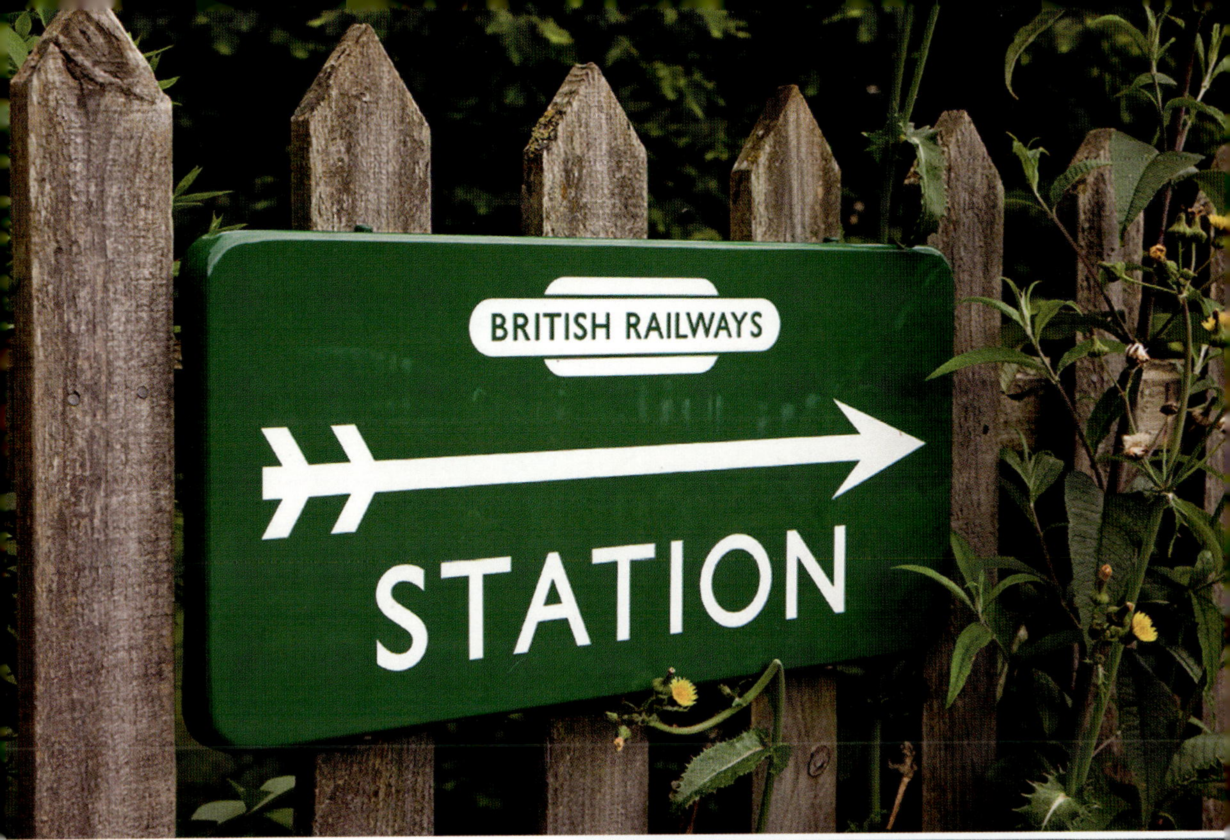

▲ At Corfe Castle on the Swanage Railway, this British Railways sign still guides the way to the station. Canon 5D, 24-105mm lens, ISO 100, 1/200 at f9.

▶ One can almost smell the steam and grease.... Close up photographs, such as a steam locomotive's valve gear, help to convey the complexity and intricacy of railway engineering. Canon 5D Mark III, 24-105mm lens, ISO 200, 1/320 at f4.

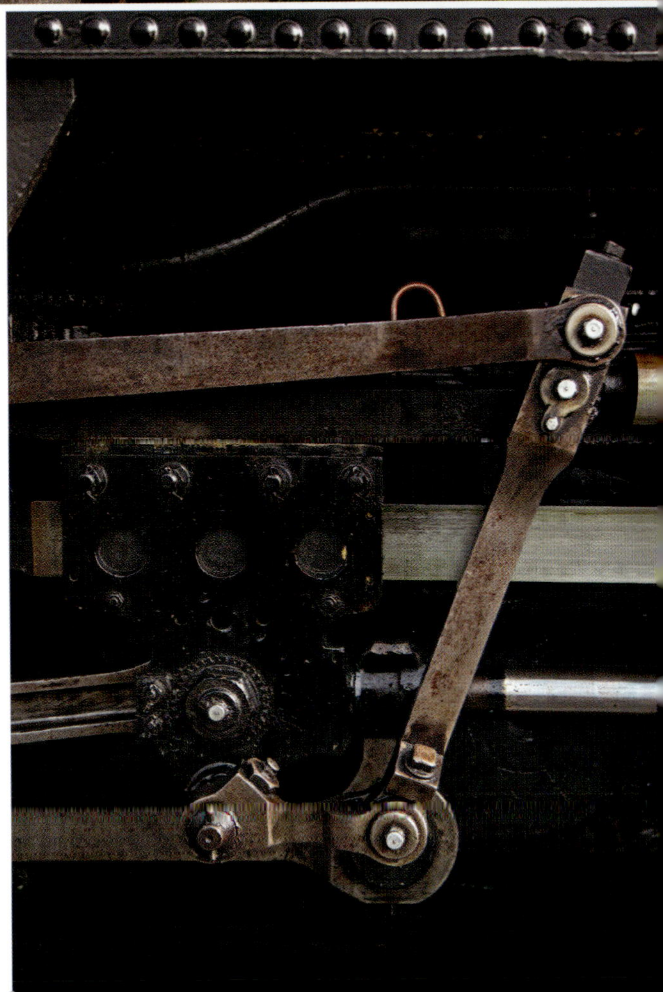

Landscape

A photograph of the railway or a train in the landscape can say as much about purpose and value of the subject as the detailed record shot. It will show the scale of the environment through which the railway passes, and perhaps the hard work of the locomotive through a plume of steam or the smoke of exhaust.

Photographically, consider the aspect and strength of the light and how it will strike your subject. An excellent free programme, www.suncalc.net, will show the direction of sunrise and sunset and where the sun will be at any chosen time of day. You just have to input the desired location through its postcode, or by clicking on the map.

For traditional results, have the sun behind you so that the train is illuminated. A test shot before the train arrives will help you ascertain whether your exposure is correct. If your camera displays a histogram evaluation of the photo, this will help you check whether the exposure is balanced.

Don't be afraid to experiment, such as seeking a wider viewpoint. The time of day may have a great effect on the quality of light in the landscape. Quite apart from the direction, the long shadows and colours of early morning or evening have a magic all of their own, and can create wonderful effects. The high summer midday sun can be flat and with high contrast. However, although shadows may be deep, an urban landscape may more suited to this, and you might find the opportunity for bright colours and abstract shapes.

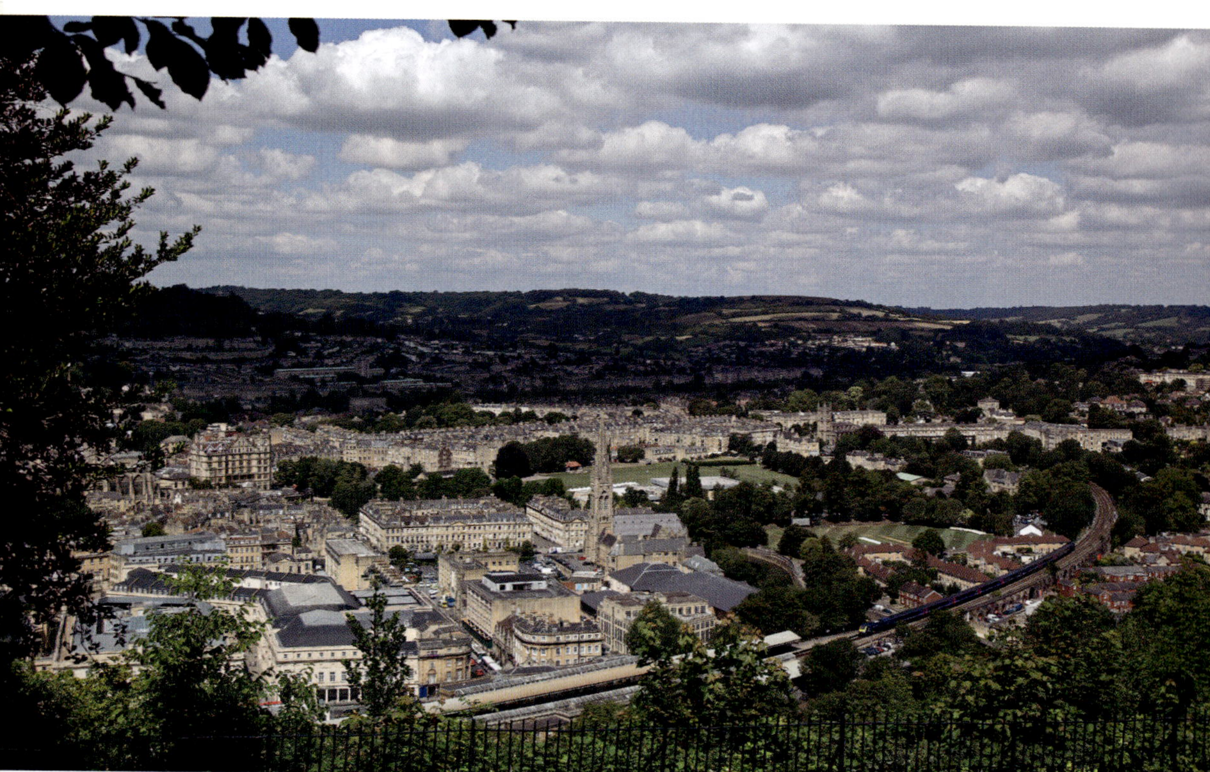

From a park high above Bath, one has a magnificent view of the city, and of course the railway's sweeping curve as it approaches the station. A First Great Western HST can be seen departing to the East towards London. Canon 5D Mark III, 24-105mm lens, ISO 160, 1/400 at f10.

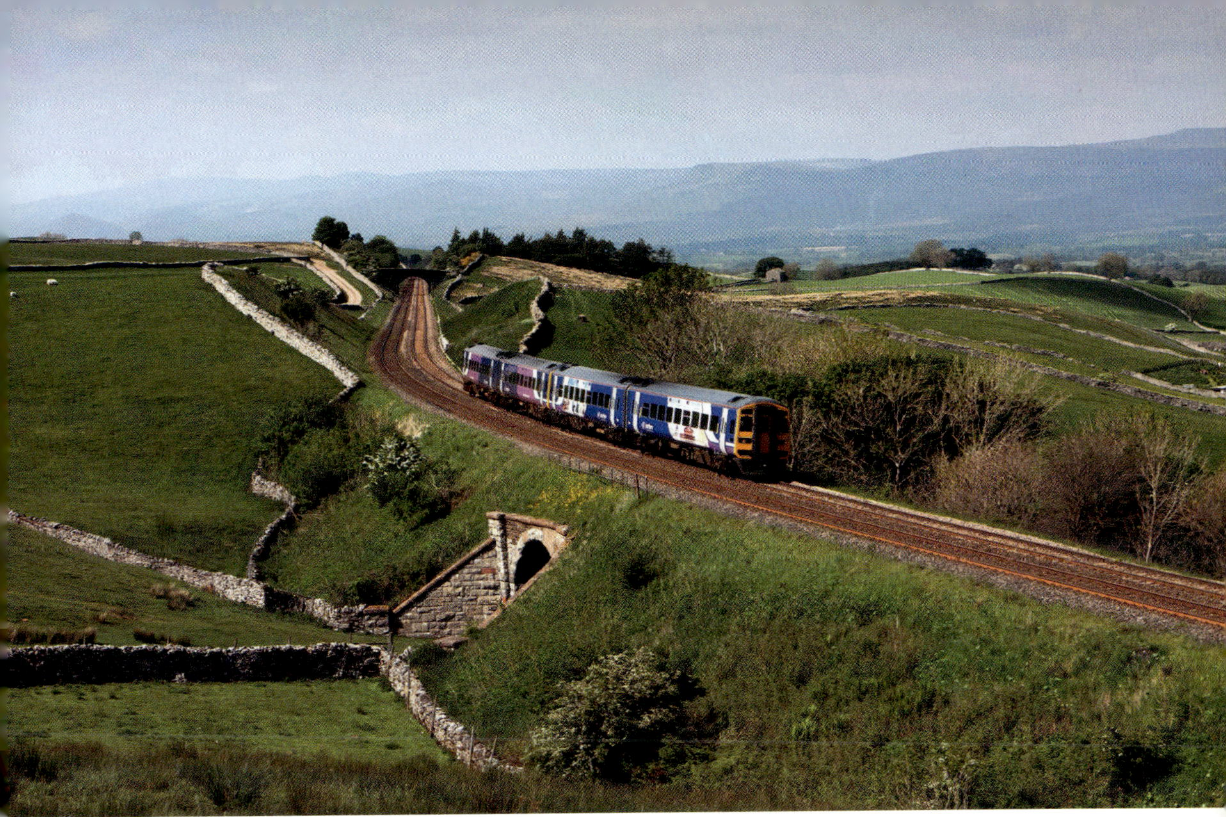

The railway in the landscape is part of our heritage, and many people correctly associate the beautiful Settle to Carlisle line with wild moors and imposing bridges. In this view, a local service led by 158 904 is climbing past Birkett Common on its journey south. Canon 40D, 50mm lens, ISO 320, 1/400 at f11.

Night or underground photography

Railway photography at night or indoors is an art form all on its own. In the days of film, one usually needed a hand-held light meter to assess exposure, and even then several exposures at different settings to get it right. The latest digital cameras have such a wide ISO capability, it is possible to take hand-held shots at night.

If you have a camera that can handle low light conditions, set the ISO to as high as you can. For shooting on a London Underground platform for example, you will need ISO 4000 to achieve a 1/250th or 1/500th shutter speed, at an extremely low f-stop. The higher the ISO rating you choose, the more noisy (or grainy) the image will be. There are propriety software programmes such as Neat Image, that can help reduce noise in the final image, but it is always best to get as best quality you can in the original image. If you are shooting on the London Underground, flash photography and tripods are banned for safety reasons, so if fitted, make sure that the autoflash on your camera is switched off.

For high quality results, and where its use is permitted, use a tripod, with a low ISO rating and slow shutter speed. Be wary of aircraft, satellites, and even stars in the night sky, as during your timed exposure, their movement will be visible as a line or light trail. Of course, you can clone this out later on your computer, but they can be confusing until you know what they are.

If your lens has image stabilisation, turn this OFF for time exposures. Your camera will attempt to stabilise the exposure when it's actually not needed, resulting in blurred images.

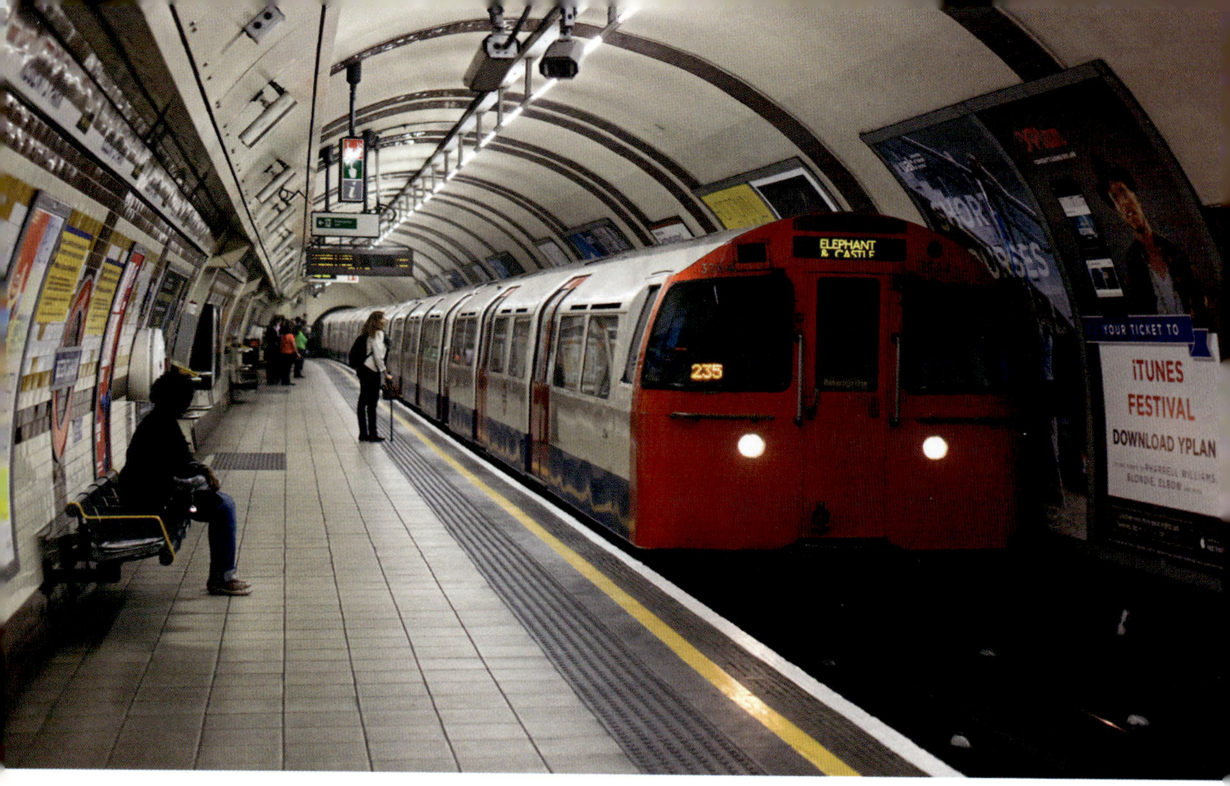

▲ Until recently, hand-held photography on underground railways was almost impossible. Advances in digital photography technology now permit high quality photography without the need for tripods. South-bound Bakerloo line unit 3264 arrives at Regents Park. Canon 5D Mark III, 50mm f1.4 lens, ISO 4000, 1/500 at f2.8.

▼ For the best results, a tripod is essential, and ideally, some lighting to illuminate your subject. During an enthusiast photographic event, GWR King class 6023 poses by the coaling stage while its fire is disposed of. Canon 5D, 24-105mm lens, ISO 100, 25 seconds at f8.

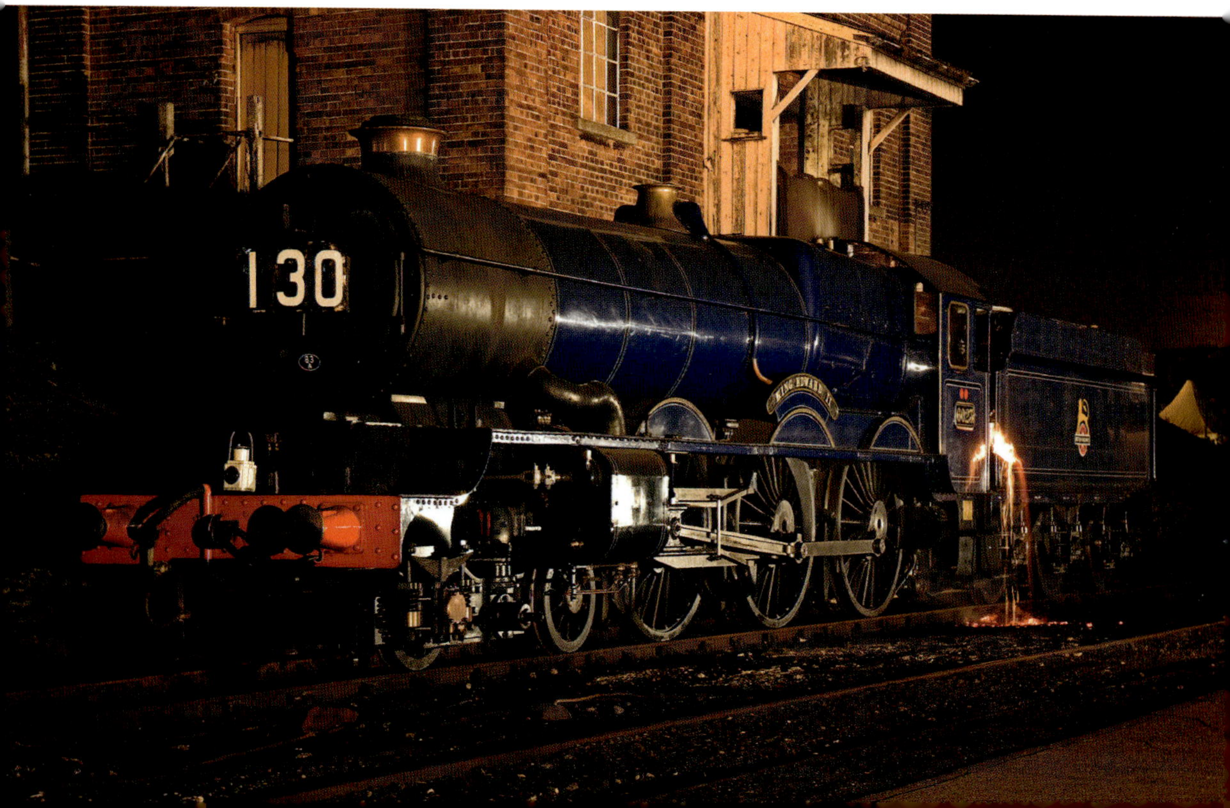

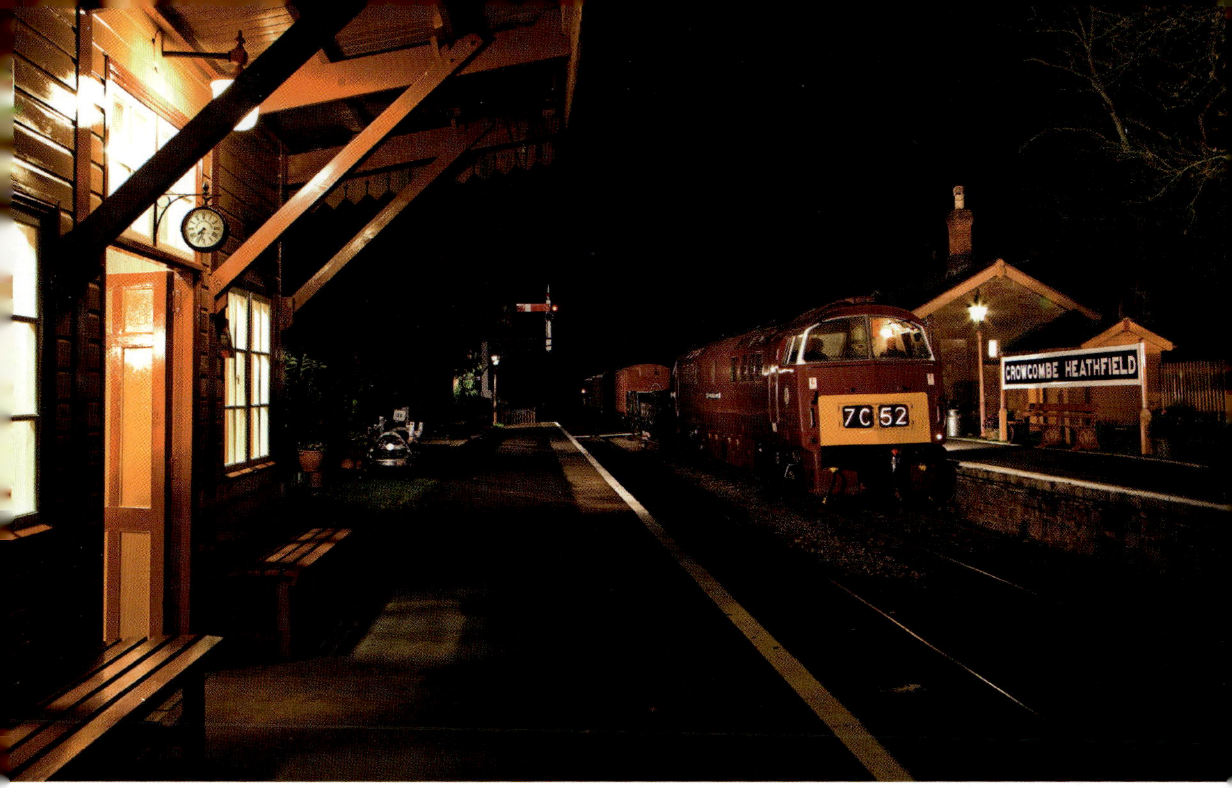

▲ With a little imagination, movement can be implied in a time exposure photograph even if all the elements are still. Western class loco D1035 'arrives' at Crowcombe Heathfield on the West Somerset Railway during such an event. Canon 5D, 24-105mm lens, ISO 100, 13 sec at f9.

▼ Where lighting is at a premium, one just as to rely on available light, and careful positioning. A locally arranged shoot at the Mid Hants Railway yielded this pleasing composition of visiting motive power during the 2013 diesel gala weekend. Canon 5D, 24-105mm lens, ISO 125, 8 seconds at f7.1.

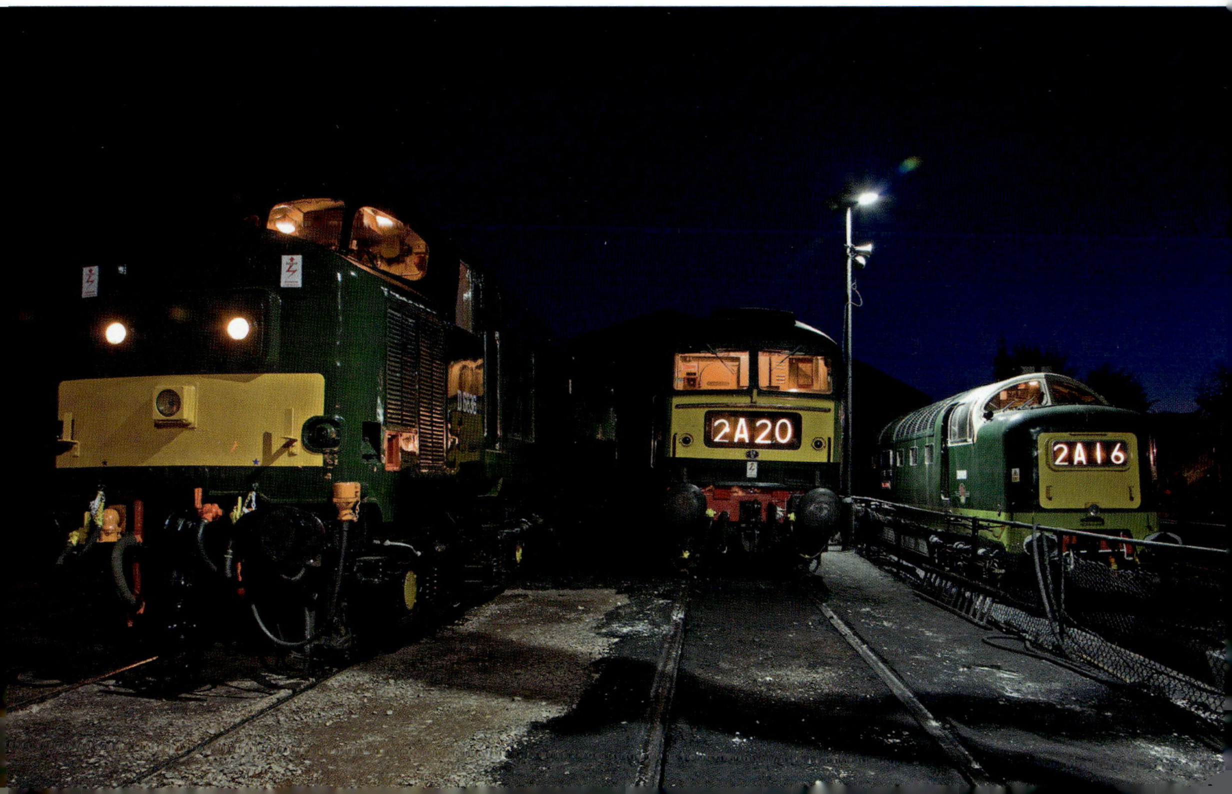

One of the newest innovations in railway photography is pole photography. Using wireless technology, a wi-fi hotspot device attached to the camera links to a tablet computer or mobile phone. The user controls the camera from a distance, and by using a sturdy decorator's pole, for example, considerable height can be gained.

For obvious reasons, NEVER attempt to use pole photography in the vicinity of overhead line equipment. Your camera will also need to be secured rigidly to the pole. There are few bespoke accessories for doing this, but some photographers have made their own.

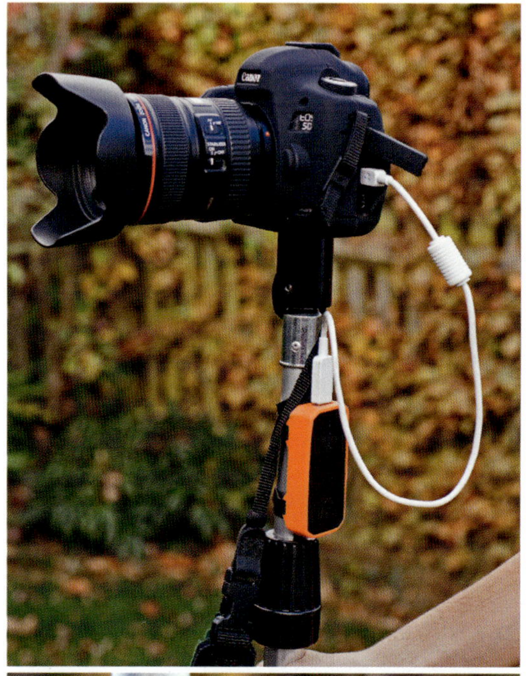

◄ This image shows a Canon 5D Mark III, mounted on a decorator's pole with a bespoke adaptor. Wireless transmission is achieved with the Weye Feye accessory, which acts as a wi-fi hotspot and allows full camera control to a mobile phone or tablet device.

▼ Control of the camera is achieved through an 'app', linking the mobile phone in this case to the image transmitter. Most camera adjustments are possible, as the live view through the viewfinder can be seen on the mobile device, and the shutter triggered remotely.

TROUBLESHOOTING

 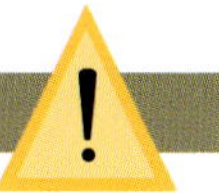

There can be little more disappointing than not securing the photo you've been planning for weeks and made a special trip for. With a little care, you can easily avoid the common pitfalls, and save the stress.

Battery flat

Make sure you have charged or fresh batteries before you set out. Camera batteries do degrade over time, losing their ability to retain the power. You may get a full indicator on your charger, only to see the strength disappear quickly on location. Always keep spares in your bag, and rotate them through your camera from time to time. Aftermarket batteries may be frowned upon by the manufacturers, but in practice they are as good as the originals, and usually a lot less expensive.

Memory card full

Have you taken the photos from your last trip off the card? To avoid arriving on location to find you only have room for a dozen shots, get into the habit of preparing for the next trip as you pack away from the last one.

Memory card not inserted

No excuse for this. Insert a memory card! Many cameras will warn you that no card is present when you switch the camera on. Keep a spare or two in your camera bag. Even if they are not large in media size, they will tide you over for a few hours and ensure your trip isn't a complete washout!

Memory card failure

Like a computer hard drive, a camera memory card can suffer a sudden fault, and become unusable. There's little you can do if on location, so make sure you have a spare, and insert that straight away. Don't throw the old card away—although you might not want to trust it in future, you can still use inexpensive software to retrieve the images.

Camera error

If your camera freezes and refuses to work—don't despair. Although never a good sign, you can try a couple of steps that may just help you to keep shooting. Turn the camera off, and then on again. If still no luck, turn off again, and take the battery and memory card out. Wait for a few minutes, and try again. The battery may be low on charge, so try inserting a spare. The camera may display a message to say what is wrong, or just remain locked. If still no luck, you have little option but to seek a professional repair. Some photographers carry a second camera body or compact in their bag on an important shoot, as a backup.

Blurred photo

This is probably the most common fault of all, and has several possible causes:

Camera shake. Press the shutter button gently, don't stab at it. Especially important in low light and where the shutter speed may be slow. If you can, use a tripod to be absolutely sure, but if not, you can do one of the following: raise the ISO setting to allow for a faster shutter speed, brace yourself against a lamppost or wall, or rest the camera itself on a stable, flat object.

Too slow shutter speed. Unless trying for a special or creative effect, increase the shutter speed to freeze the action. The depth of field may fall off into the background, but pre focusing on the position where you want the train to be will help. Increasing the ISO rating will also help.

Auto white balance/colour cast

The time of day, and different light sources, produce variations in the colour of light, which can have a noticeable effect on photographs. These differences are referred to on a colour temperature scale (in degrees Kelvin, or K). The lower the colour temperature, the more red light predominating, and therefore the 'warmer' the light will appear. As the colour temperature rises, the more blue light is prevalent, and the 'cooler' the light we observe.

Artificial light sources will produce strong colour casts due to the predominance of light at certain colour temperatures, giving your pictures excessively orange or red hues for example. A camera is normally set as a default to assess the colour temperature automatically. Some have settings to adjust for cloudy or interior locations. These are fine in most cases, but if you are planning a shoot where the quality of the results are critical to you, and your camera allows, consider a custom white balance to get things 100 per cent right. Take a colour temperature reading from a white or mid grey source (e.g. a sheet of paper) and use this setting for your shoot.

Specks on your photos, also known as 'dust bunnies'

These are small, often circular grey marks visible on your image when viewed on your computer screen. They're caused by small pieces of dust or other materials that have got into your camera and settled on your camera's sensor.

NEVER try to remove them with your fingers, or blow them away with your mouth. No matter how clean you think your fingers are, you will end up leaving a greasy residue on the most sensitive part of your camera. If you blow, you will possibly leave microscopic moisture droplets on the sensor.

Some cameras have an auto sensor clean function that vibrates the sensor to dislodge any unwanted materials. You can also get a blower brush that will gently direct air over the sensor. Don't be tempted to use compressed air—it's usually icy cold and will condense on the sensor. If you're confident, you can buy specialist fluids and cleaning swabs for your camera. These are effective, but require care in use and a steady hand. If the problem is bad, you may find it easiest to send the camera to its manufacturer or a specialist repairer, for a service and clean.

'Noisy' photos

In digital photography, noise is the equivalent of grain in the film world. The latest cameras have stunning low light capabilities that will allow for a reasonably noise-free output in conditions that would have been impossible just a few years ago. Always go for the lowest ISO rating possible to minimize the effect.

Deleted images

All is not lost if you have deleted the images from you memory card by mistake. SanDisk's RescuePro is a simple programme you can purchase cheaply that will carry out a scan of the card, and unless you have formatted it, it will usually find images you thought were gone forever. Another is the aptly titled iRecover, which does a similar job.

Magnetic fields

Whichever type of memory card you use in your camera, remember that, just like your credit cards or even railway ticket, it is a magnetic storage item, and will be affected by strong magnetic fields. Keep them away from transformers, loudspeakers, and similar devices, which have strong fields around. Bringing the card too close will corrupt the data (i.e. scramble the image), and you will not be able to recover the file.

Caring for your equipment

Your camera will hopefully be one of your most treasured possessions, and it is common sense to look after it. Protective rubber 'skins' are relatively cheap and available for most DSLRs. They can be kept on the body permanently and as well as providing basic impact protection, help make your valuable item less conspicuous to prying eyes. Delkin and Camera Armour have a wide variety of choices for most cameras currently available.

Your camera's rear screen is a vital part of the body whether you use a DSLR, CSC, bridge or compact. Protective glass protection can be obtained cheaply that will stick to the glass of your screen permanently and help you avoid scratches and moisture.

Insurance should be considered in case of theft or damage. Many home insurance policies now include cover for personal possessions, even when used away from the home. These are excellent value for money and in many cases you do not have to itemise the equipment as long as the value is not excessive. If you own a high end camera body or lenses, notify the insurer about these specific items and cover can be arranged for only a few pounds more. If the worst does occur and your equipment is stolen or badly damaged, keep a note of serial numbers (in advance!) so that a police report can be filed, and a claim made.

Location Techniques

PANNING

Normally in railway photography, freezing the action with a crisp, sharp shot is the primary objective, but there are occasions when you may deliberately want to show blurring. You may want to specifically illustrate a sense of movement, which can be by either through a carefully composed shot with movement, either of people or the train, shown through blurring of the subject, or by panning, so that the subject is sharp and the background is blurred.

In both cases, focusing and shutter speed control are key. By utilising the shutter priority mode, the camera will look after the aperture value. For people walking, a shutter speed of below 1/15th second will show blurring. Moving trains will obviously be travelling faster, so 1/200th or below may give the effect you desire. For a composed static shot, a tripod or other solid base will support the camera, and take the photo as the subject passes across the frame. A few practice shots will help you decide on the optimum balance of exposure and framing.

Panning is definitely a technique that requires practice. Firstly, set your camera's autofocus points so that all are active. This will increase your chances of a sharp shot. With a lowish ISO and shutter priority value selected, set your camera to continuous autofocus mode. This will ensure the camera tracks the moving train. Most important of all, however, is the way you move the camera to follow the subject.

Stand with your feet apart and hold the camera firmly. Have an idea in your head of the position at which you want to take the shot. As the train passes across your viewpoint, follow it

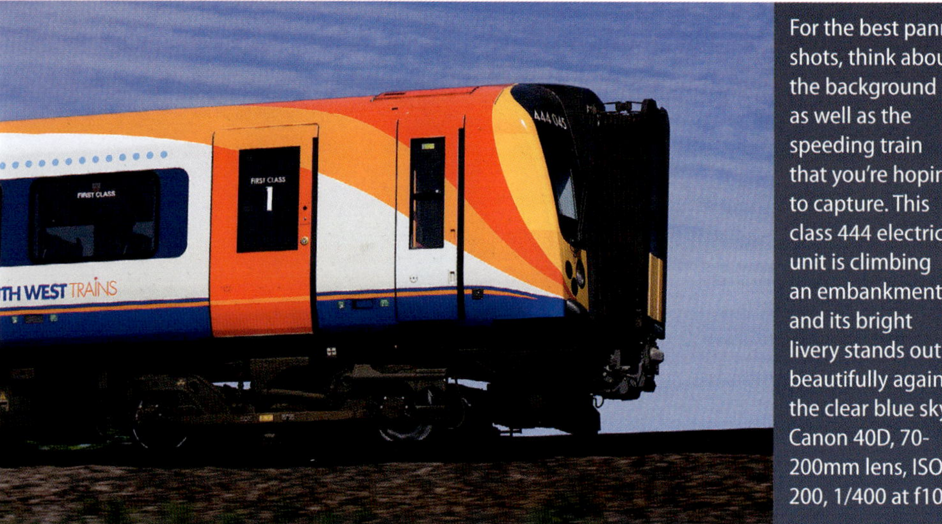

For the best panned shots, think about the background as well as the speeding train that you're hoping to capture. This class 444 electric unit is climbing an embankment, and its bright livery stands out beautifully against the clear blue sky. Canon 40D, 70-200mm lens, ISO 200, 1/400 at f10.

with the lens, and at the desired spot, take the photo. Continue to follow the subject through the lens in one fluid movement. This smooth panning motion will help you to achieve a sharp subject against a blurred background.

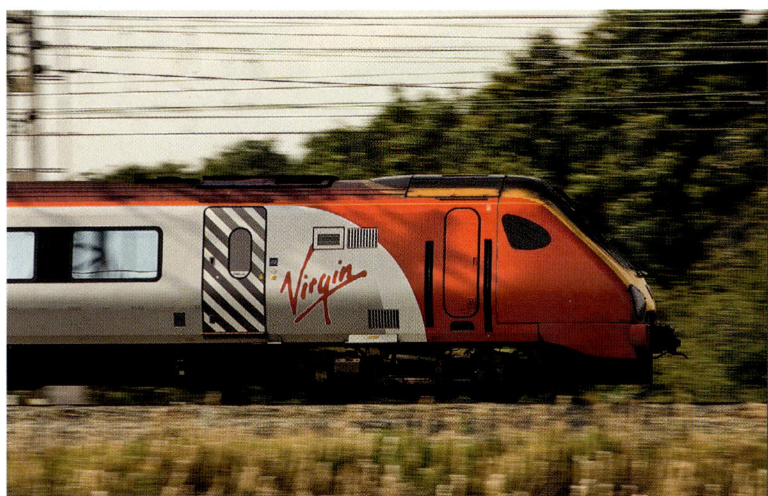

Movement against a detailed background, such as the trees behind this Virgin Voyager unit, calls for a slow shutter speed, and the panning technique helps to keep the train sharp while the leaves appear blurred. Panning also heightens the visual impression of speed. Canon 40D, 70-200mm lens, ISO 160, 1/200 at f10.

OVER OR UNDER EXPOSURE

A strongly lit background, or deep shadows, can sometimes fool a camera into overcompensating, resulting in a picture that's too light or too dark. You may want to create a special effect, but for an accurate exposure, there are a number of ways to override the camera's meter reading and still get a good exposure.

Almost every digital camera will have an exposure compensation control. Depending on your camera, you should be able to adjust the exposure by increments of ½ or ⅓ of a stop. It works logically, so adding a '+' value will make the image lighter, and adding a '-' will make it darker. For example, if you are shooting a snowy scene, apply a value between -1 to -2 EV. Remember to reset normal when you have completed your adjusted scene shoot.

Another useful tool is the Autoexposure Lock (AE-L) control. This doesn't adjust the camera settings, but allows you to hold an exposure reading while you compose, rather than the camera assessing the focusing and exposure when you press the shutter button. It's best used in the spot or partial metering mode, as you will be taking a reading from a part of the scene that you want to have the 'correct' exposure, and holding that value for the wider view. The AE-L button is usually indicated by an asterisk symbol, and placed near the shutter button for ease of use. It's really easy to use and particularly useful for silhouettes or scenes with large areas of bright sky.

Finally, some cameras have an AutoExposure Braketing (AEB) facility. The camera can be set to take images at different EV values (often +/- three stops). Those with cameras that have an auto Higher Dynamic Range (HDR) control will be familiar with this process as this is how the camera takes three shots at different exposures and then merges the results into one. As with HDR photography, as three shots are taken in rapid succession, it's not really suited for moving subjects and best used with the camera on a tripod.

Back Home

AFTER THE IMAGE IS TAKEN

Once you have returned home from your successful trip, you will want to review the images obtained. What looks outstanding on the camera may not be so wonderful on your PC monitor, but don't make any rash deletions. Download the images from the camera's memory card to your computer. You can always edit out the rejects later when you have looked at them on your PC screen.

Editing the images is easily done in a couple of ways. When you bought your camera, you received with it some basic software, and a connection lead between camera and computer.

If using a USB card reader, don't skimp. As it's the main interface between your camera and computer, and will be used regularly, buy a robust model that will last. The memory card reading speed will be noticeably faster as well.

You will need software to review, edit, and rename your images. There are plenty of options available in addition to that which comes with the camera. The current brand leader is Adobe Photoshop, an extremely powerful, and very expensive, image manipulation tool. Unless you are really going to get into photography in a big way, it is possibly a step too far. 'Lite' versions such as Adobe Photoshop Elements have most of the tools that you will need, and are literally a fraction of the cost. Adobe's Lightroom is a good compromise between the two, with straightforward 'photographer-friendly' editing tools.

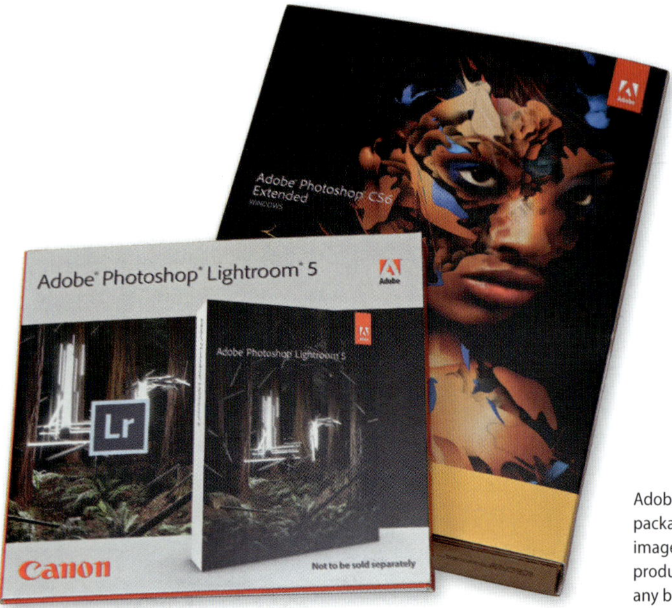

Adobe's Lightroom and Photoshop software packages are among the most popular for digital image processing. There are many comparable products from other manufacturers that will suit any budget and technical requirement.

Few people enjoy filing, but it makes sense to create a simple plan for where you will store your images. If your railway photography is just part of your other creative outlets, create a folder called 'Trains' or 'Railway Photography'. Next, create subfolders for each year. Windows will automatically file folders in numerical order ahead of alphabetically, so use the date of the shoot and the location as the folder title. A trip on 25 May 2014 to the Severn Valley Railway might be saved as '20140525 SVR'. This is only a guide, but the format works well.

BACKUP

So far, your images have been copied from your camera memory card onto your home computer. Sooner or later, you will delete the images from the card, so that you can use it again and again—one of the benefits of digital photography! What remains on your computer is your precious digital photo collection.

Before you sit back and relax, think about the unthinkable…. If your computer was to suffer a malfunction, would all of your images be lost? It's foolish to think it won't happen, but there are a few simple steps for protection.

A surge protection socket/adaptor will protect the computer against variations of mains electricity. Next, consider how you will back up your images. The easiest and cheapest option is to save the material onto a CD or DVD. This is not a long term strategy, as despite their seeming robustness, both degrade over just a few years, eventually becoming unreadable.

It's far better to save your material onto a resource that is external to the computer itself, so that if anything happens to the PC, the content is untouched. External hard drives are relatively cheap and can easily accommodate your whole photo collection. Copy new shots onto the backup at the same time as you save them onto the computer. Even this is not without risk, however. For total peace of mind, backup your backup onto a second external drive, always handling them carefully to protect them from knocks.

If you don't want to have the images at home at all, consider a 'cloud' back up. For an annual fee, your images are automatically saved onto servers at a data centre. This is an effortless option and ideal for a growing collection. Whenever you turn your computer on, they will scan your image file to see 'what's new' and save the latest files automatically. JustCloud offers an excellent and reasonably priced service and is well worth considering.

Whatever method of backup you choose, don't put it off. It only takes a few minutes of your time, and will save a huge amount of heartache.

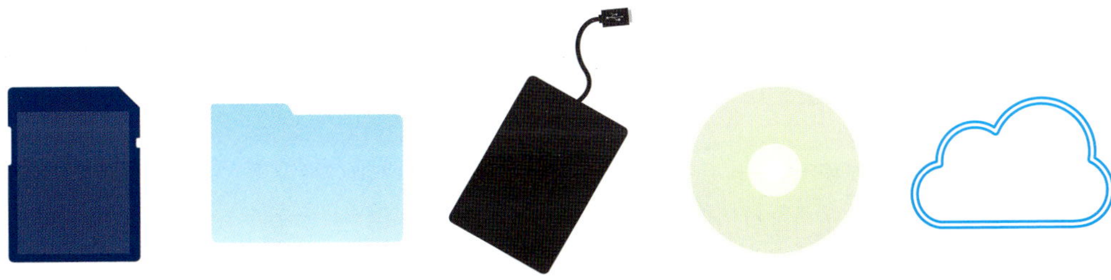

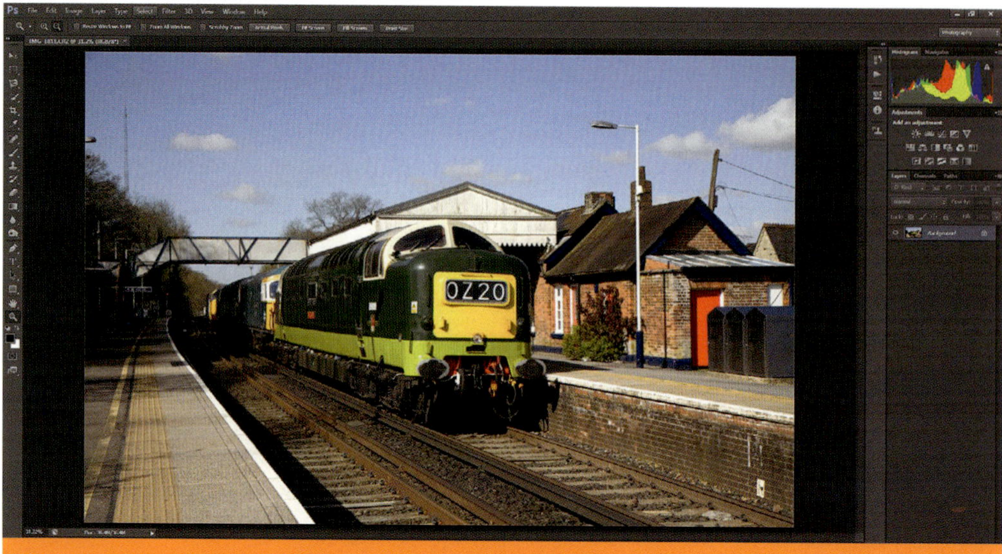

This is the original image of D9009 as opened up on a computer in Adobe Photoshop CS6.

Once you are back at home, you may want to make some initial adjustments to your photos. With any image manipulation, always make a copy of the shot to start with and work on that copy. If a mistake is made, you can always start again without fear of having ruined the precious original.

Straightening

One of the easiest remedies is to straighten the horizon. It's all too easy to take a photo and then realize that the shot is leaning a little to the right or left. Once you have selected your image, choose **Image/Image rotation**, and choose the degree of rotation that you want to apply. Once you are happy, click on the tick/ok button.

Cropping

Cropping will allow you to select a section of your image and save it as a separate file. Look for the **Crop** tool—usually two overlapping L's. As you make your selection on the photo, the area to be removed is usually greyed out, allowing you to get a sense of what the finished result will look like. Click on the tick/ok button to confirm your choice. As well as a regular vertical or horizontal selection, you can also rotate the crop selection to give a dramatic slant to the photo.

Colour balance

Different types of weather can give a picture a slight colour cast. Our eyes compensate for these so we never notice the variations in normal life, but back on your home PC, you may notice sometimes that a photo has a slight tinge. This is easily remedied. In Photoshop, go to **Image/Adjustments/colour balance**, and move the sliders to give you a result that you are happy with.

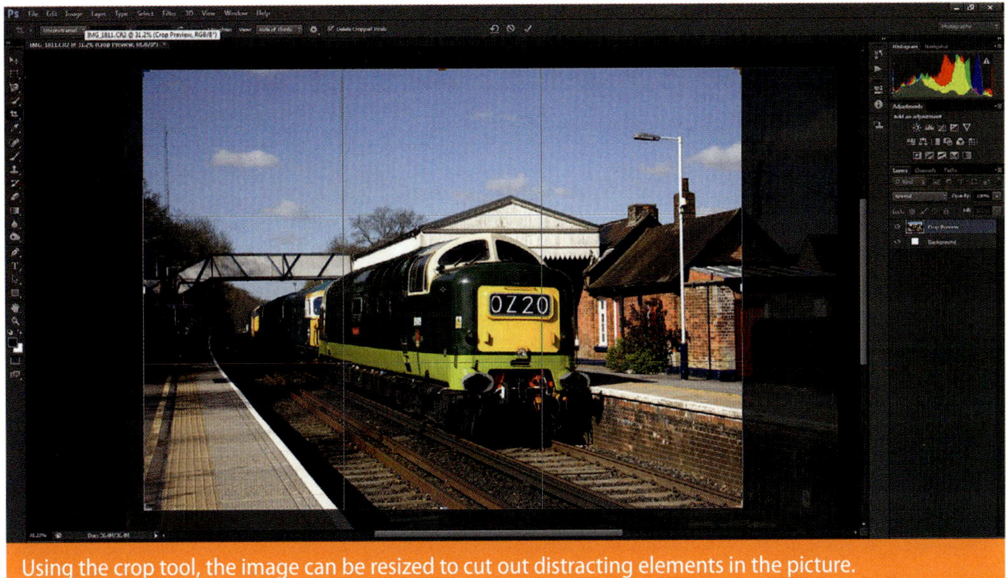

Using the crop tool, the image can be resized to cut out distracting elements in the picture.

Saturation

A strong colour image can be made to almost jump out of the screen by skillful adjustment of the saturation control. As long as the original image is relatively colourful, such as in bright sunlight, use the **Image/Adjustments/Hue/Saturation** control to bring an image to life. Make the changes in small increments, as overdoing the impact can turn a strong shot into something garish.

Contrast

Contrast can be heightened or reduced using **Image/Adjustments/Brightness/Contrast** control. The degree of application will be visible on your chosen image. Take care not to overdo the effect

Sharpening

One of the cleverest tools in digital photography is the ability to sharpen an image. Although the camera carries out some processing of your photo, the data on your memory card is still a digital 'negative', and careful sharpening can add real impact to an image.

Although confusing terminology, sharpening is done using a tool called the Unsharp Mask. You will find this under **Filter/Sharpen/Unsharp Mask**. The amount of sharpening carried out, like other adjustments, is always a matter of taste. Usually, a value between 50–100 will suffice, keeping the Radius setting on 1.0 and the Threshold on 0.

Converting to black and white

On a cloudy day, when the colours are muted, converting your image to black and white can create a dynamic effect. There are several ways of creating a black and white image, but the easiest in Photoshop is to choose **Image/Adjustments/Desaturate**, as this will take all of the colour out of the image in one go. Then choose **Image/Adjustments/Brightness/Contrast** to select the level of impact you desire.

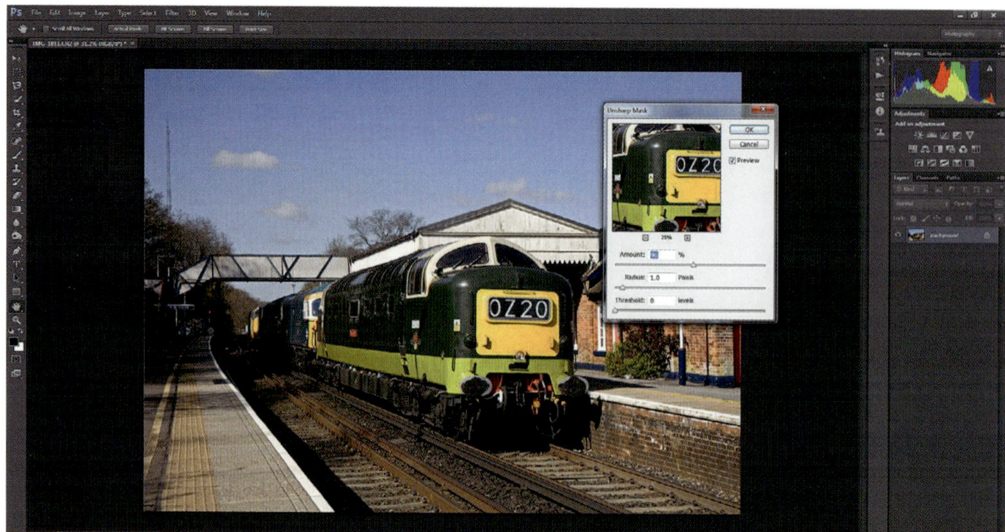

Although your photograph will of course be in sharp focus, some digital sharpening is required on the computer to give the final image real 'bite'. The degree applied is a matter of personal preference and should not be overdone.

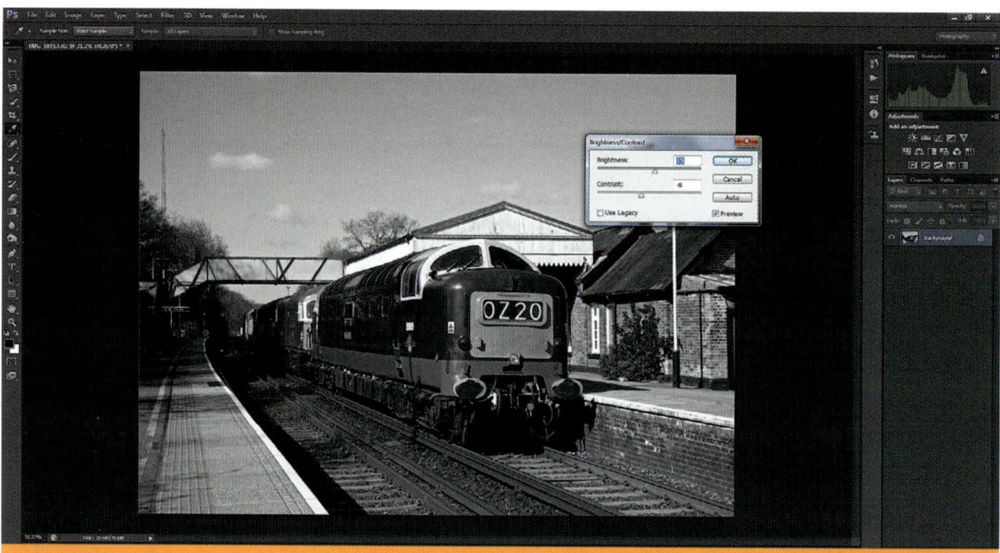

To simulate a bygone scene, the Desaturate tool allows for the colour in a picture to be removed, and create a black and white image.

In UK law, the copyright of a photographic automatically rests with the photographer, unless agreed otherwise in advance. Sadly, it is all too easy to copy an image for one's own uses, good or bad. There are some simple steps that can be taken to provide an element of protection. Your cameras may allow for ownership data to be saved as each photo is taken, such as 'Copyright photograph John Smith'. Although not seen in the displayed image, the text resides within the technical data buried within each frame.

If printing a photo for display, or saving to a website, you can assert your copyright by adding your name to the image. In Photoshop, click the horizontal type tool, and use your mouse to draw a rectangle on your image in a prominent area. Don't worry too much about the final position, as it can be moved later. Choose the font you wish to use and the size of the lettering. Before you start typing, hold the Alt button on your keypad down and type 0169—then press enter. This will insert the universal copyright symbol ©, after which you can type your name. By saving the photo file, this will be set into the image.

DISPLAYING YOUR IMAGES

If you are proud of your photography, why not share your excellent work with your friends, family, and the world at large. Your home computer printer will be able to offer good, basic results. Don't use plain writing paper for the prints—the quality will be very poor. Most local supermarkets stock photographic paper for home inkjet printers—just choose the size and finish you require (glossy, matt, etc.), and get printing!

For a special event, or perhaps to record the best shots each year, consider a photobook. Most of the suppliers online offer free software to help you put your book together, and all you need to do is to 'drag and drop' the images onto the page templates provided. If you haven't cropped or otherwise tweaked them yet, some offer basic image editing capability, but remember that what you decide to include is what you will get back, so make sure you are happy with the pictures before you press 'send'.

TABLET COMPUTING

If you have a mobile device like an iPad, it's very easy to copy your collection over, so that you can share your masterpieces with your family and friends.

With many different makes and models, it is impossible here to offer detailed advice on the ways of transferring photos for each one, so the following guidance is necessarily only of a general nature.

Using Apple's iTunes software, for example, allows the easy transfer of whole folders of images. You will need to set up a destination folder on your iPad, but once you have instructed the programme to start 'syncing', you can relax. Once it's complete, you can effortlessly swipe through your favourite images on your tablet device.

Digital photography has opened up a completely separate industry in photo gifts. You can have your favourite photo saved onto a mug or t-shirt, or a wide variety of gifts. A useful option is to create a calendar. Save the best photo each month and at the end of the year, create a calendar. The international firm Vistaprint offers a speedy and reasonable service with lots of excellent ideas for presentation and delivery.

The growth of digital photography has also led to a wide variety of book publishing opportunities. Simply choose the size, layout, paper quality and number of pages you require, and choose the photos you want to include. As one might expect, the better quality the photo file, the better the reproduction in the book will be. In many cases, the retailer will offer a template onto which you can simply drag and drop your pictures into position. You will also have the option to add captions and other narrative if you wish. If you need the item for a special event, check delivery dates as some books are compiled at central printing facilities in Europe and can take days, if not weeks, to arrive.

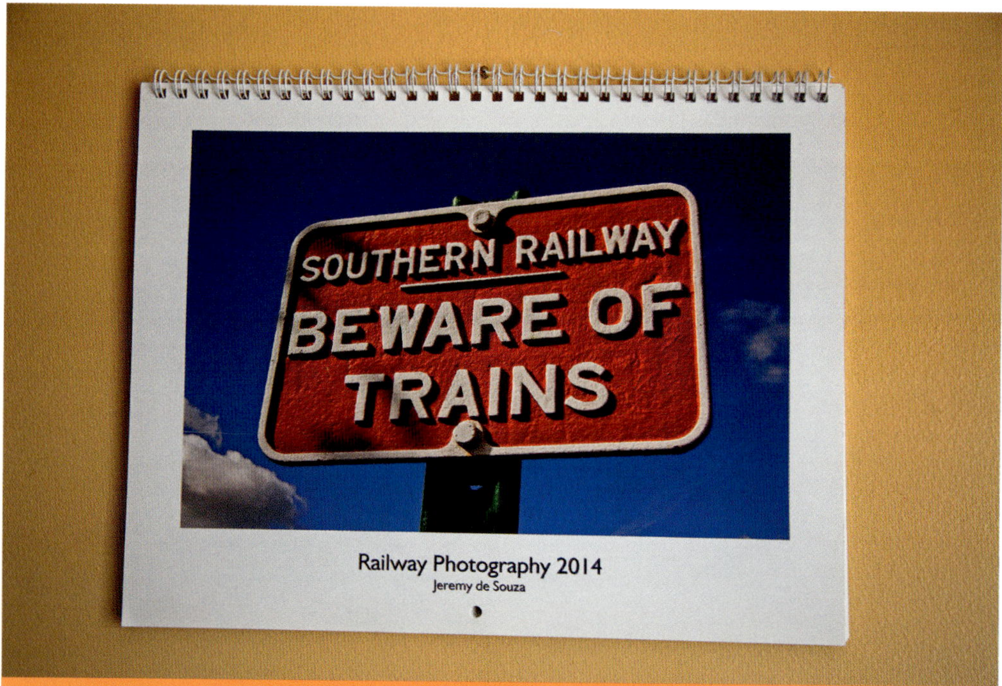

Calendars are just one of a wide variety of gifts that can be easily created from a digital photograph. Make a selection of your best shots throughout the year to ease the choice.

To exhibit your work to a truly worldwide audience, you can even set up your own website. Although sounding daunting, it can be done at virtually nil cost, with websites such as Flickr, Weebly, and many others offering free sites for you to exhibit your images on.

If you are willing to invest a few pounds each year, more display functionality can be added, and more advanced sites such as Zenfolio and Smugmug will allow you to exhibit your work like a professional. They can even be enabled to allow viewers to buy copies of your photos through the website.

There are a few points to remember when uploading images to a website for display. Despite high capacity broadband across most of the UK, a large image file may take a few minutes to upload to your chosen website host. Consider reducing the file size (of a copy image—not the original!) and uploading that instead. When viewed on a screen, the quality difference will be marginal. If your website host offers security options, be sure to enable these. Unless you are happy for others to copy your photos, take steps to ensure this can be done easily. As the photographer, international copyright rests with you, but just to make sure, enable protection that prevents anyone 'right-clicking' on your photo to copy it for themselves. Some sites will display a security message if this is attempted. You may also be able to add a watermark (visible or otherwise) as further protection.

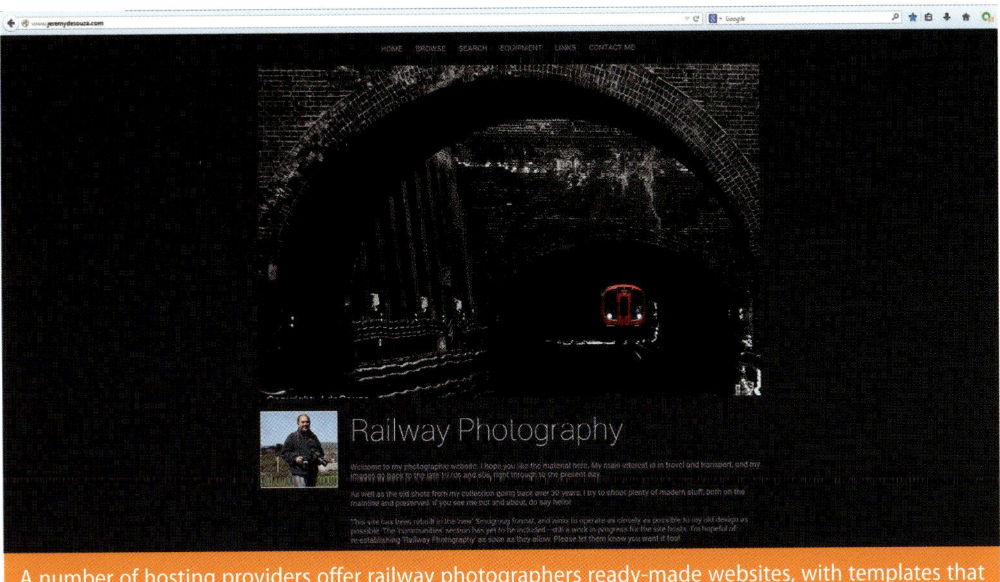

A number of hosting providers offer railway photographers ready-made websites, with templates that images can be added to quickly and easily.

Digitising Your Collection

Digitising film images—what to do with your old slide/negative collection

Many older railway enthusiasts have amassed a large collection of 35mm or 120 film slides and negatives. It's sadly an unavoidable truth that the film stock deteriorates over time, and they should be copied onto a digital medium to preserve the images for the long term.

A dedicated slide/film copying tool will allow them to be processed in a relatively fast and straightforward manner.

For simplicity, a table top scanner like the ION Film 2 SD Plus is convenient, as it's a standalone unit that can be used without connecting to a computer. The scans are saved onto the SD card, which can then be transferred onto your computer at a later date. Although suited to 35mm only, it is a reasonable device for home use.

If you prefer higher quality scans, or have other film formats such as 120 to copy, invest in a flatbed unit. There are several on the market from manufacturers such as Canon, Epson, and Nikon, and they have the ability to scan negatives, transparencies, and prints to different sizes, and to very high quality.

Whatever scanner you use, remember that it will not perform miracles, and can only scan what is on the slide, including any existing dust, fungus, or finger marks. You will need to use image processing software to sharpen and 'clean up' imperfections.

Choice of scanner

Choosing your scanner, like your camera, will be a matter of personal preference. Try to go for the best unit you can afford, as it will help ensure your photos are scanned to the highest quality possible. They come with all cables and software, and you should be set up and ready to go fairly quickly.

Using a scanner

As with handling any photographic media, take care touching slides or negatives. Static electricity may cause them to attract small amounts of dust, so use a gentle puff from a camera blower brush to clear these. Do not blow as you may cover your precious slide with minute moisture droplets. Compressed air canisters are also to be avoided as the gases contained are cold and cause a similar problem. The sheer force of the compressed gas could also damage the slide or negative.

For the scanner glass surface, use specialist lens glass wipes before use, to ensure that the surface is free from any blemishes or finger marks. Keep a dust cover on your scanner when not in use.

Typically, having loaded the source media, you can preview each image before a detailed scan is made. You will have the chance to crop the area to be recorded, so that you can avoid the slide mount in the recorded image. You will also be asked to select the resolution of the scan. A setting of 800 dpi or above gives a high quality image with only a few minutes duration for each scan. If the image to be scanned has blemishes—scratches or other marks—several scanners include software that will remove these automatically.

CHOOSING THE RIGHT OUTPUT AND SAVING THE RESULTS

As with categorising the output from your normal photography, think in advance about how you want to file your images electronically. You may want to set up a system for year taken, location, loco class, etc., but make sure that you stick to the structure as your collection of scans grows. Remember also that you will be post-processing your images after scanning and possibly resizing if you intend to show them on a website, so make allowances for that in your naming structure. Finally, remember that these are all extra demands on your computer and hard drive memory, which will fill up the more scans you make!

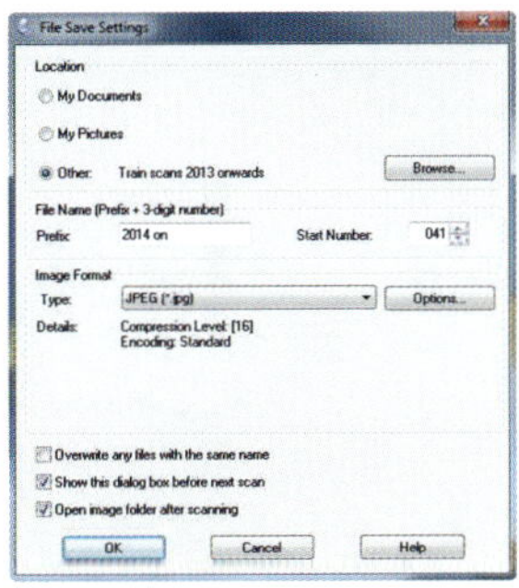

Another high-quality scanner is the Epson Perfection 4990, shown here with a 120 rollfilm carrier ready to be loaded. The lid is closed during operation.

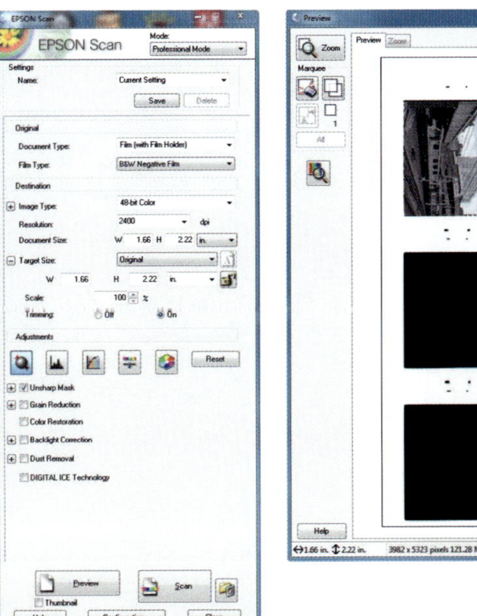

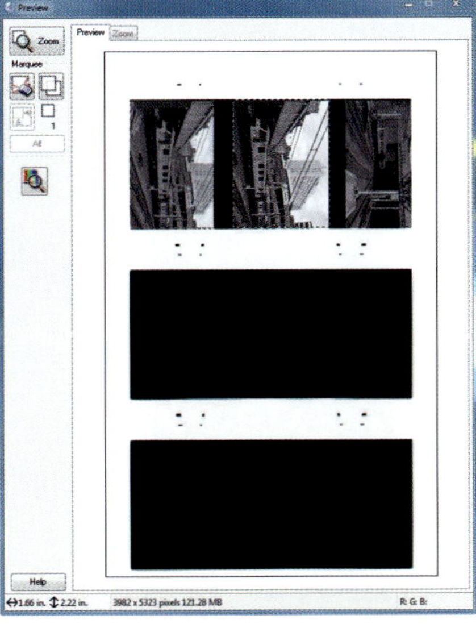

Once a scan has been made, the unit will ask where the user wants the image saved. Sequential numbering should be enabled as it will help manage your growing digital image collection.

Previous page: The CanoScan 9000F flatbed scanner provides high quality results from 35mm or 120 rollfilm formats. (*Courtesy Canon UK*)

Gallery

Here is a selection of images to demonstrate some of the techniques explained in this book.

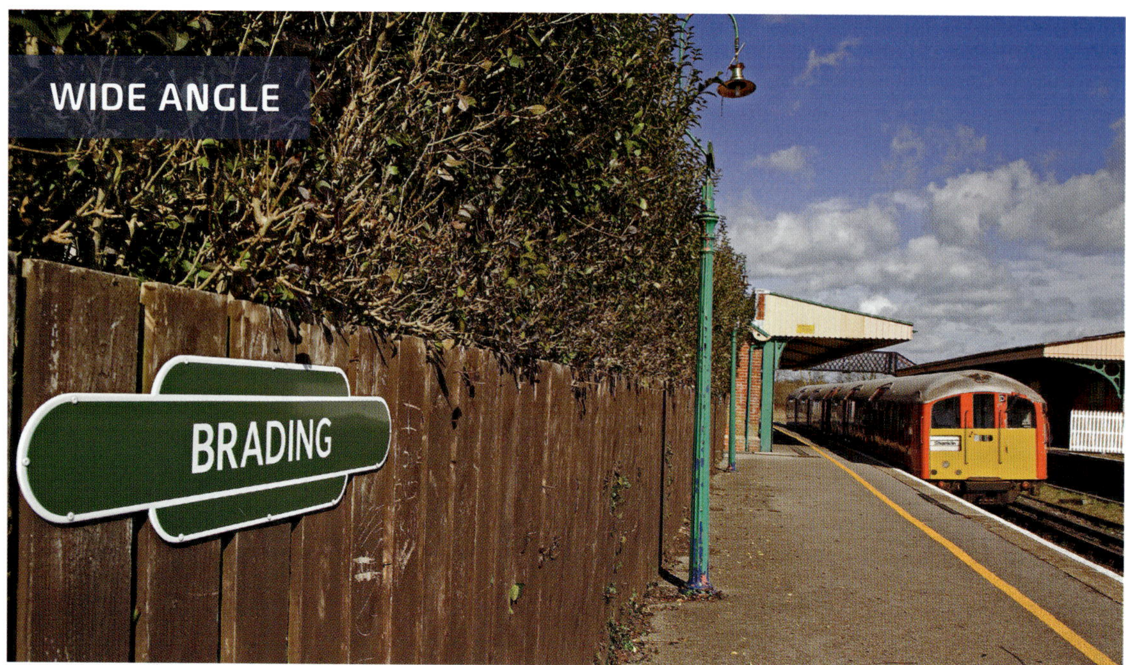

With the sun on the other side of the train, a creative wide-angle view at Brading station on the Isle of Wight sets the scene for this shot of the former London Underground stock. Canon 5D, 24-105mm lens, ISO 250, 1/250 at f11.

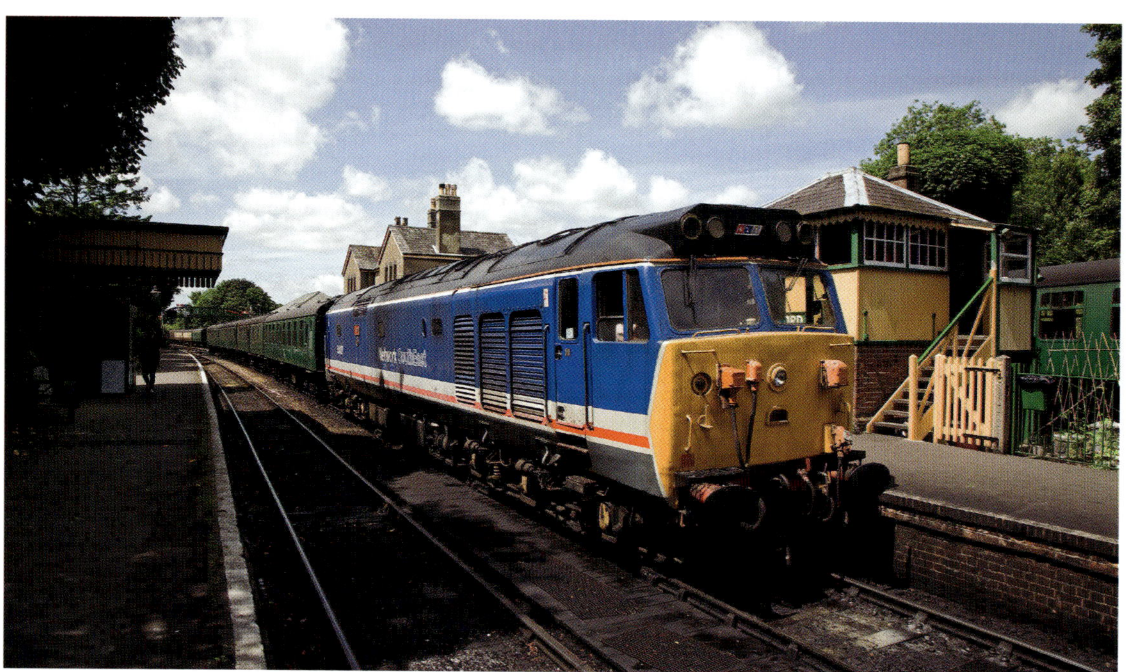

50 027 Lion at Arlesford is given the wide-angle treatment. The viewpoint accentuates the perspective of the train behind the loco, and is boosted by the blue sky and white clouds. Canon 5D, 24-105mm lens, ISO 160, 1/160 at f9.

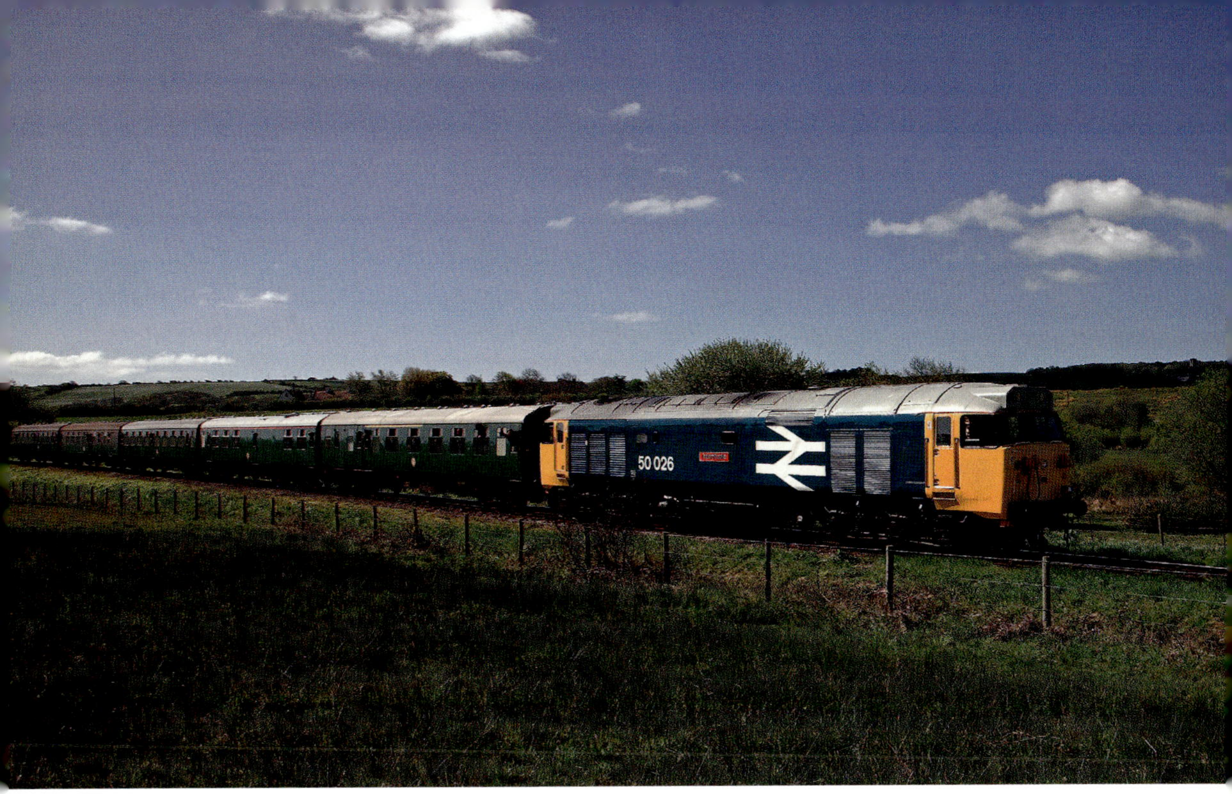

▲ Another class 50 image, but this time of 50 026 beneath the big Dorset sky during the Swanage Railway's 2013 diesel gala. Canon 5D, 24 105mm lens, ISO 250, 1/500 at f10

▼ The meeting of six Gresley A4 pacifics at the National Railway Museum in York was inevitably extremely popular, and with the crowds, photos were hard to obtain. By seeking an alternative viewpoint, this angle gave a sense of perspective for all six locomotives, the crowds, and the museum itself. Canon 5D, 17-40mm lens, ISO 400, 1/160 at f7.1.

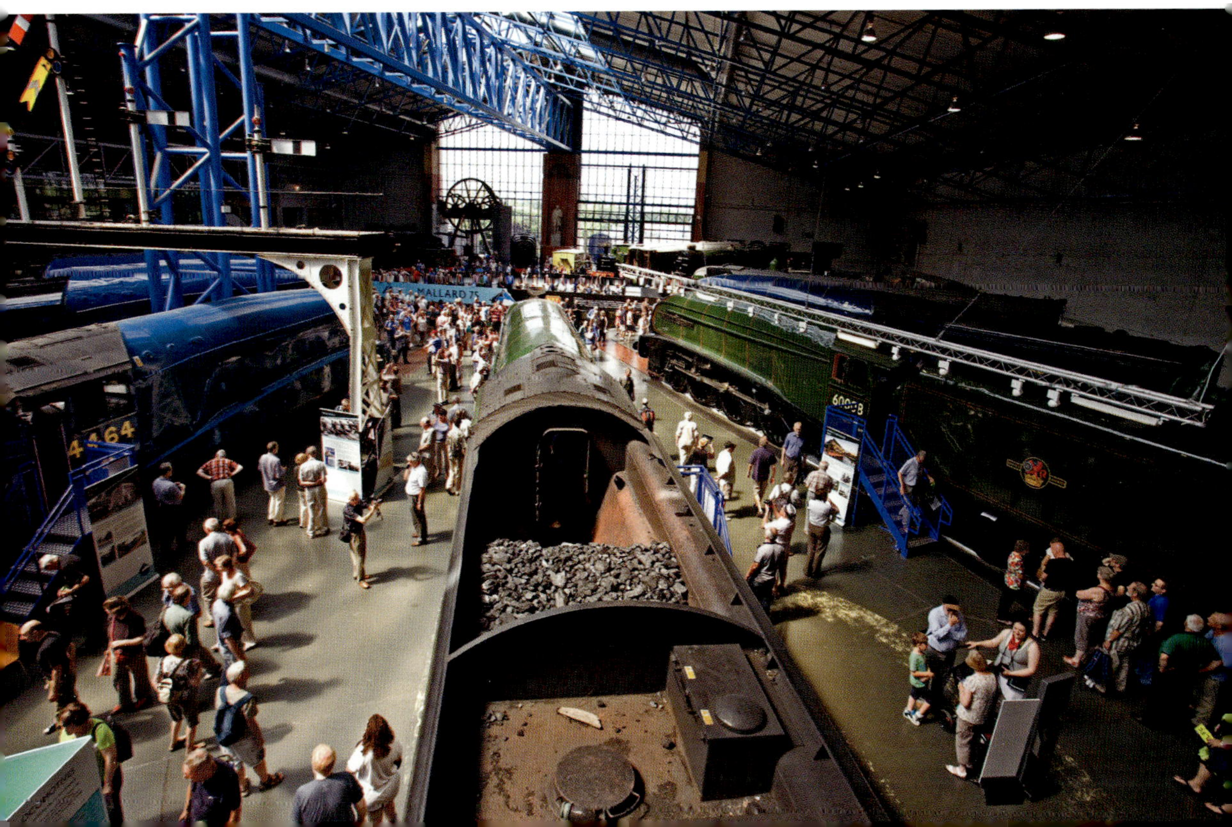

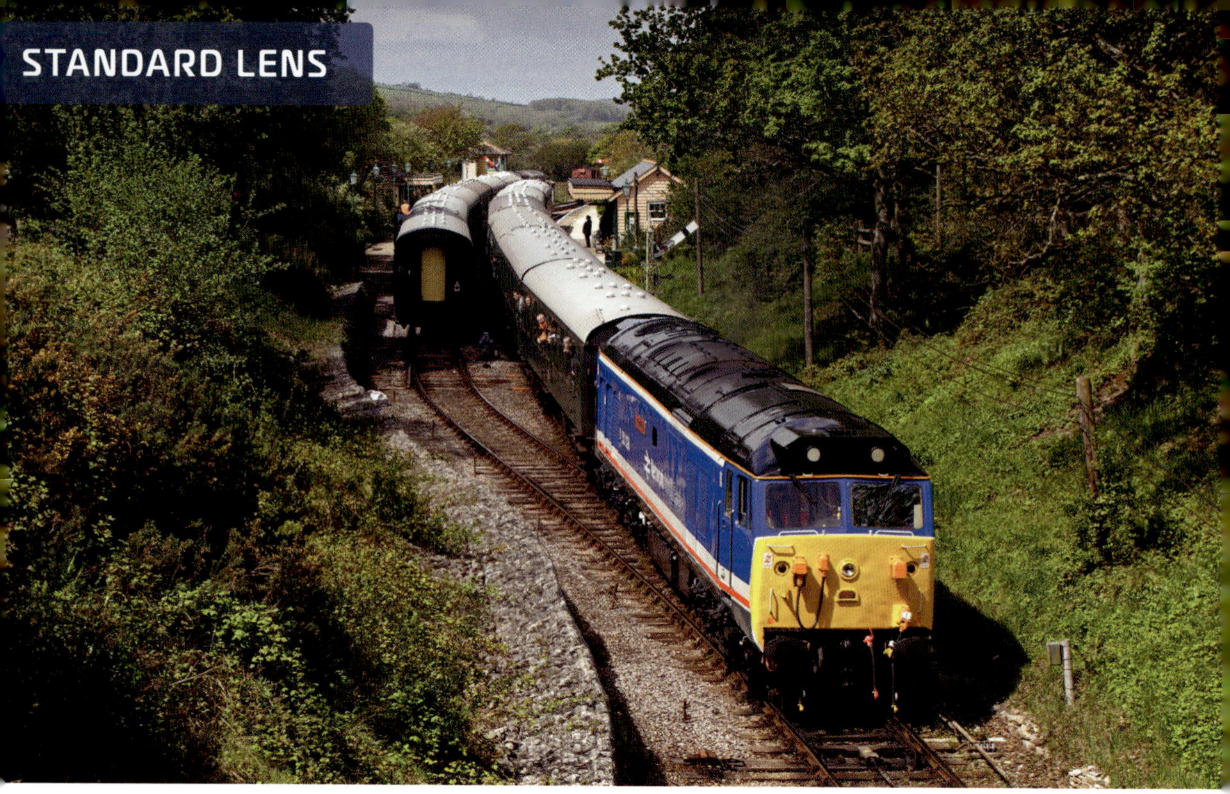

▲ A classically standard, sunny railway photograph. 50 026 departs south from Harmans Cross on the picturesque Swanage Railway in Dorset. Canon 5D Mark III, 24-105mm lens, ISO 320, 1/500 at f10.

▼ A big country with big scenery demands a big train. In this summer 2007 view, the triple-headed 'Canadian' slows to a halt at Jasper, *en route* to Vancouver. It was a stroke of luck to get this sharp image as the shutter speed had mistakenly been set too low. Canon 10D, 24-105mm lens, ISO 200, 1/125 at f8.

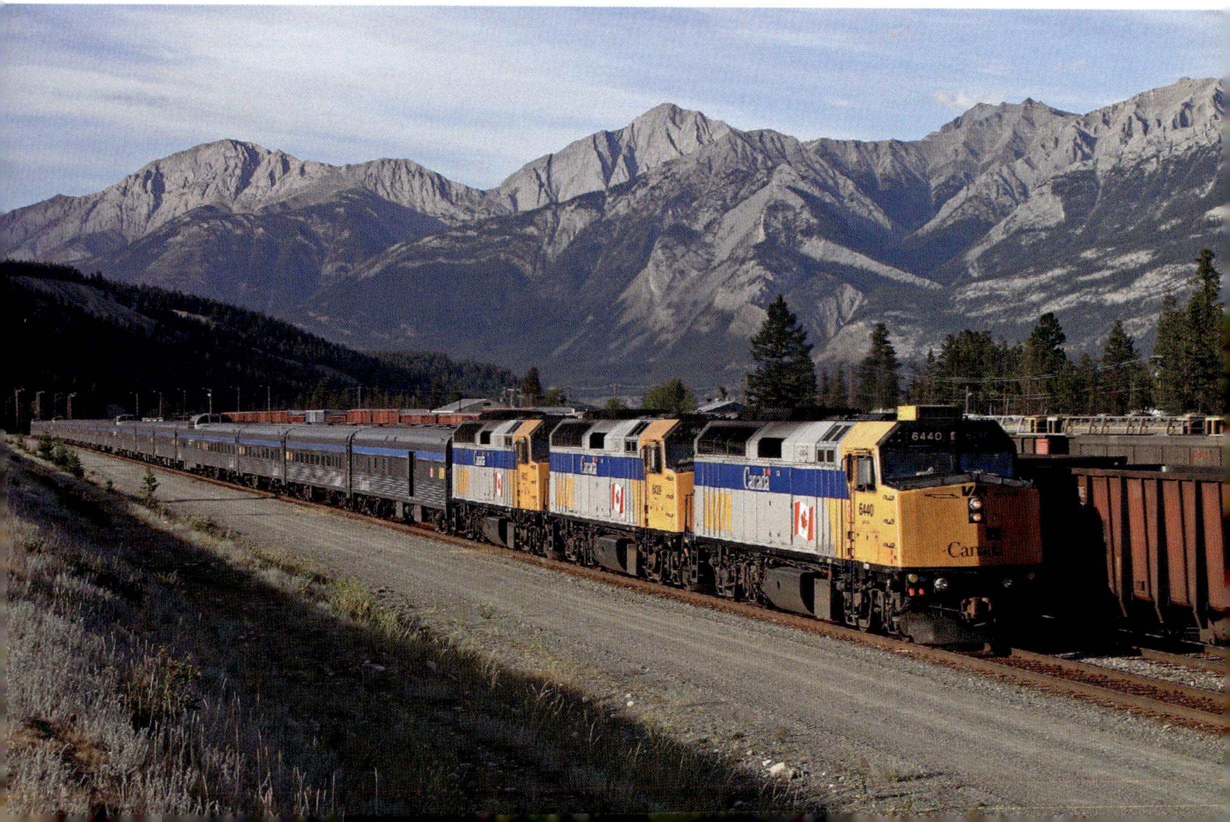

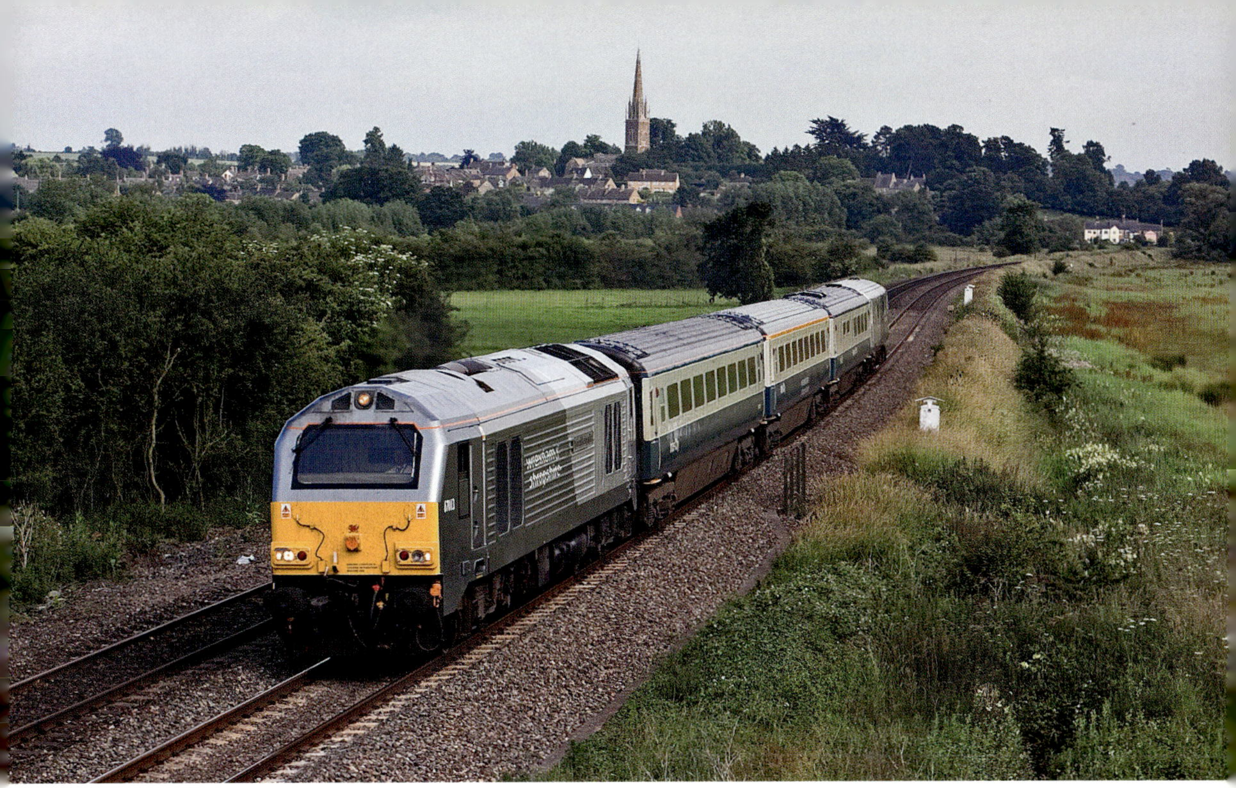

▲ The well-known location of Kings Sutton near Banbury provides the setting for 67 013 as it heads north with an afternoon service from London Marylebone. Canon 40D, 24-105mm lens, ISO 400, 1/500 at f6.3.

▼ 150 281 pauses in the warm September sunshine at Betws-y-Coed on the Conwy Valley line in North Wales. The miniature tracks of the Conwy Valley Railway Museum can be seen in the foreground. Canon 10D, 28-80mm lens, ISO 100, 1/125 at f9.5.

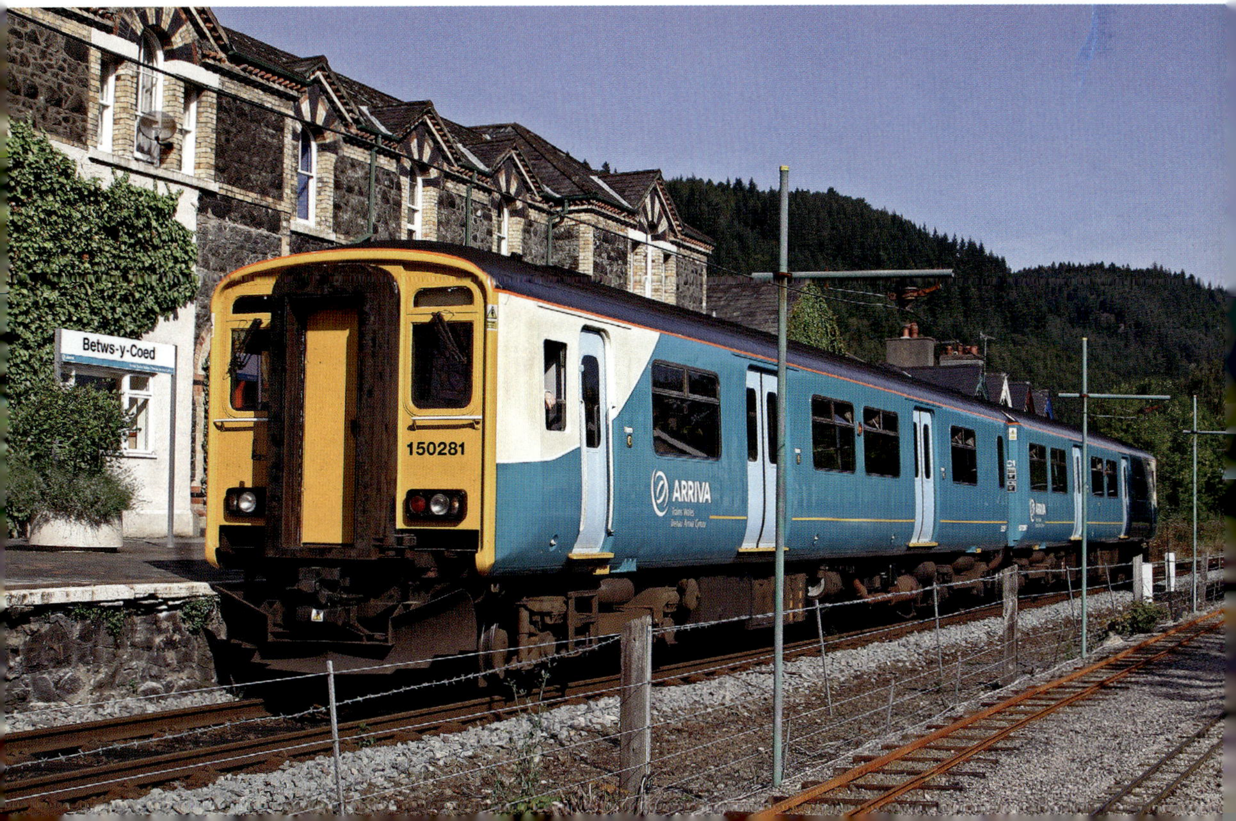

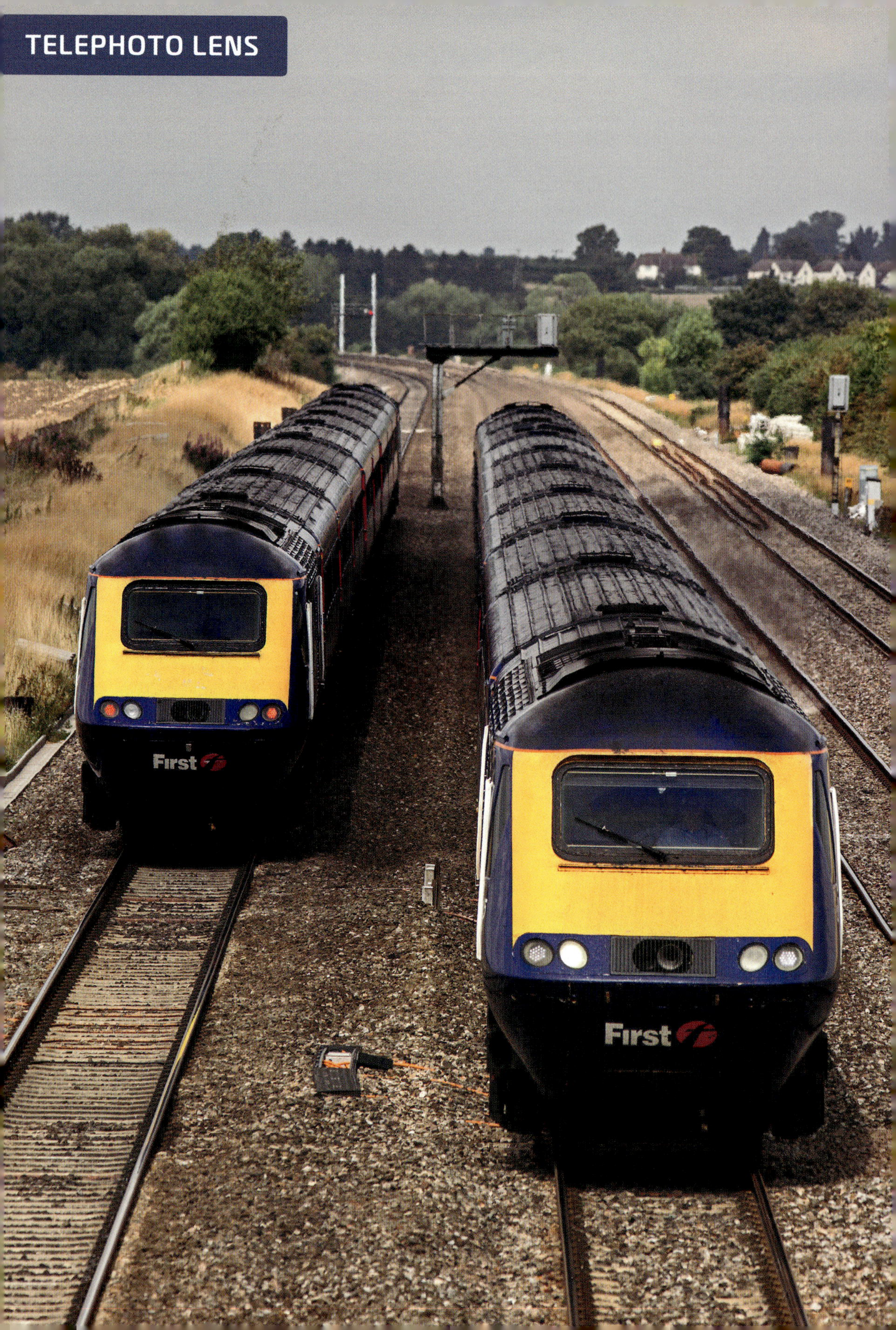

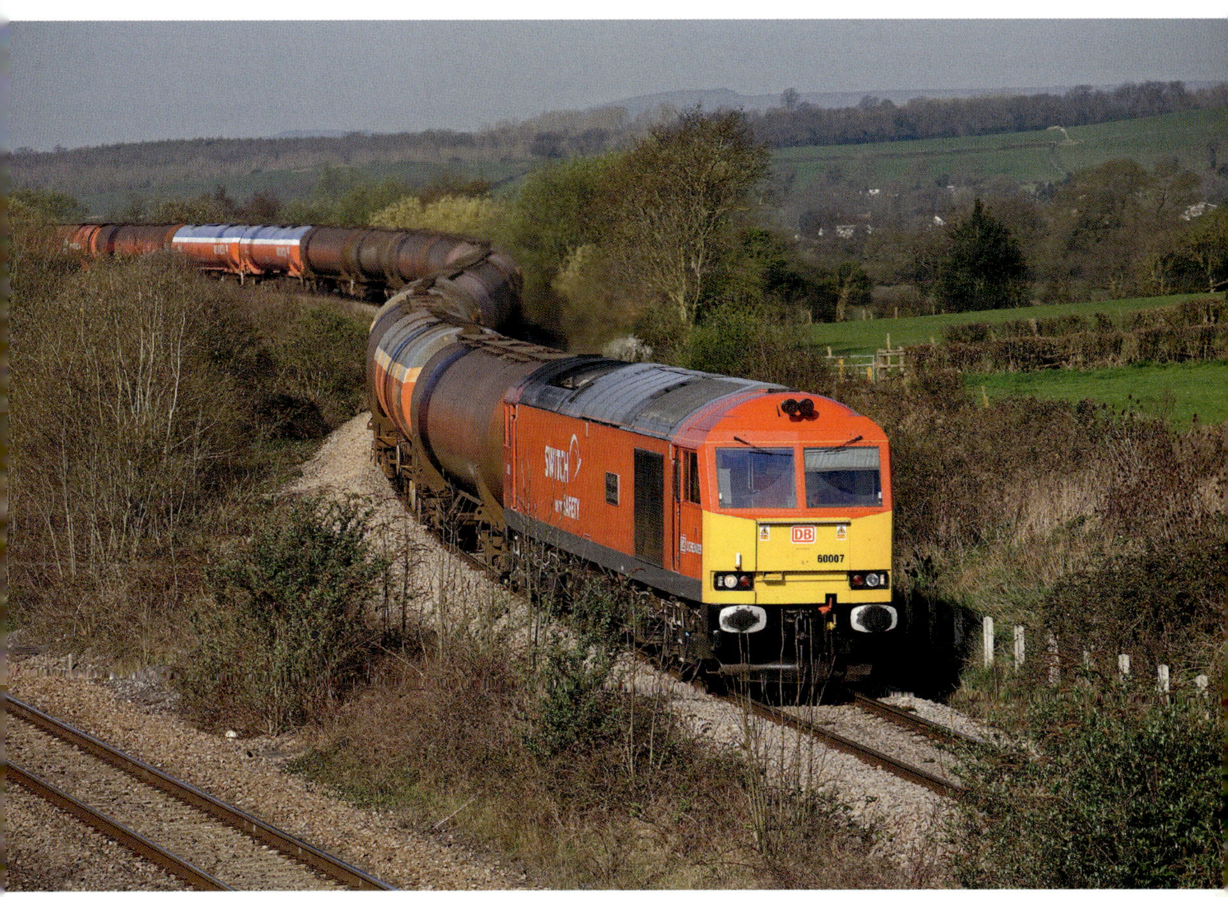

▲ A telephoto lens compresses the oil train behind 60 007 as it descends from the Bishton flyover to regain the South Wales mail line near Newport. Canon 5D, 70-200mm lens, ISO 320, 1/800 at f8.

◄ Split-second timing was needed to capture this shot of two HST passing at Cholsey, between Didcot and Reading. A high shutter speed ensured that the movement of both trains was frozen. Canon 5D Mark III, 300mm lens, ISO 400, 1/800 at f8.

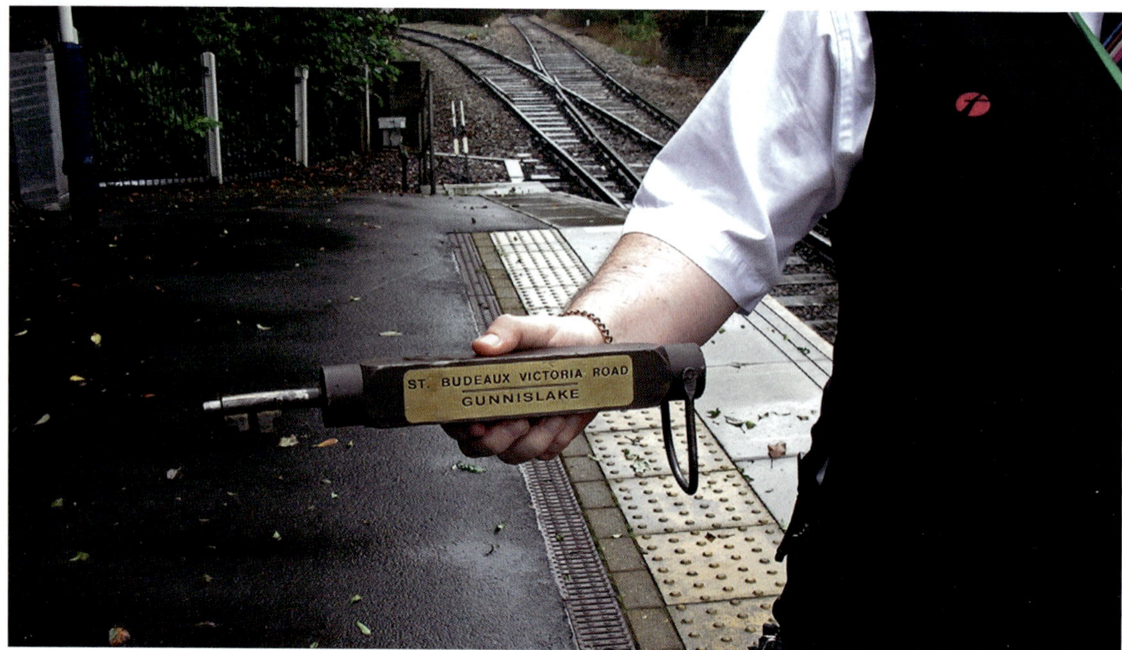

A wonderful piece of railway history that's in use every day. The guard helpfully shows the single line token to the photographer, before placing it into the interlocking apparatus at Bere Alston on the Tamar Valley line. With it in place, the train will be able to continue its journey towards Plymouth. Canon PowerShot G9, ISO 200, 1/320 at f10.

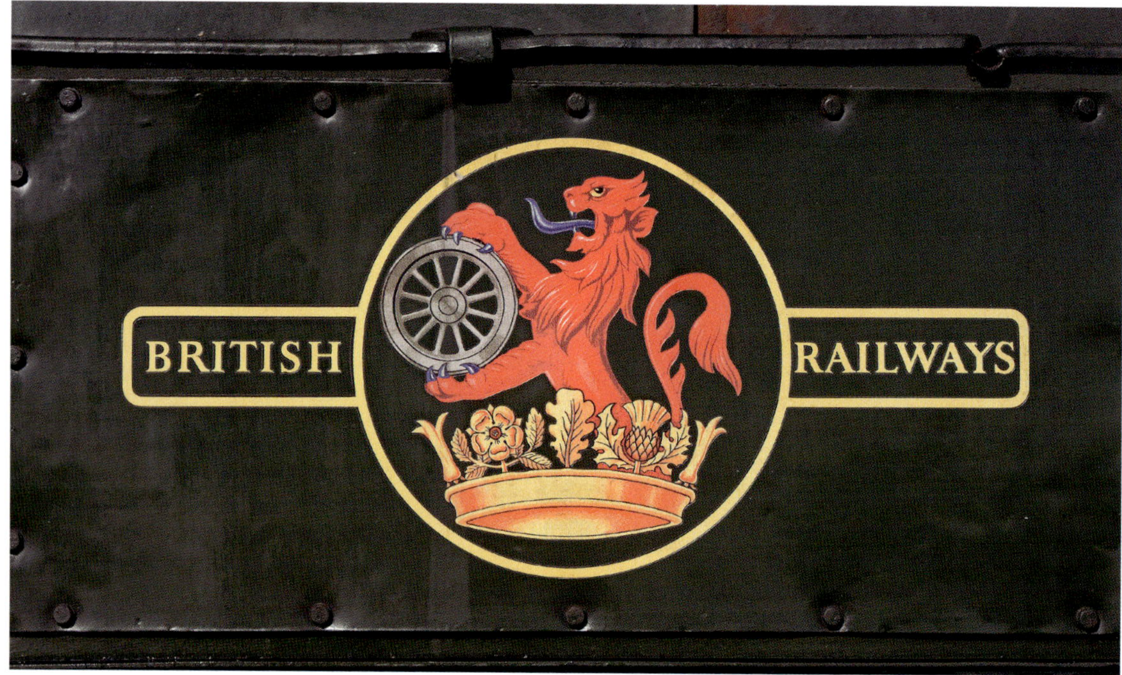

A design classic. The British Railways 'Lion & Wheel' emblem as carried by steam and diesel locomotives alike—in this case, a preserved shunter. Canon 40D, 24-105mm lens, ISO 250, 1/400 at f10.

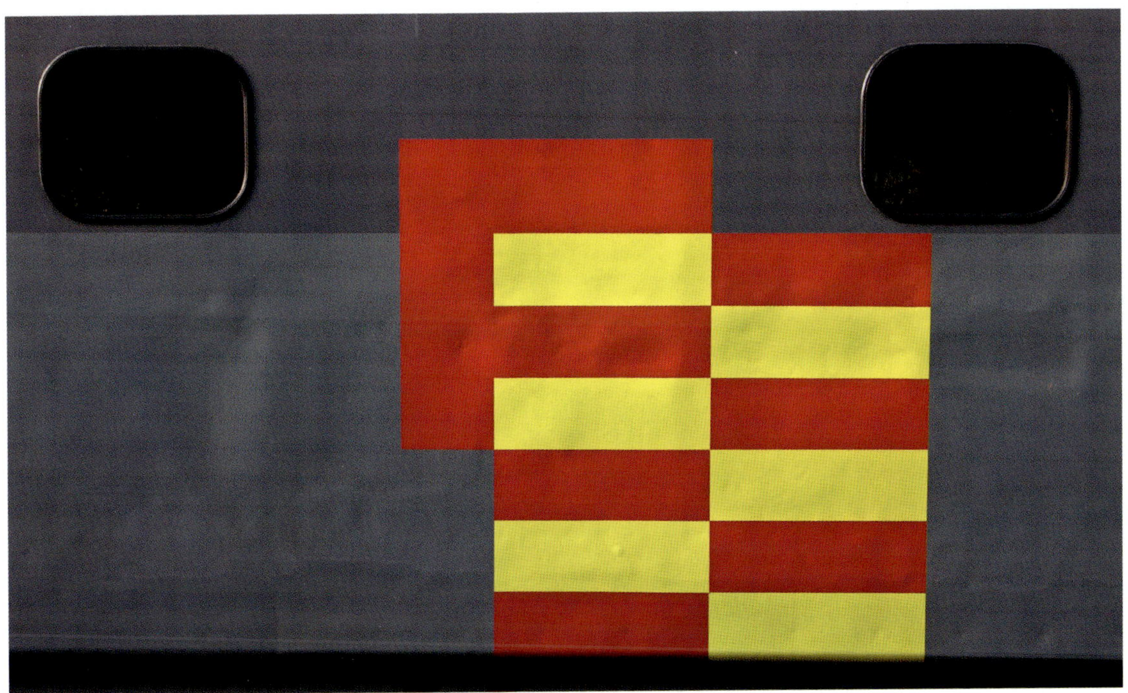

33 063 on the Spa Valley line in Kent carries the colourful Railfreight Construction insignia. The bold colours make for an interesting abstract composition. Canon 40D, 24-105mm lens, ISO 400, 1/80 at f6.3.

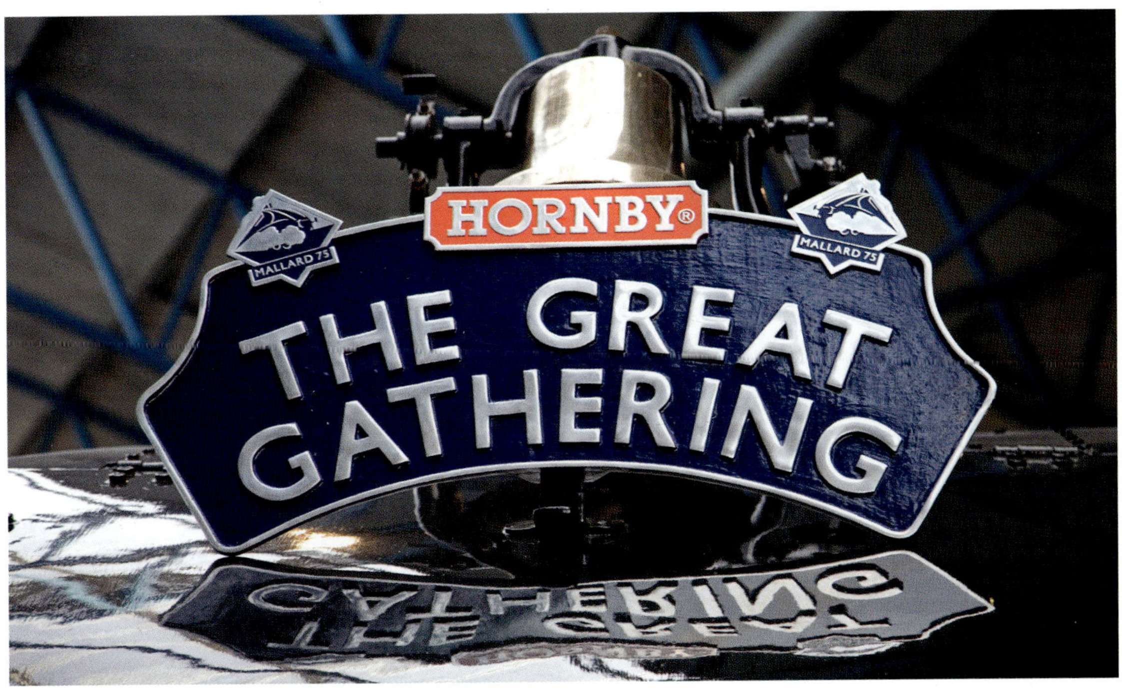

A fitting headboard for the historic event at York in 2013, when six Gresley streamlined A4 locomotives were brought together for a unique gathering. Canon 5D, 24-105mm lens, ISO 400, 1/40 at f6.3.

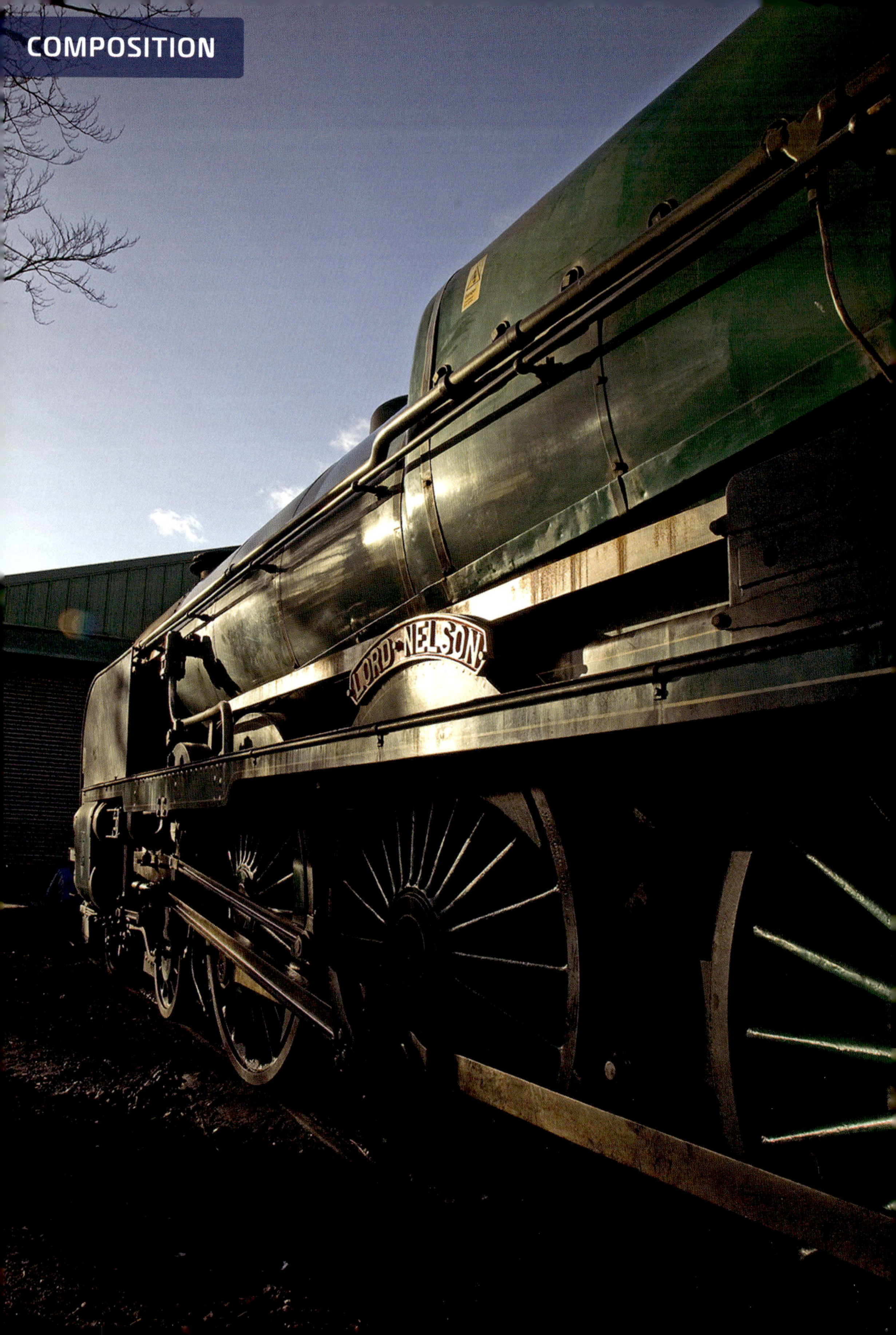
COMPOSITION
LORD·NELSON

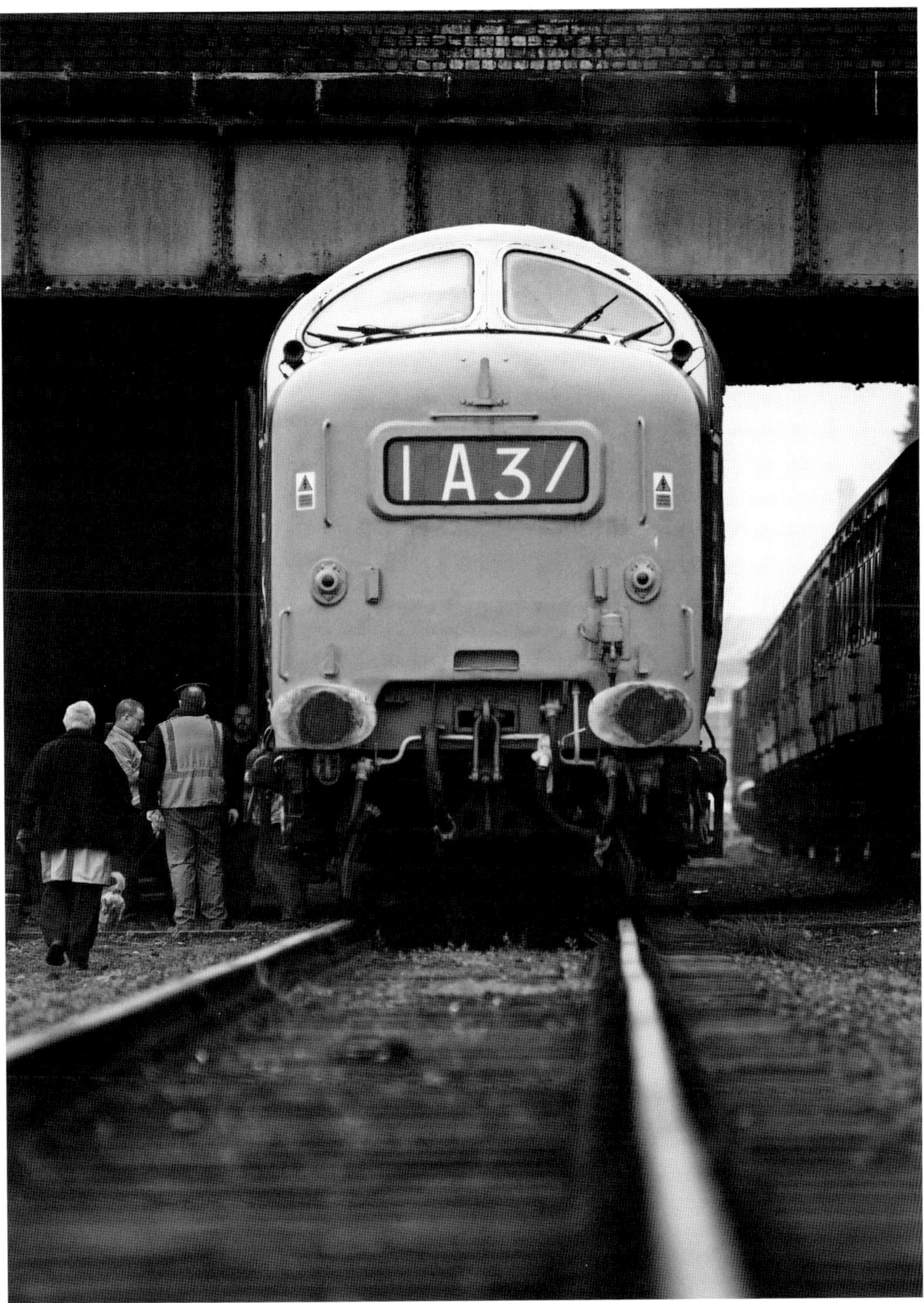

▲ 9016 at Loughborough during a photo charter. Use of a 300mm lens and a low viewpoint allows the eye to be drawn along the rail toward the locomotive. Canon 5D Mark III, 300mm lens, ISO 400, 1/400 at f4.5.

◄ The sun reflecting off the boiler and the position of the loco's connecting rods all contribute to lead the eye into the photograph. Canon 5D, 24-105mm lens, ISO 160, 1/250 at f10.

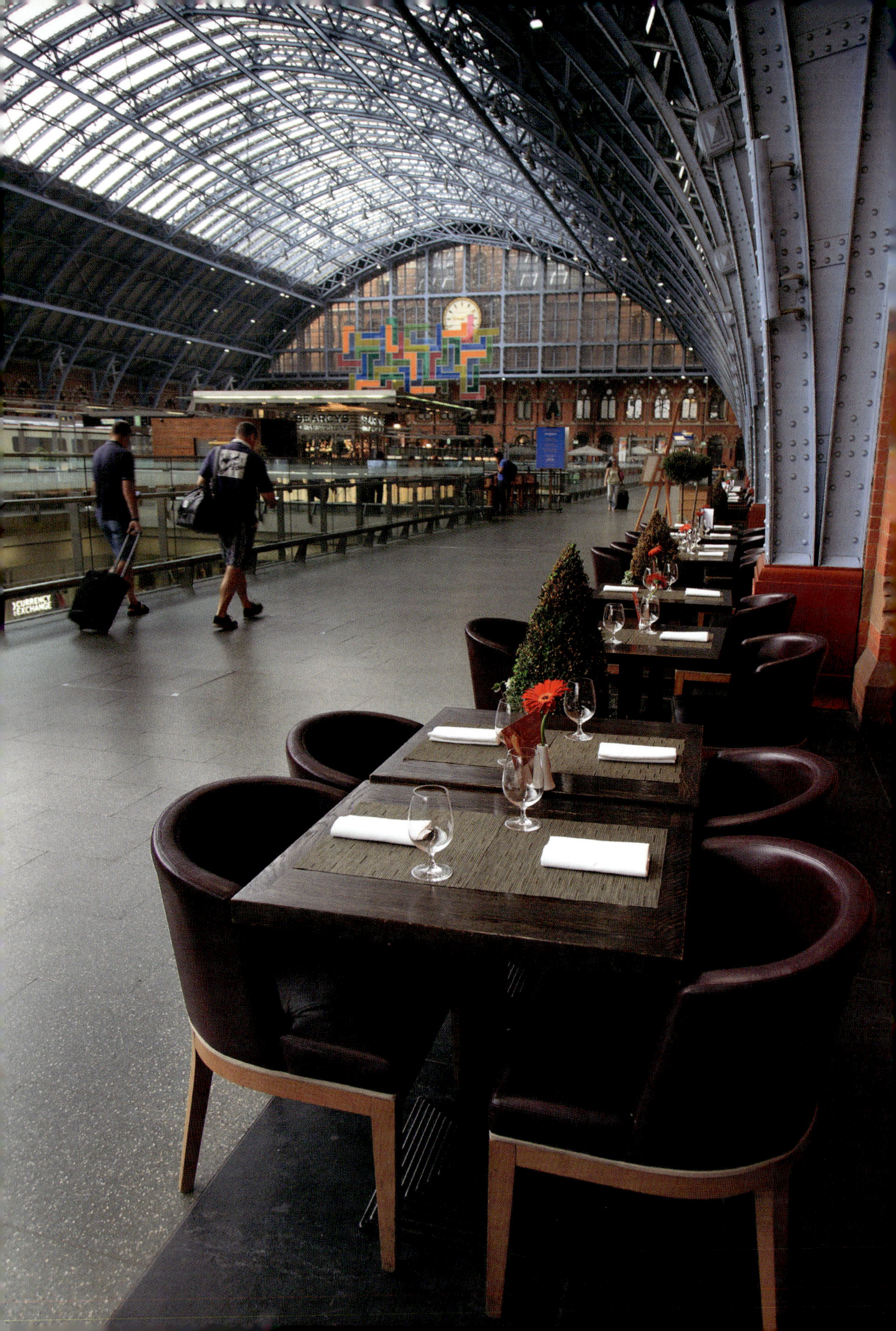

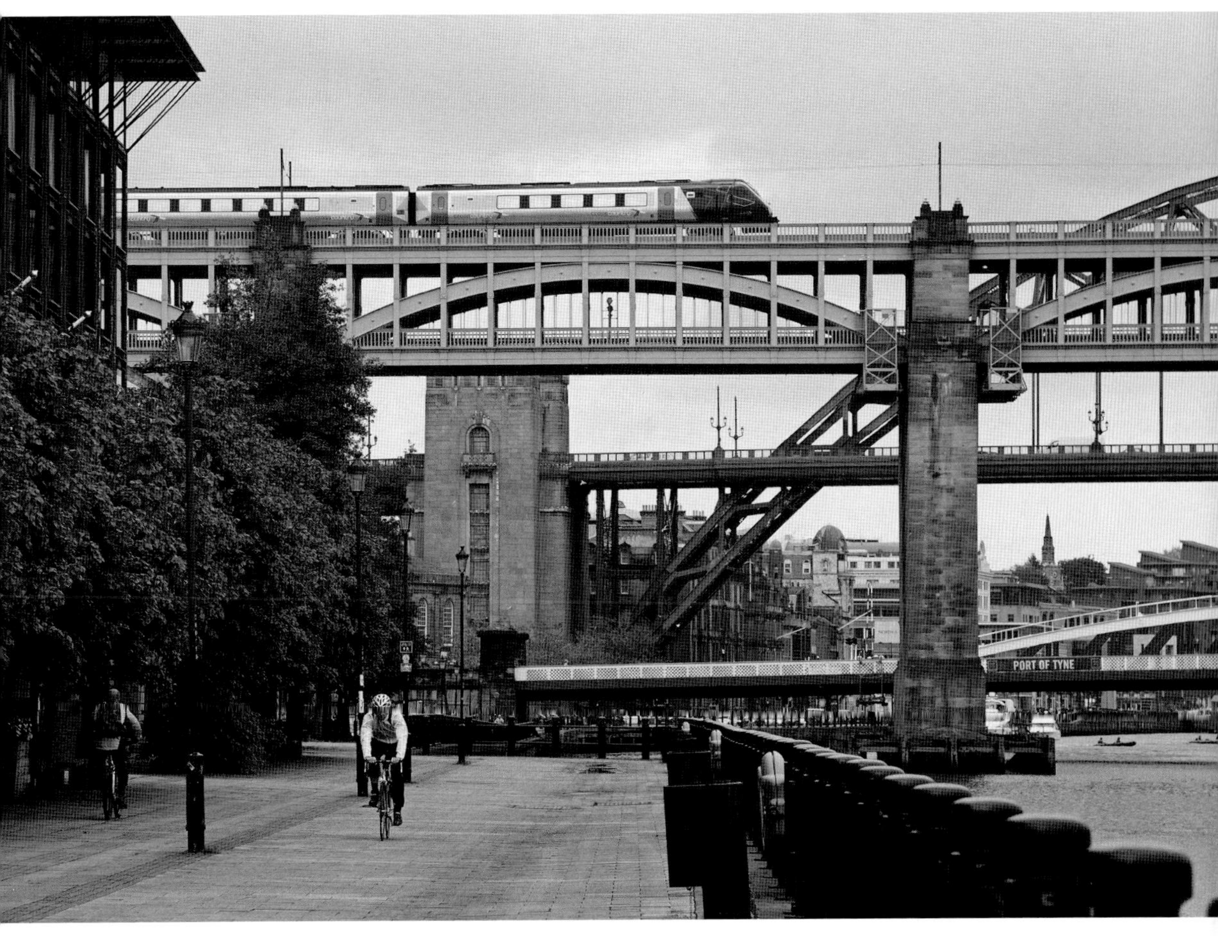

▲ With a Voyager passing on the high-level rail bridge, a cyclist provides much-needed foreground interest on the banks of the Tyne in Newcastle. The dull weather meant that conversion from colour to black and white was imperative for this shot. Canon 5D Mark III, 24-105mm lens, ISO 320, 1/320 at f7.1.

◄ What was once a grimy and dark station is now a thriving restaurant venue. Passengers and their luggage complete the wide-angle composition at St Pancras in London. Canon 5D Mark III, 24-105mm lens, ISO 400, 1/30 at f4.5.

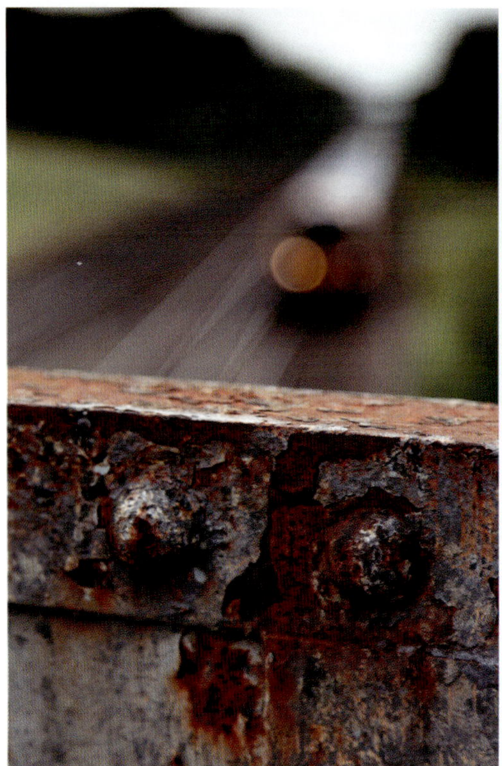

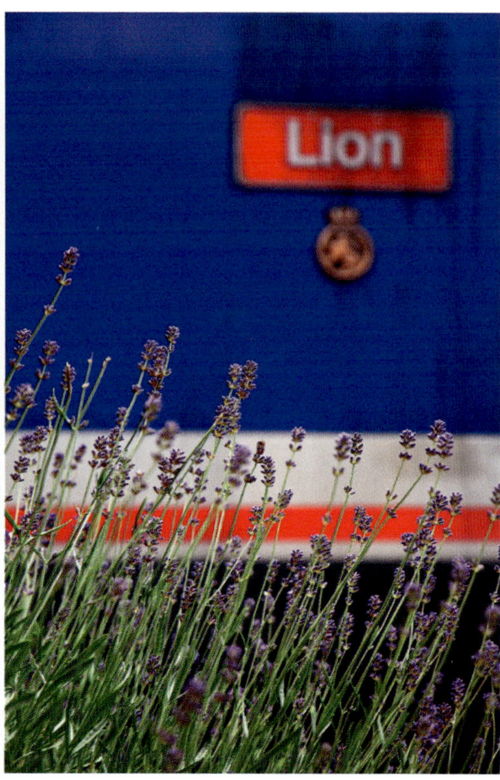

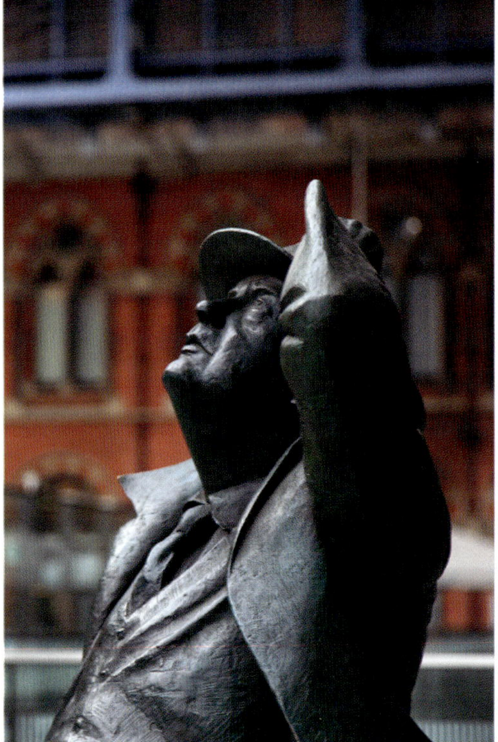

▲ Selective focusing is an interesting option, either in its own right or in poor lighting conditions when a 'traditional' image might not be possible. Using the narrow depth of field of a low f number, the foreground can be sharp, as in this example, while the passing train in the background is blurred. Canon 5D Mark III, 24-105mm lens, ISO 320, 1/800 at f4.

▲ In a similar vein, the lavender dominates the foreground while 50 027 Lion sits calmly in the rear. Canon 5D, 24-105mm lens, ISO 160, 1/100 at f5.

◄ To have had the building behind the statue of Sir John Betjeman in focus as well would have been very distracting. Placing the wall out of focus ensures that the eye concentrates on the subject. Canon 5D Mark III, 24-105mm lens, ISO 400, 1/40 at f4.5.

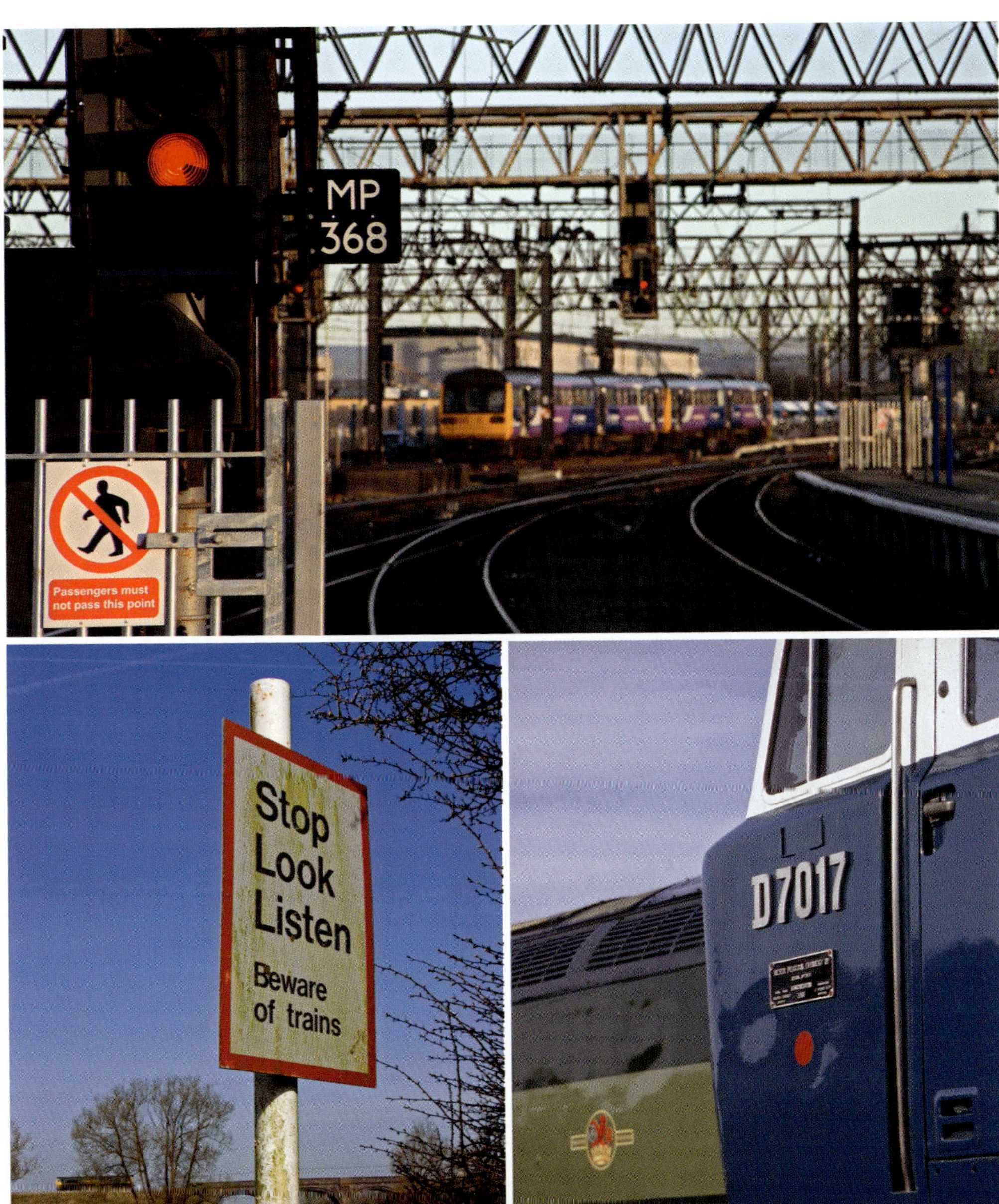

▲ A slightly busy image visually, but selective focusing helps to balance the dominance of red in the image from the signal, the sign, and the sun's cast on the departing train. Canon 5D Mark III, 24-105mm lens, ISO 400, 1/400 at f6.3.

◄ The sign in the foreground dominates this image on the Westerleigh branch, of course, but by looking into the background, one can see a passing light Class 66 on the GW main line. Canon 40D, 70-200mm lens, ISO 200, 1/320 at f14.

► Heritage diesel colours. Hymek D7017's vivid blue livery contracts with the two-tone green of the Class 47 in the background. 120 film transparency scan.

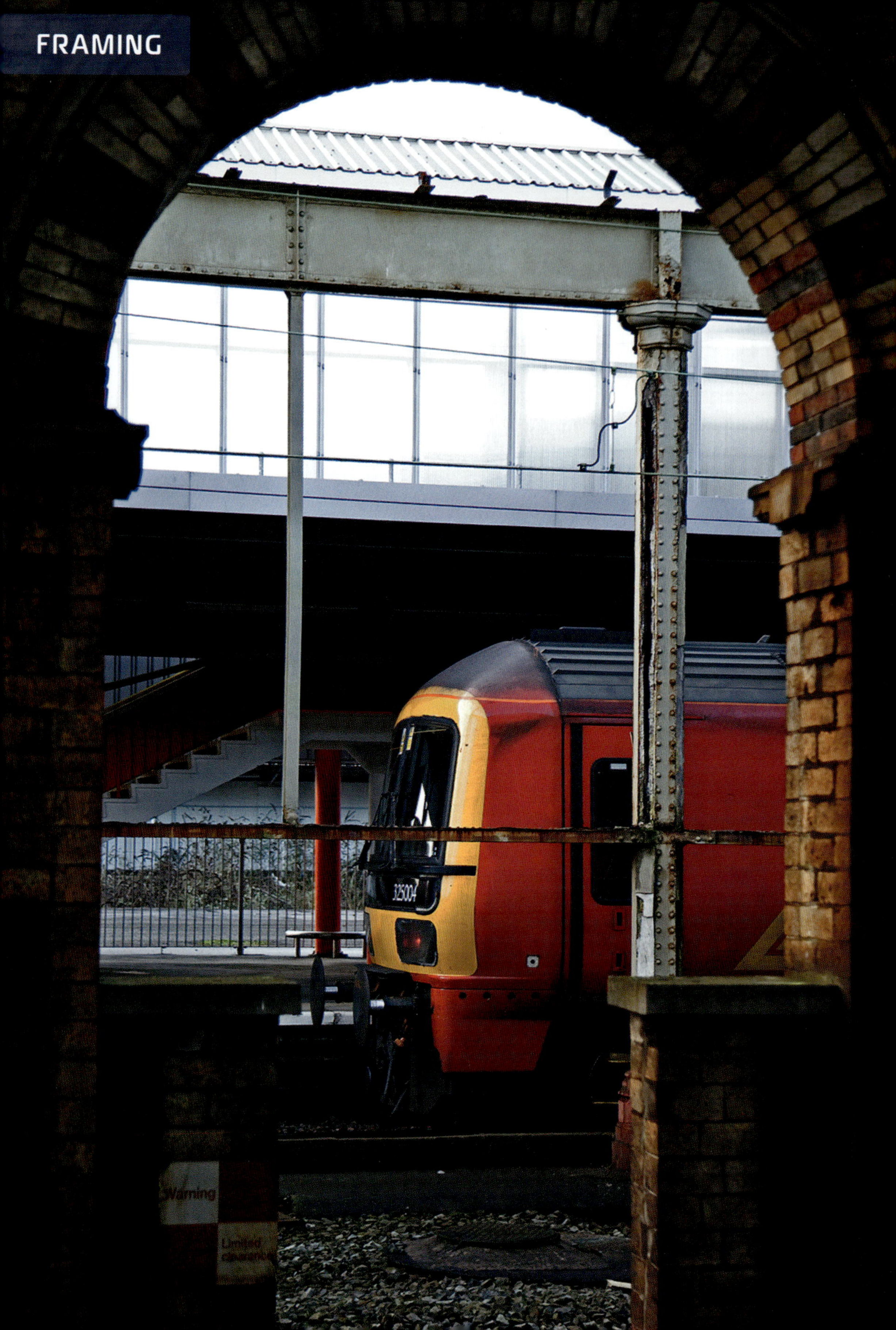
FRAMING

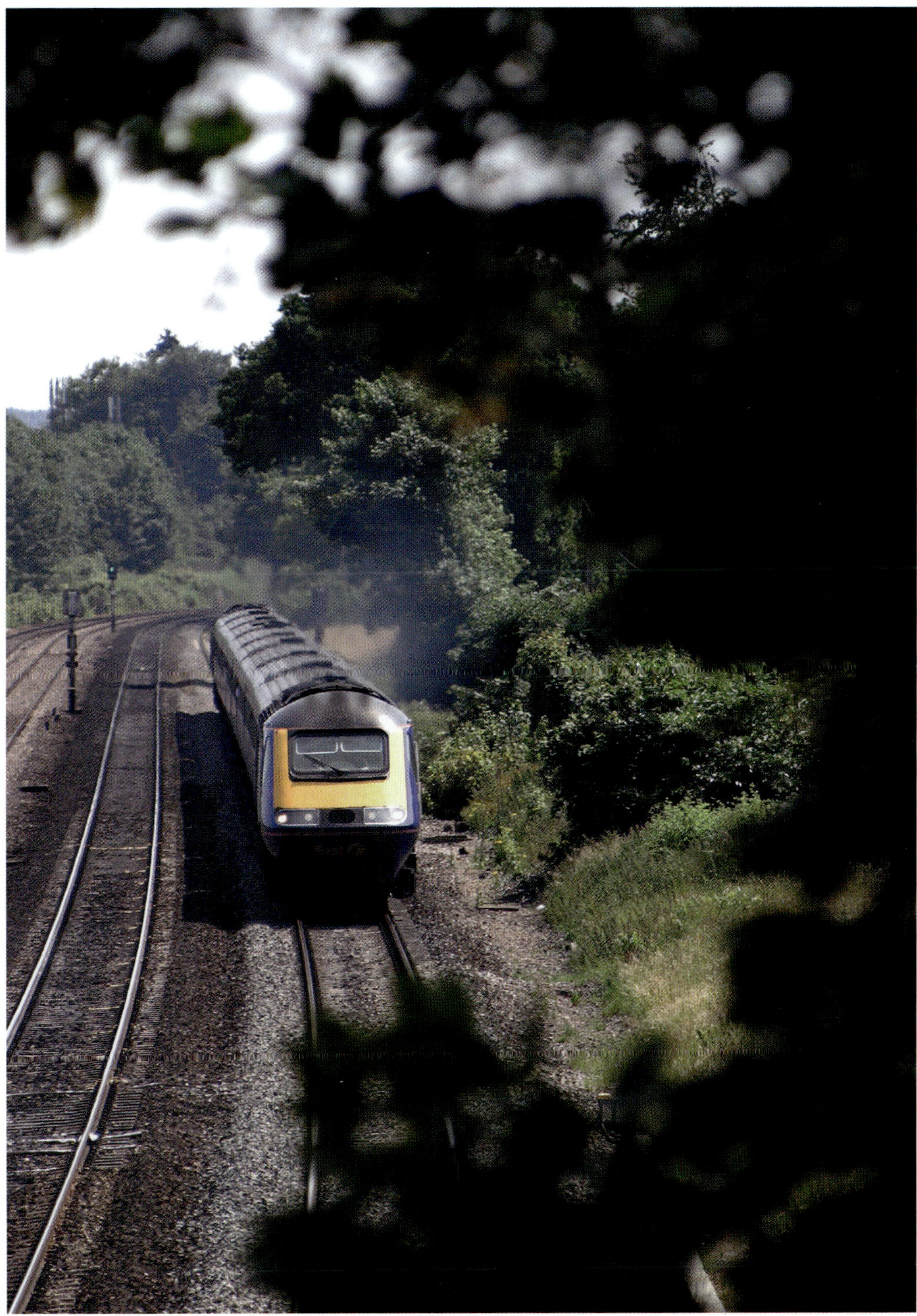

▲ A handy gap in the trees provides a convenient viewpoint for a passing down HST at Lower Basildon, between Reading and Didcot. Canon 10D, 80-200mm lens, ISO 400, 1/1000 at f5.6.

◄ Postal unit 325 004 is framed by this brick archway at Crewe station. Canon 5D, 24-105mm lens, ISO 250, 1/50 at f4.

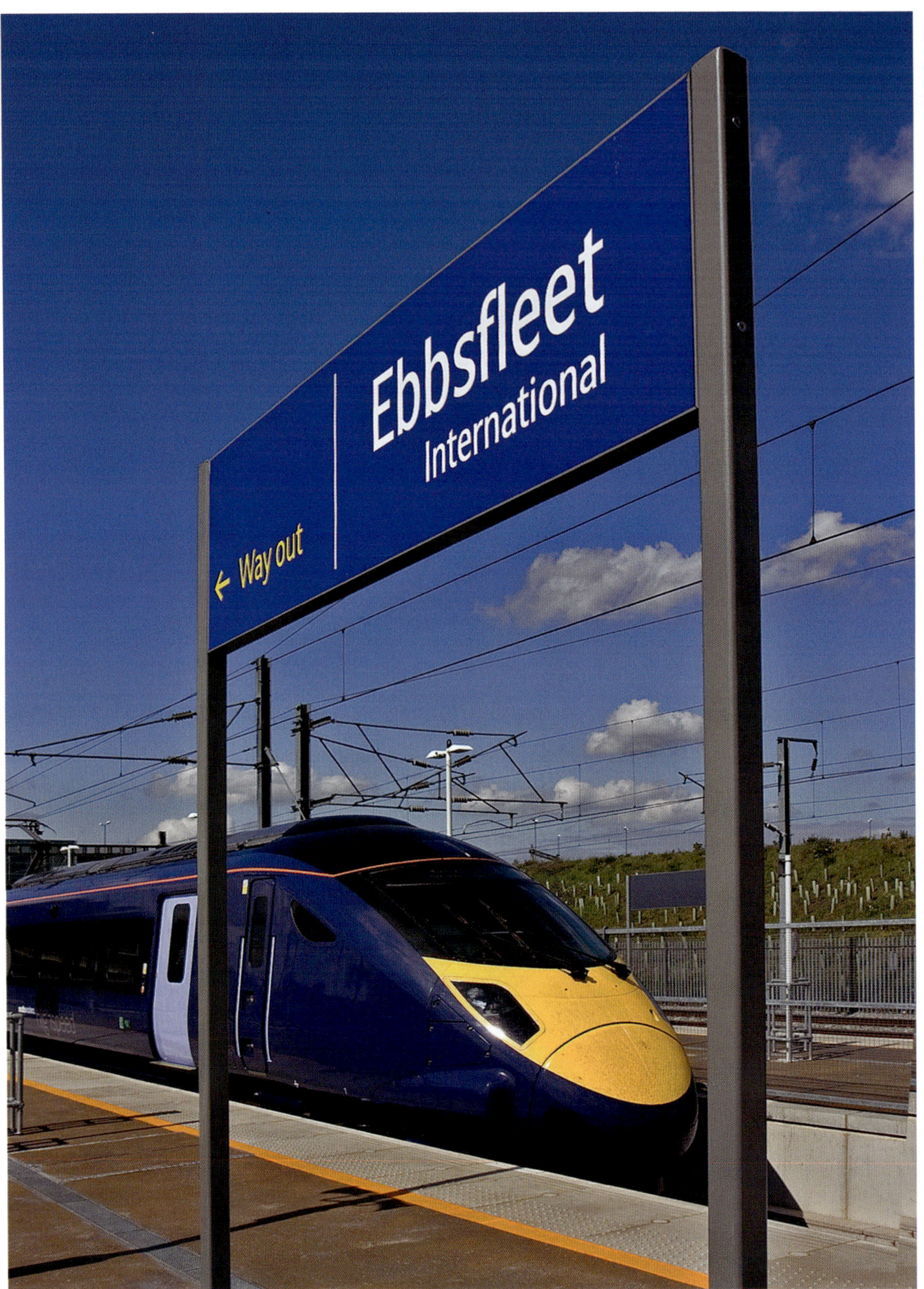

Ebbsfleet
International
← Way out

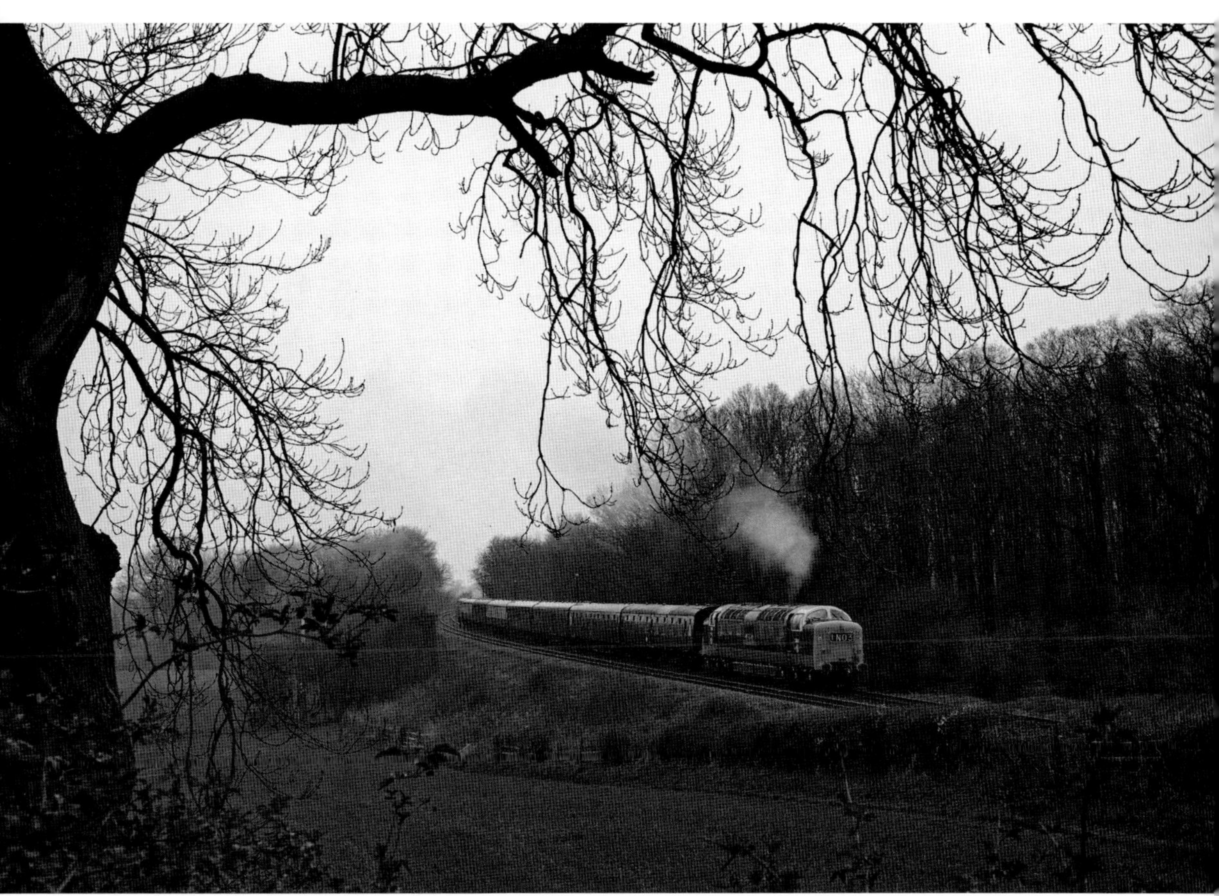

▲ In dire weather, this tree provides a welcome frame (and shelter from the rain) for 9016 during a 2014 photographic charter on the Great Central Railway. Canon 5D Mark III, 24-105mm lens, ISO 500, 1/400 at f8.

◀ In this image, the nose of this high-speed Javelin unit is framed perfectly by the station sign at Ebbsfleet International. Blue dominates the photo, but the yellow warning provides a powerful contrast. Canon 40D, 17-40mm lens, ISO 250, 1/400 at f14.

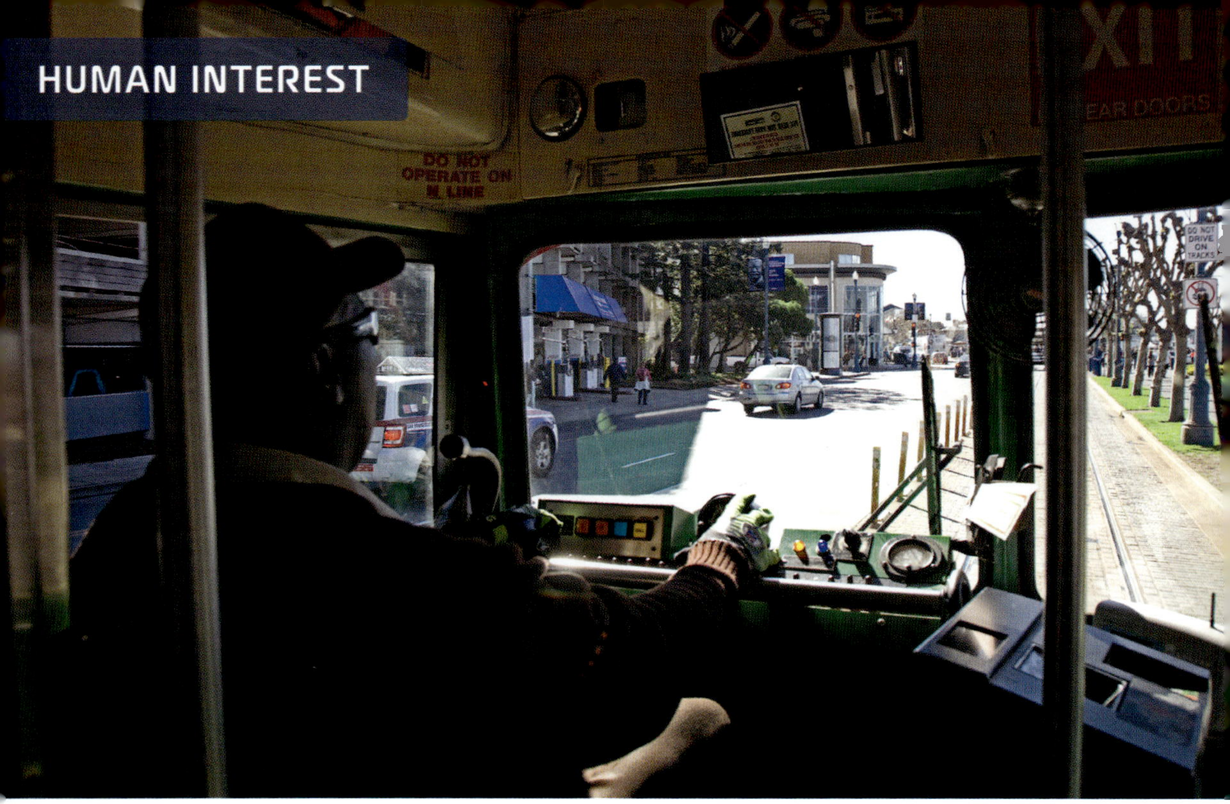

▲ The front seat of a San Francisco streetcar offers a drivers-eye view of the road ahead. Canon 5D, 24-105mm lens, ISO 160, 1/100 at f7.1.

▼ This was not a posed photograph! The dad is question was explaining the intricacies of 37 901's braking system to his young son. Canon 5D Mark III, 24-105mm lens, ISO 125, 1/400 at f8.

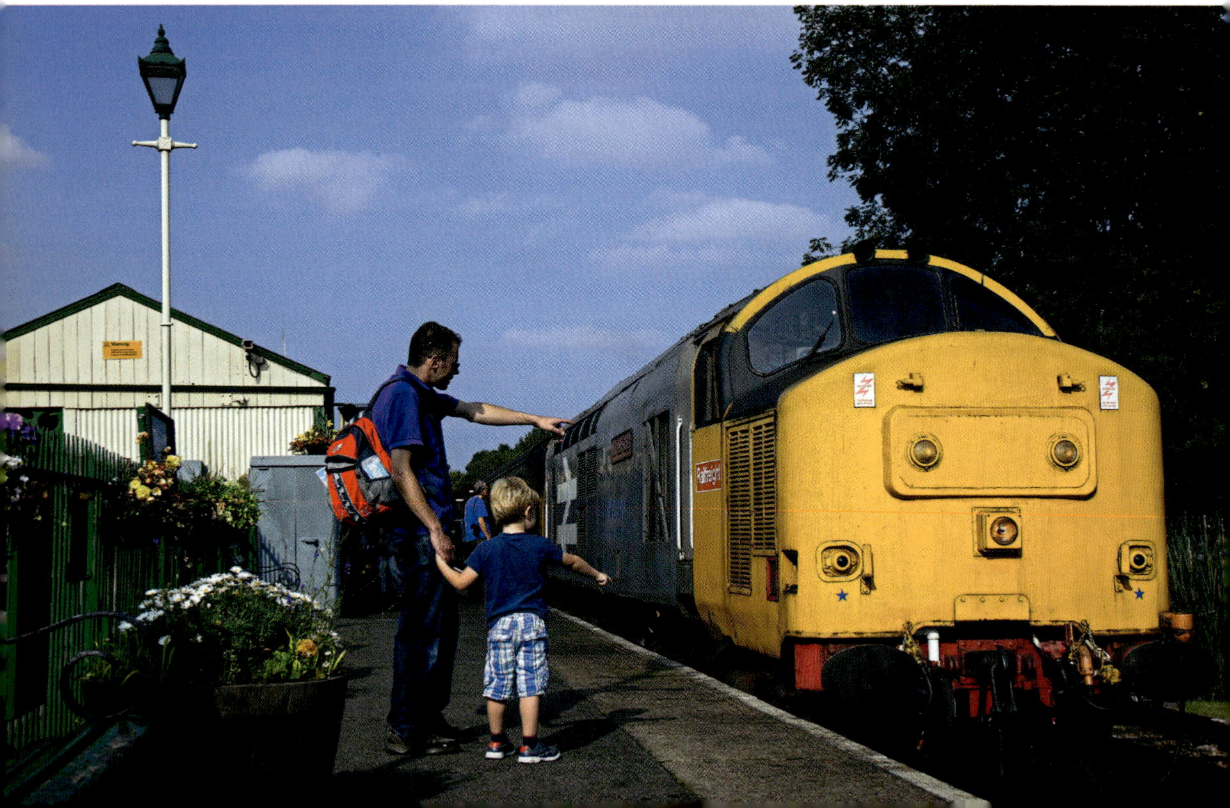

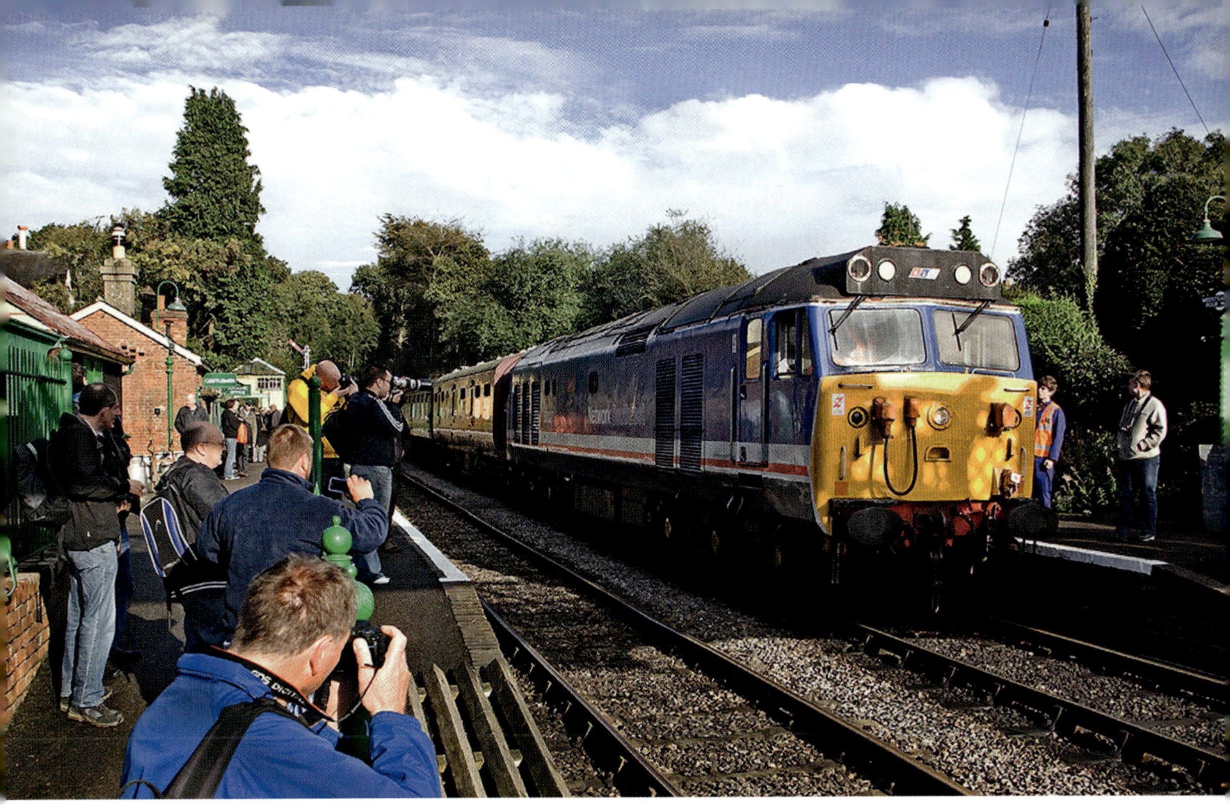

▲ The arrival of 50 027 back at the Mid Hants Railway after a lengthy spell away was met with plenty of photographers keen to record its first run. Canon 5D, 24-105mm lens, ISO 320, 1/320 at f8.

▼ Great Western pannier tank loco 3738 is topped up with water at Didcot Railway Centre. A fast shutter speed freezes the water droplets in mid air. In retrospect, a slower speed would have been a better choice, allowing them to blur a little. Canon 5D, 24-105mm lens, ISO 400, 1/200 at f8.

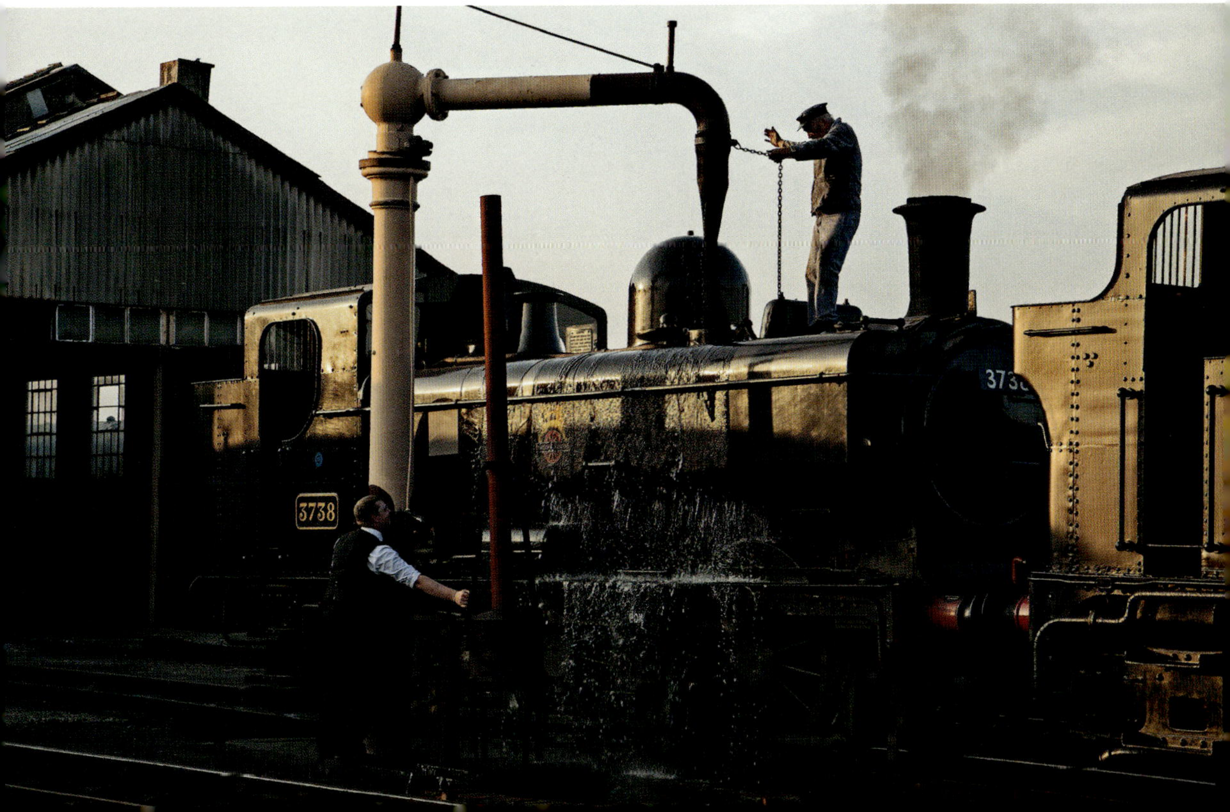

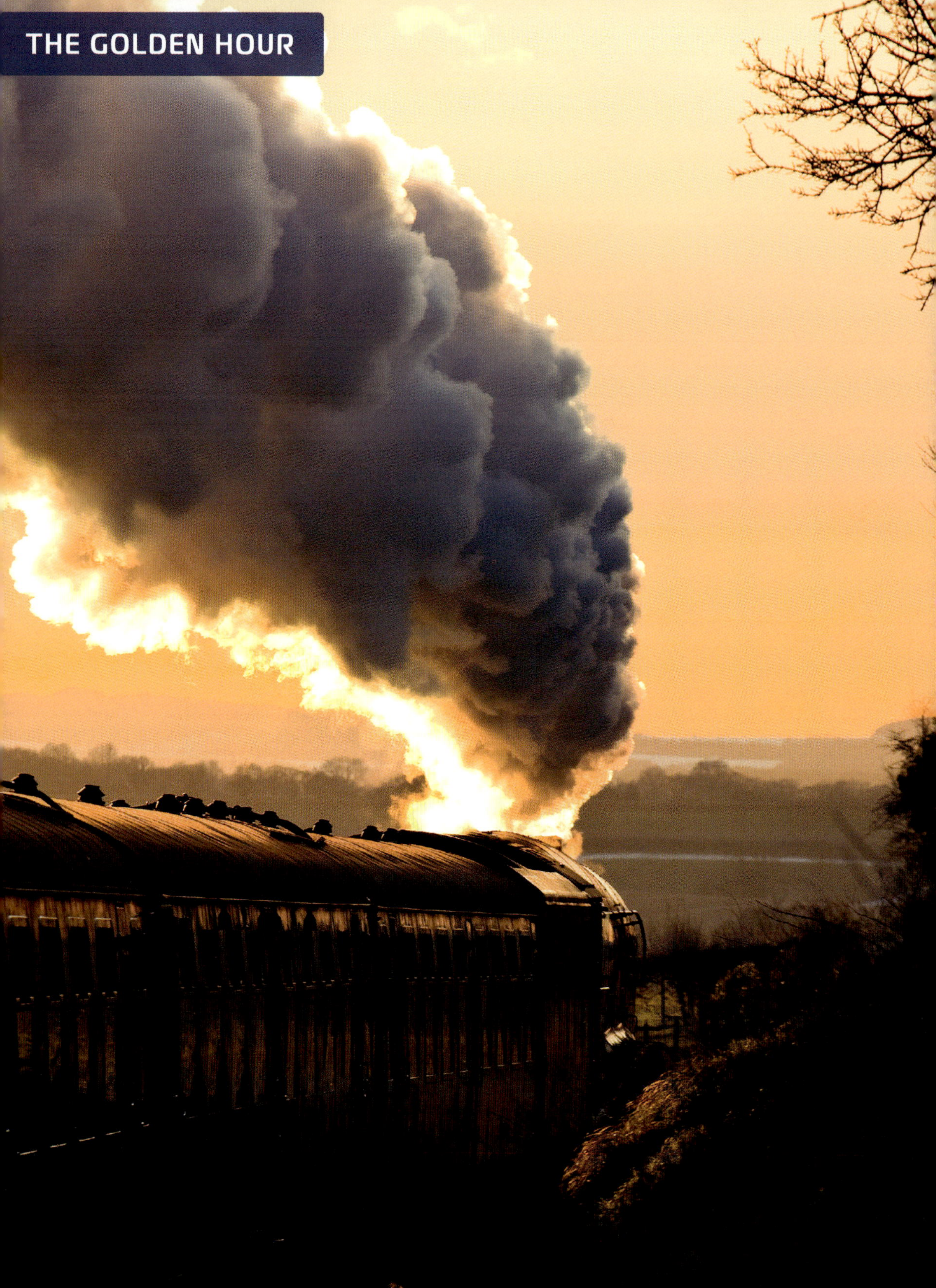

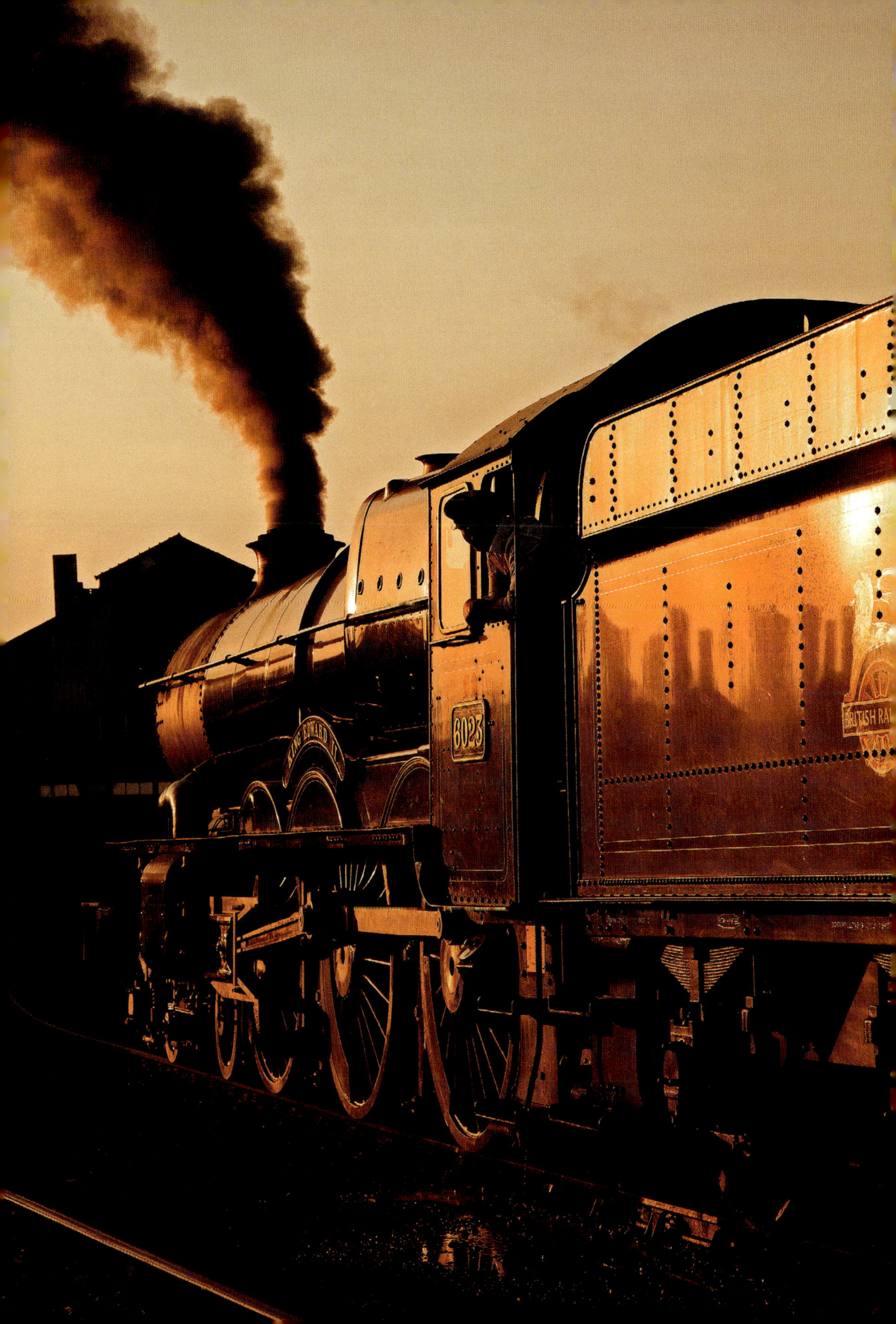

VIEWPOINT

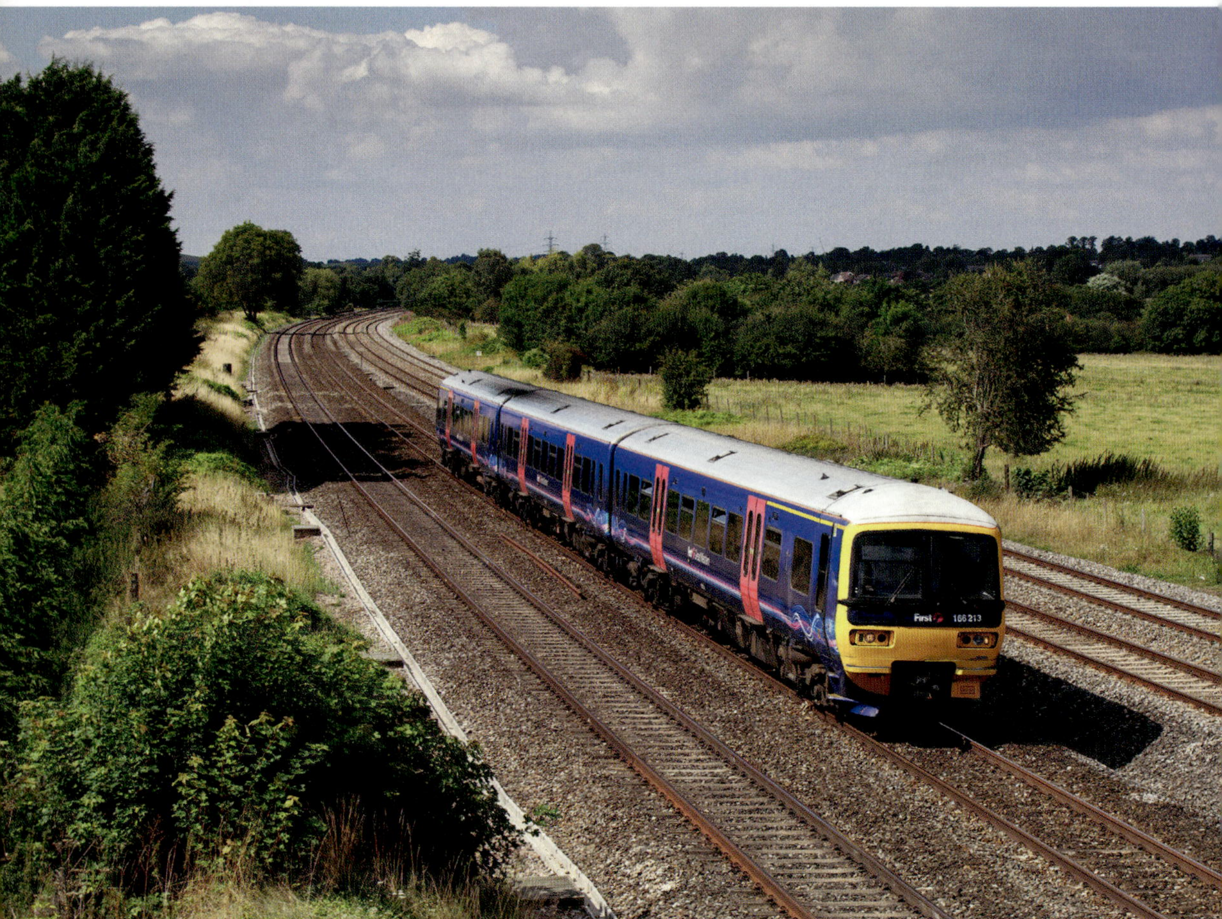

▲ A raised viewpoint offers the photographer a chance to see a broader perspective. In this view at Lower Basildon in the Thames valley, it was important to show the catenary-free location in its full glory, as imminent electrification will spoil the classic shot forever. Thames Turbo 165 213 speeds past on the fast line on a glorious 2014 summer afternoon. Canon 5D Mark III, 24-105 lens, ISO 400, 1/1250 at f7.1.

► A unique viewpoint on a unique trip. The first Eurostar unit to venture to Bourg St Maurice in the French Alps was exciting enough, but I could not turn down the (escorted) invitation to climb one of the station lighting towers for this photograph. Not for the faint hearted, and only possible under official supervision. 35mm slide scan.

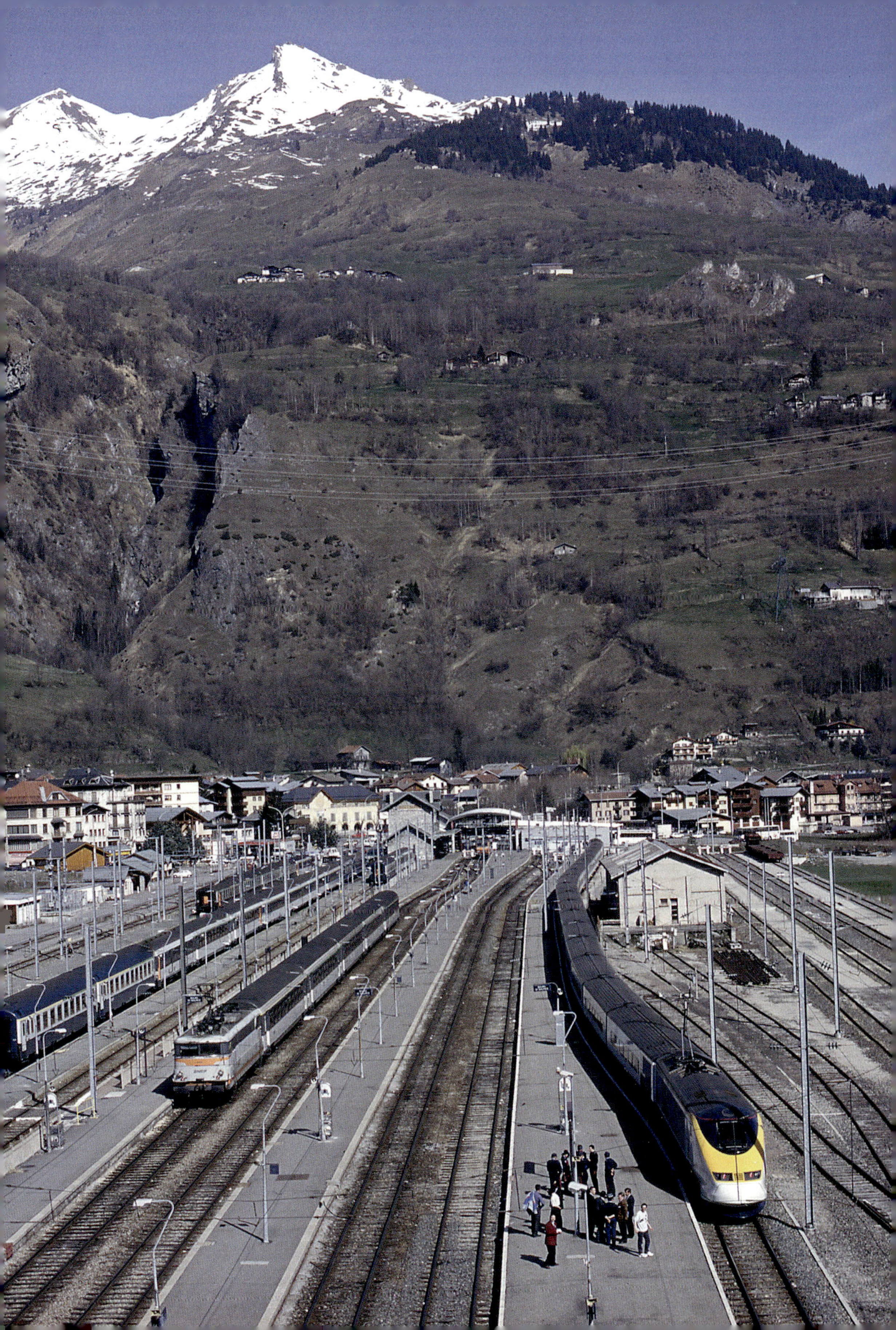

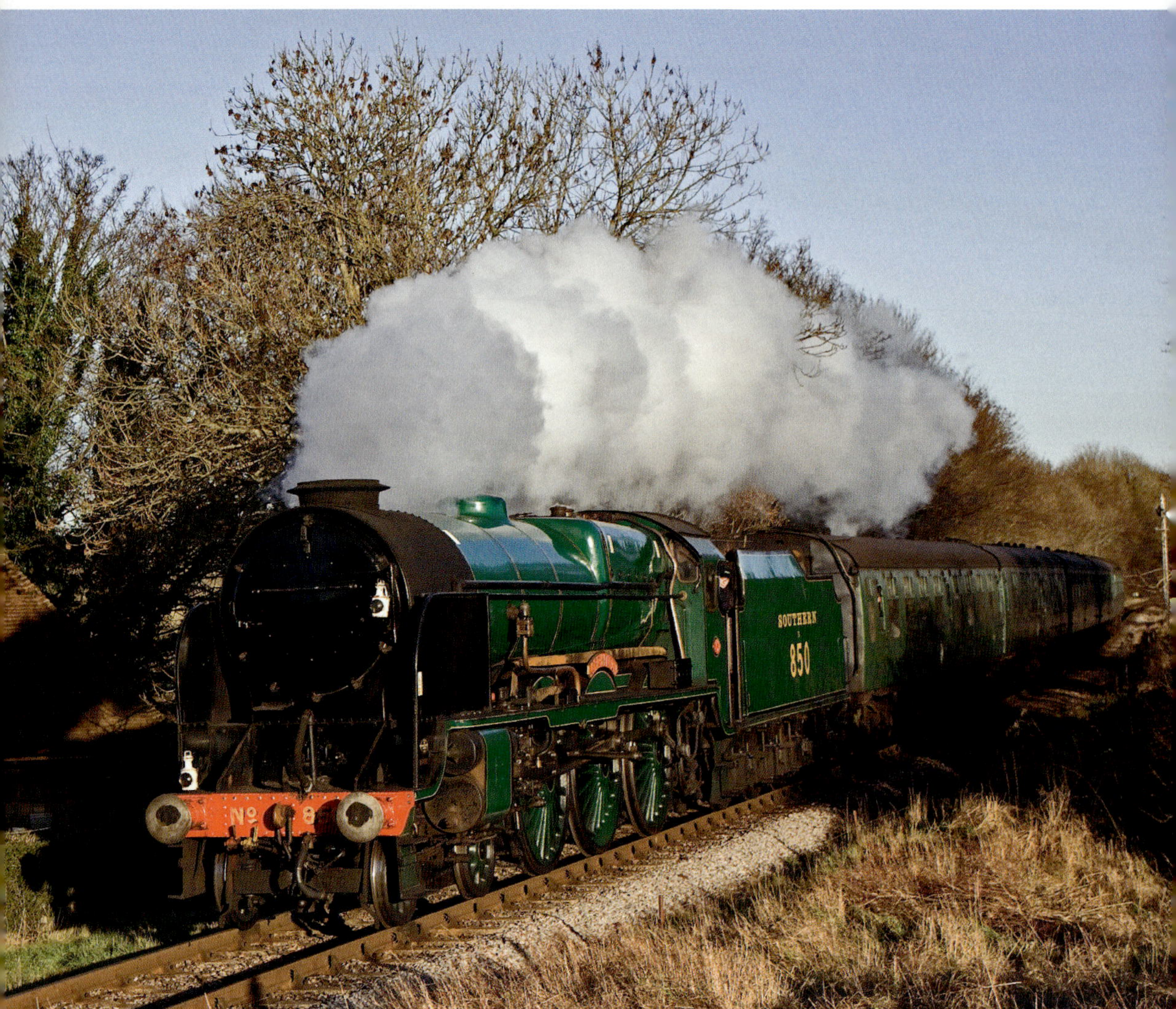

▲ Sometimes it all just comes together. Crisp winter air encourages a good head of steam from 850 Lord Nelson as it approaches Arlesford. Canon 5D, 24-105mm lens, ISO 320, 1/640 at f5.6.

▲ Very much a grab shot, but one that definitely worked. D9009 leads D1062 and D821 through Stafford *en route* to the North Yorkshire Moors diesel gala in 2013. With seconds to get a camera out and ready, familiarity with the controls and settings paid dividends. Canon 5D, 24-105mm lens, ISO 320, 1/800 at f4.

▼ This was just a matter of being in the right place at the right time. Adelante unit 180 110 overtakes Thames Turbo 165 116 at Lower Basildon. Canon 10D, 80-200mm lens, ISO 400, 1/750 at f8.

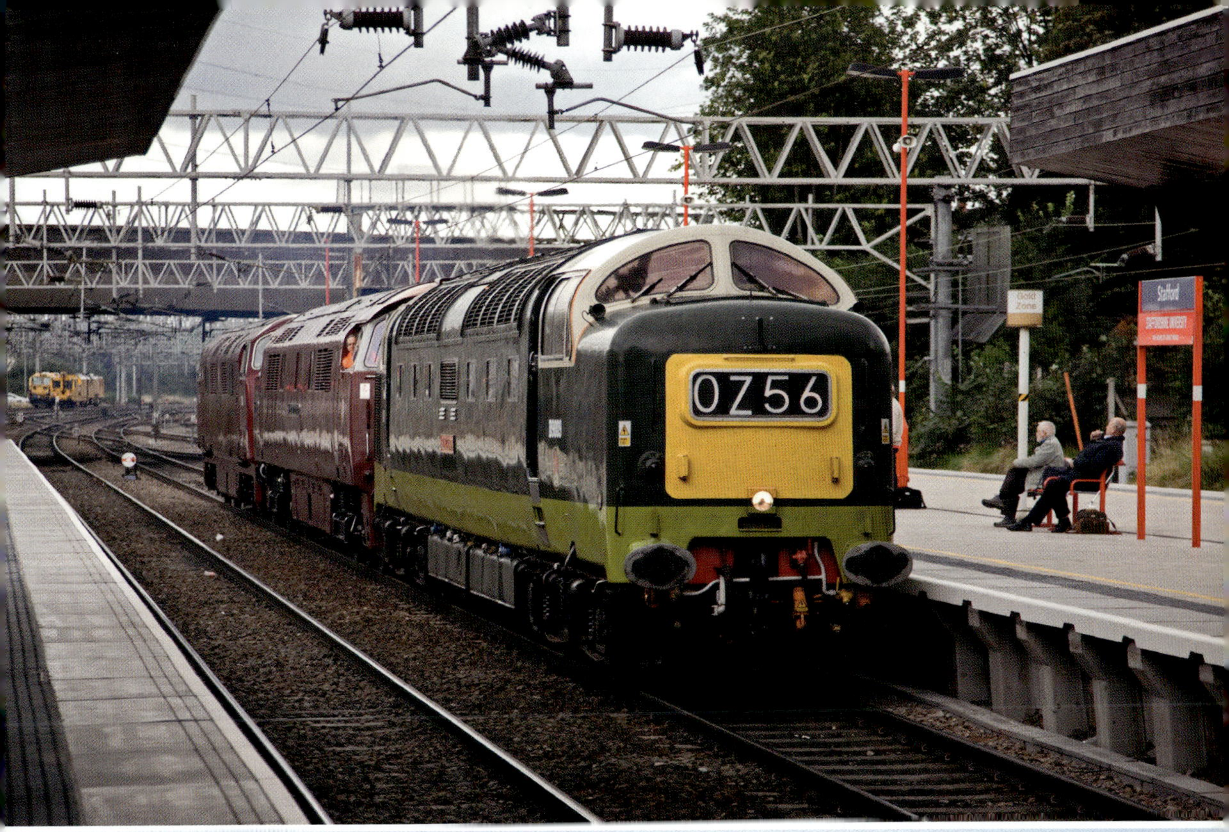
0Z56
Stafford

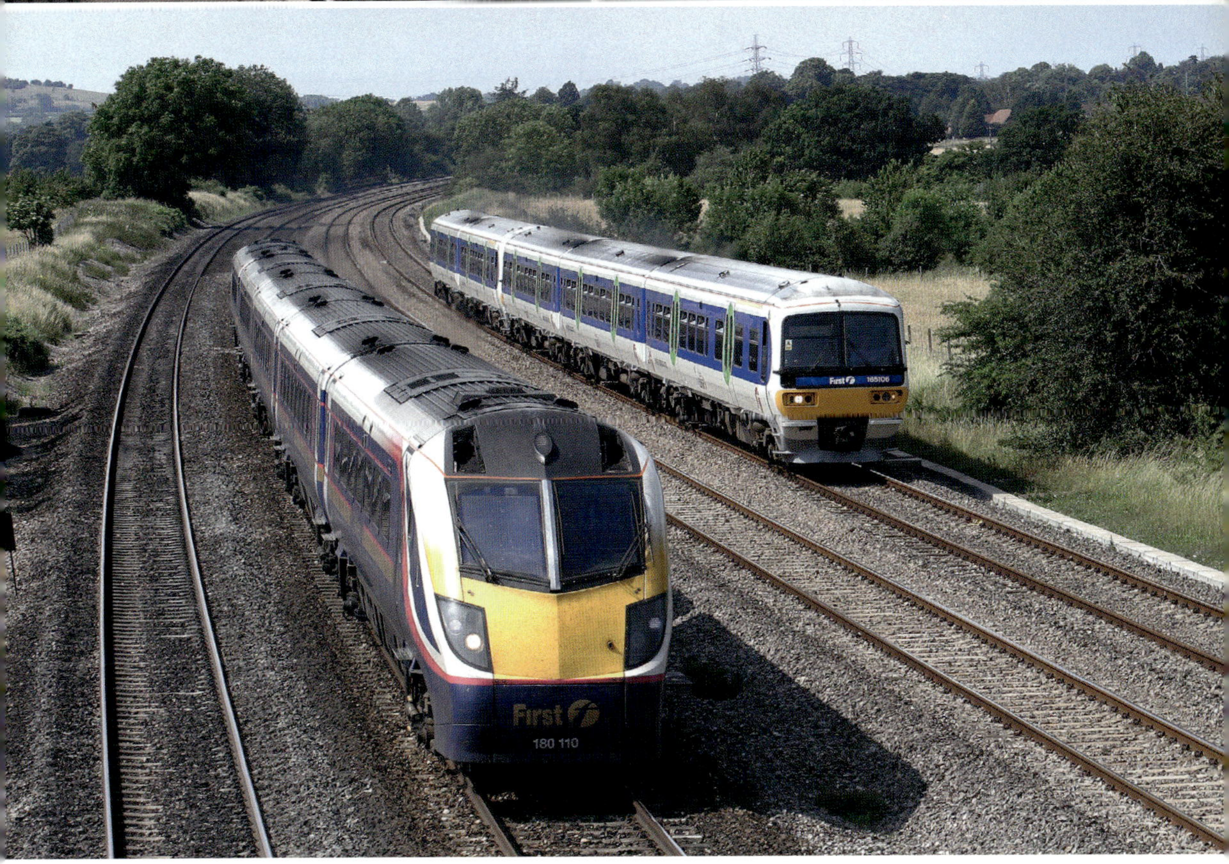
First
180 110

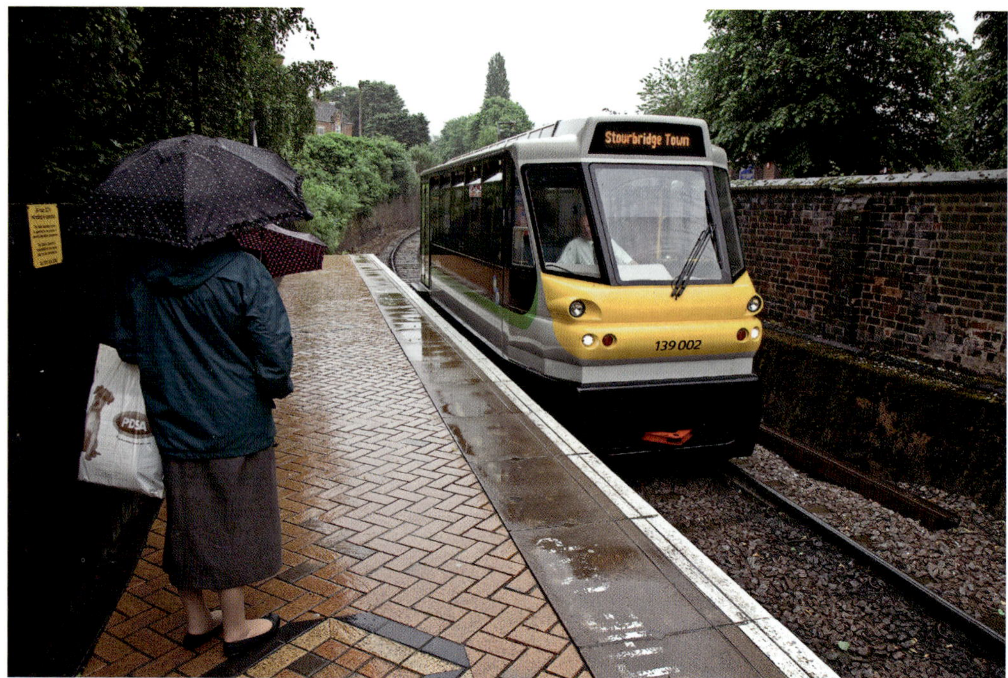

A rainy afternoon in Stourbridge Town. The wonderful Parry People Mover has been providing sterling service on the short branch from Stourbridge Town for several years now. An elderly passenger awaits the arrival of 139 002. Canon 5D, 24-105mm lens, ISO 500, 1/125 at f7.1.

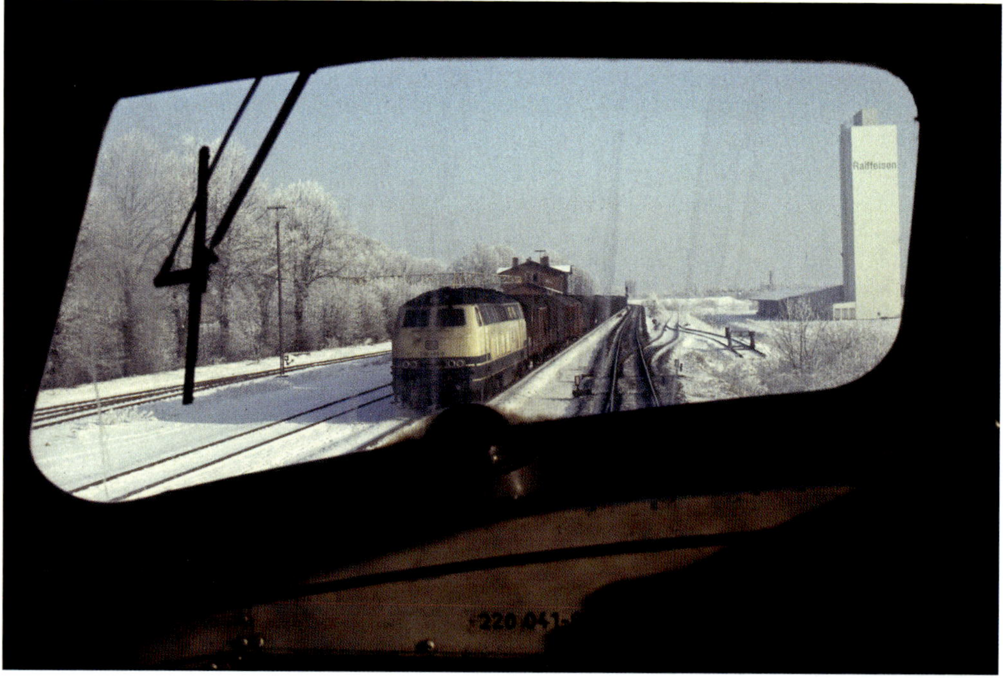

Many enthusiasts travelled to Germany in the early 1980s to ride behind the last of the German V200 diesel hydraulics, and one would occasionally be offered the chance of a ride with the driver. From the cab of 220 041, a passing freight is glimpsed near Lubeck, hauled by a DB class 218. 35mm slide scan.

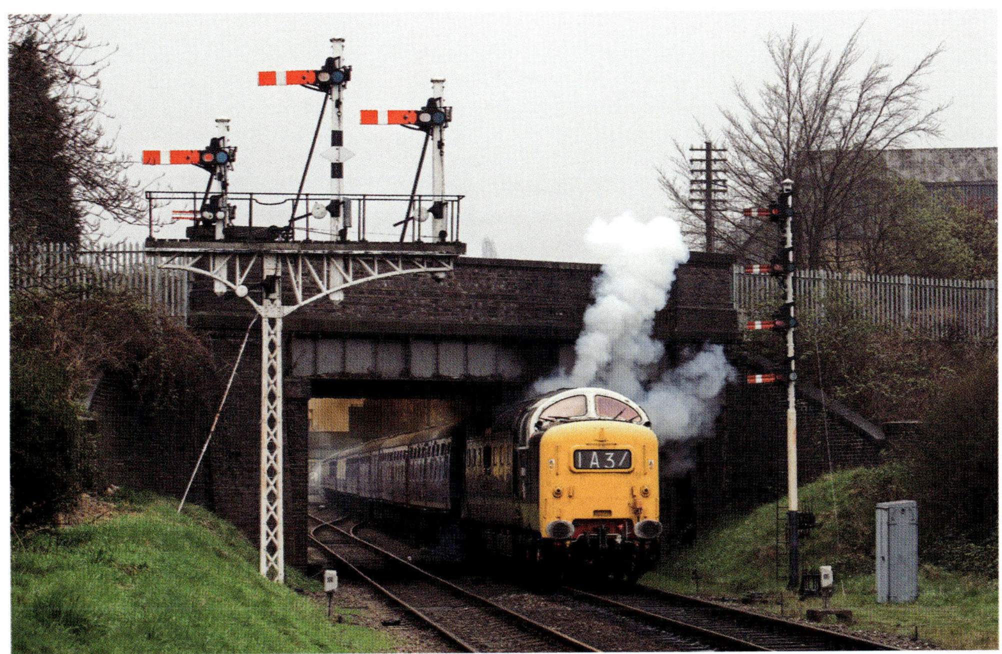

Any fan of the Class 55 Deltics will be familiar with this sight. As power is applied, a plume of exhaust lays a smoke trail behind D9016 as it departs from Loughborough. Canon 5D Mark III, 24-105mm lens, ISO 640, 1/640 at f5.

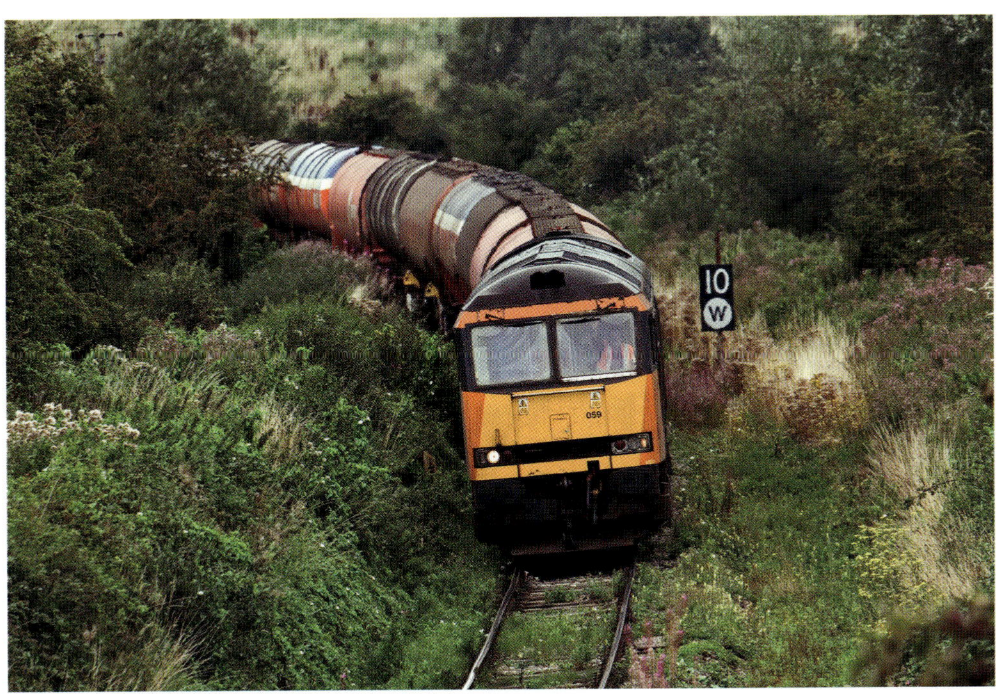

60 059 creeps slowly along the Westerleigh branch with its loaded oil tanks from the Robeston refinery in Wales. The train seems almost lost in the undergrowth, although appearances can be deceptive—the location is almost right in the middle of the village. Canon 40D, 70-200mm lens, ISO 250, 1/500 at f5.6.

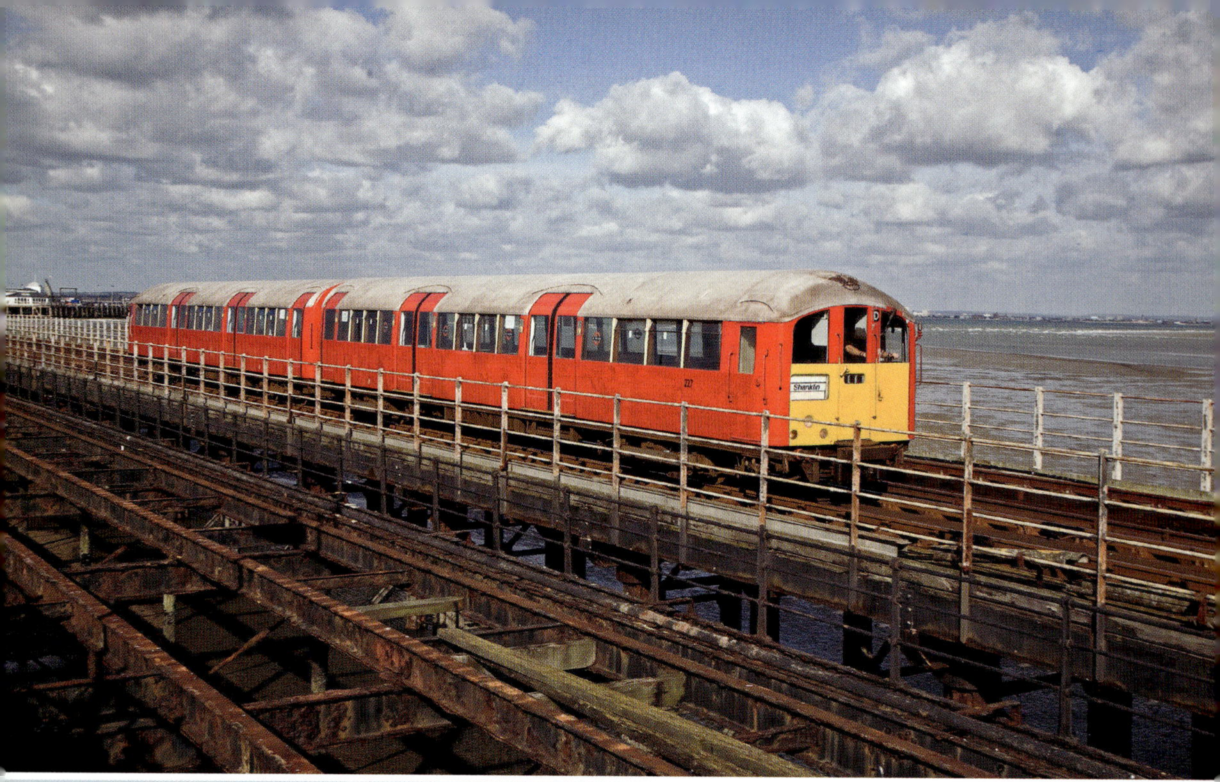

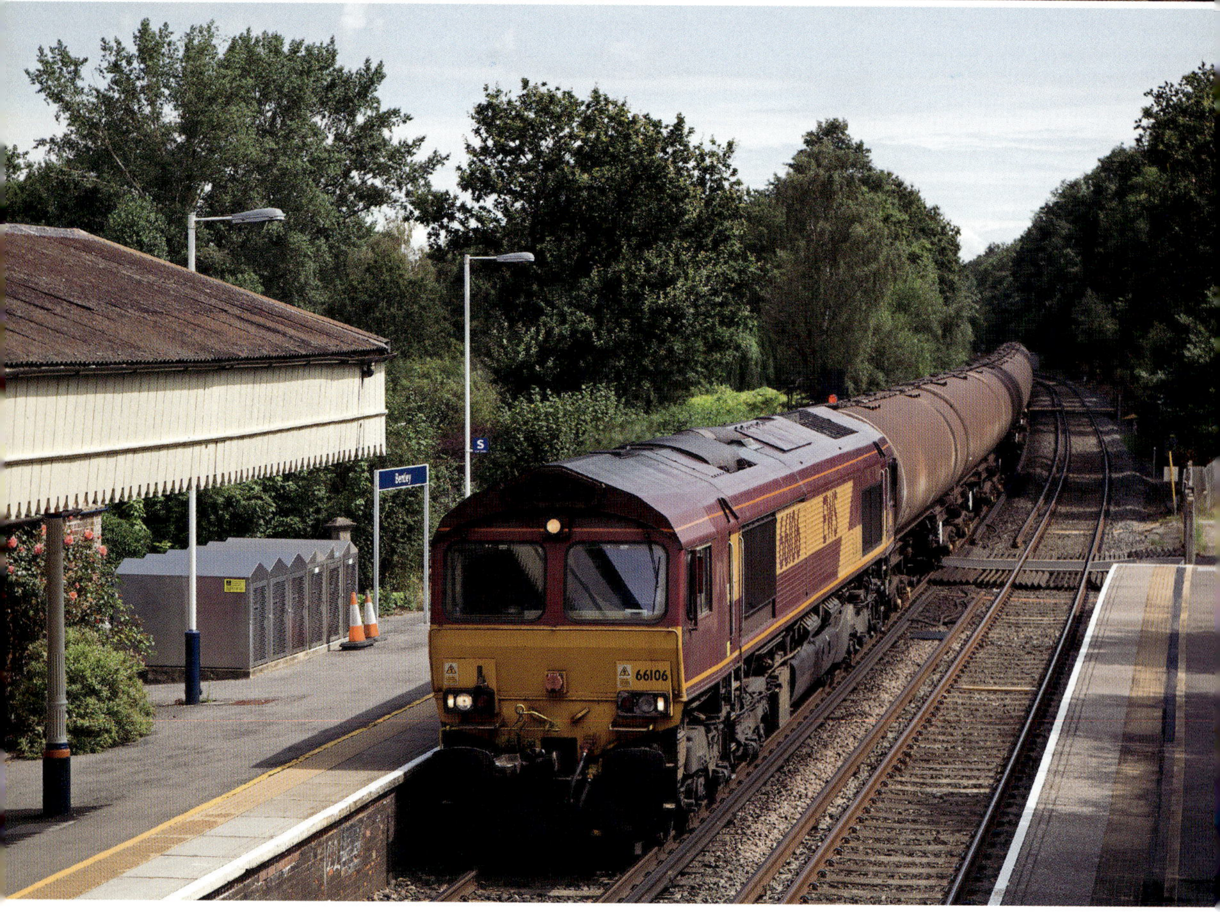

 Gallery

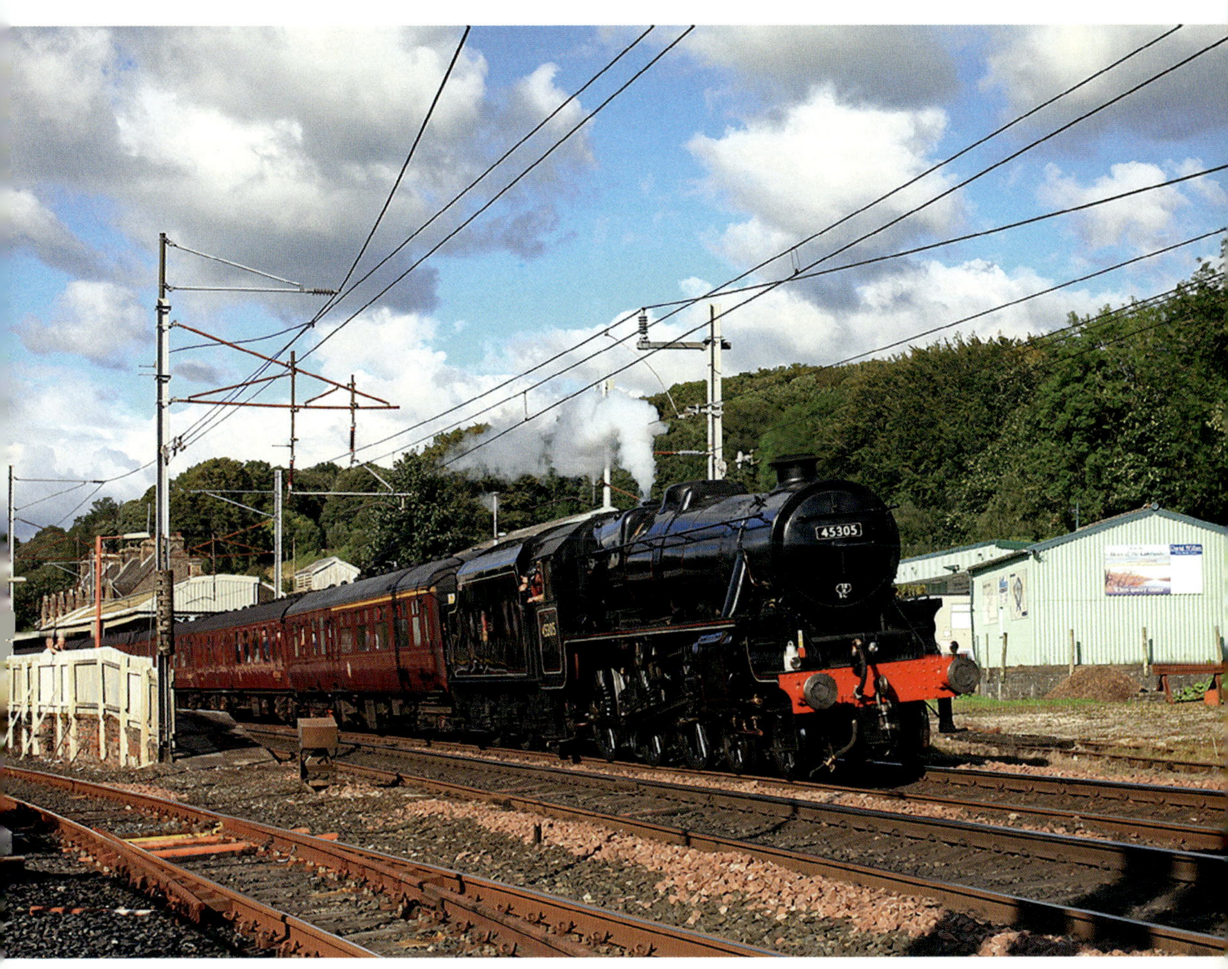

▲ Hot weather in the summer is of course welcome, but it does mean little visible exhaust smoke from steam engines. Fortunately, the safety valves blowing as the train sped through Oxenholme gave a momentary white steam plume. Canon EOS 5D, 24-105mm lens, ISO 250, 1/640 at f8.

▲ Ex-London Underground unit 229 rattles along the pier at Ryde on the Isle of Wight on a glorious day in March 2012. The city of Portsmouth can be seen in the distance across the Solent. Canon 5D, 24-105mm lens, ISO 250, 1/320 at f13.

▼ Perhaps just another photo of a Class 66 on a freight, but personally, this was six years in the making. The Fawley to Holybourne oil tanks only run three days a week, and the coincidence of a day off work, the train running, and the sun shining was an opportunity not to be missed. 66 106 passes Bentley on the Alton branch in summer 2014 just a few miles from journey's end. The branch is a single line with a passing loop at Bentley, hence the train appearing to be running 'wrong line'. Canon 5D Mark III, 24-105mm lens, ISO 320, 1/800 at f6.3.

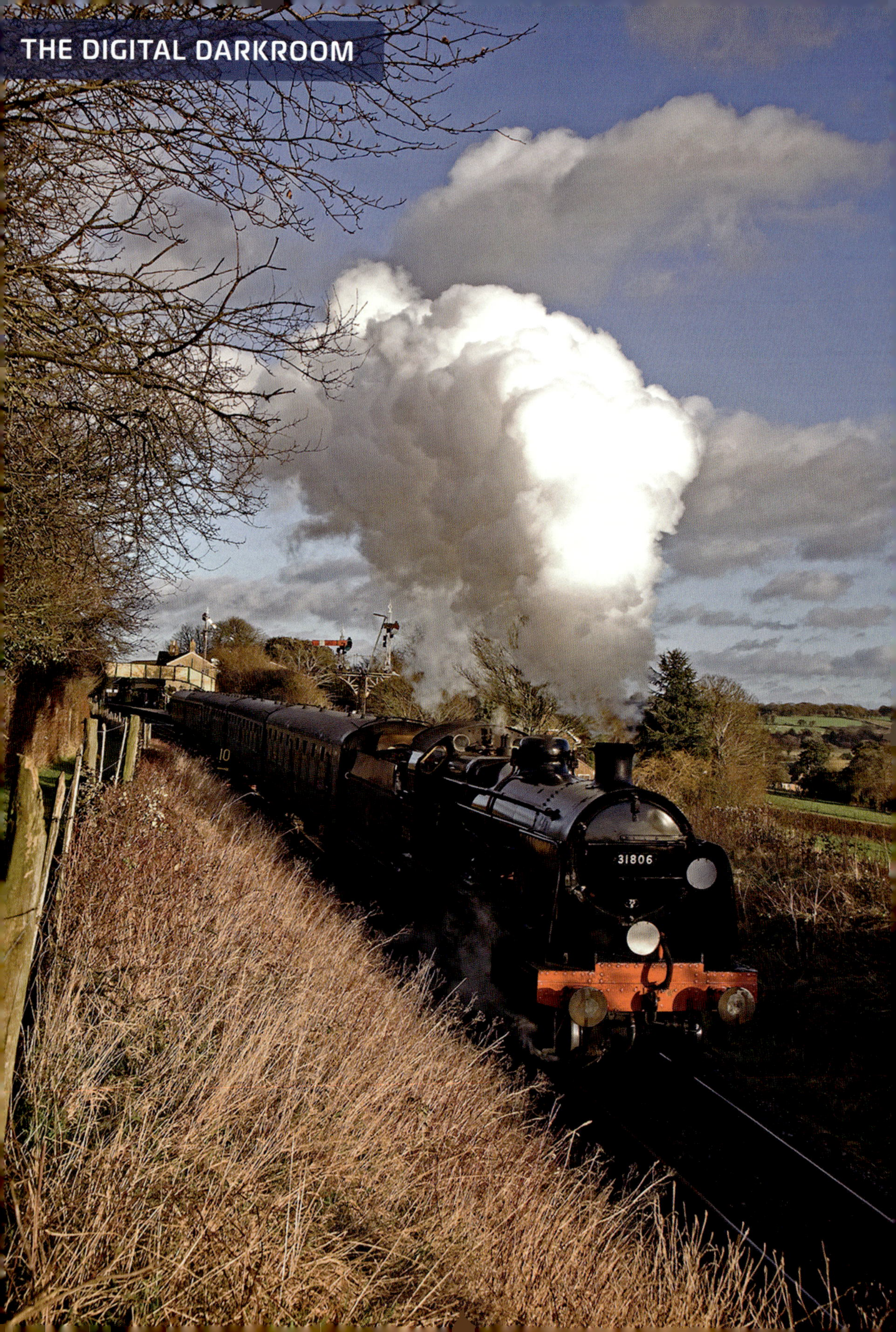
31806
10

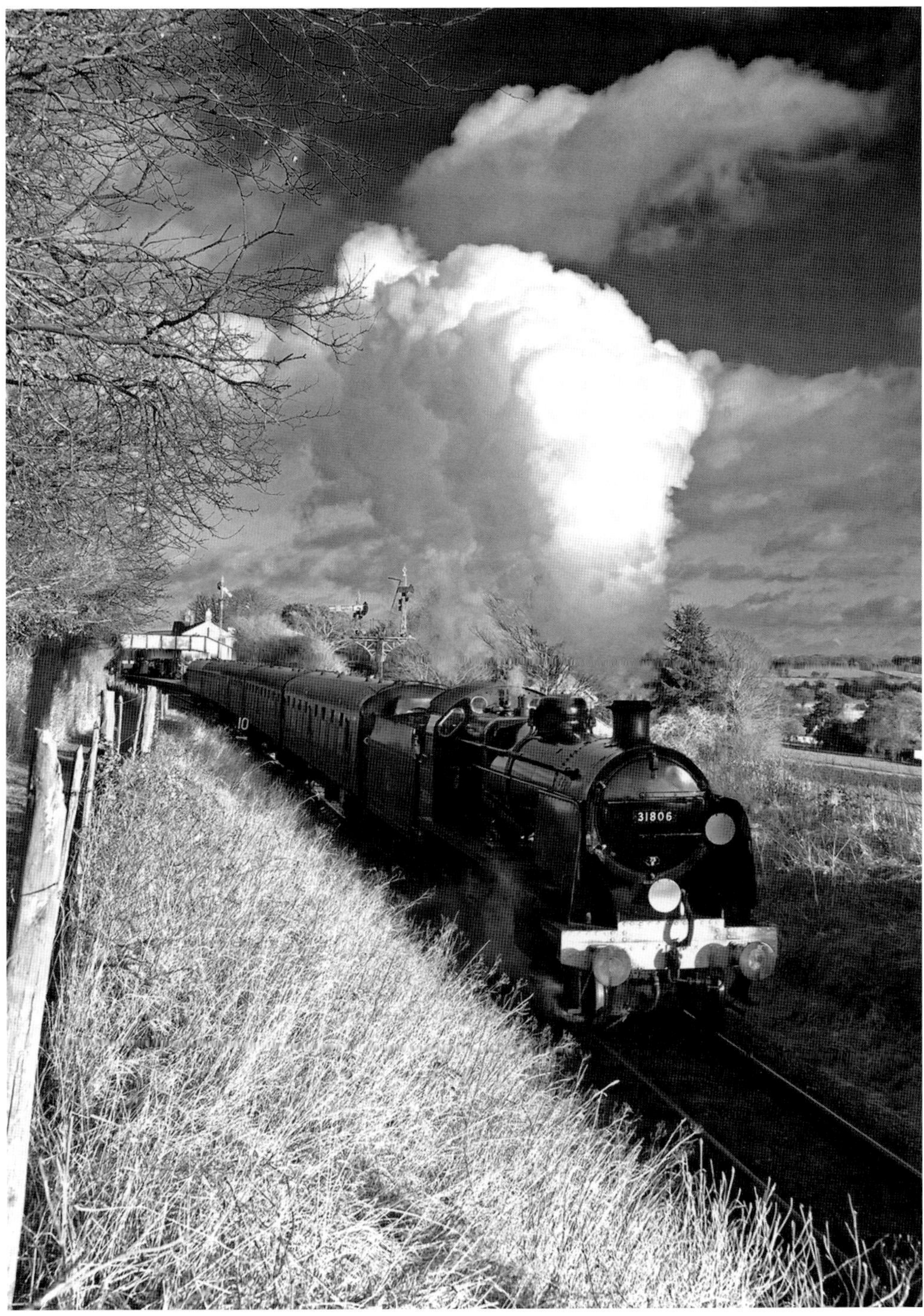

◄ 31806 makes a lively departure from Ropley towards Arlesford on a cold winter's day. Canon 5D, 24-105mm lens, ISO 200, 1/200 at f10.

▲ Using Photoshop's brightness and contrast adjustments and converting to black and white, the image is transformed to give an almost infra-red effect.

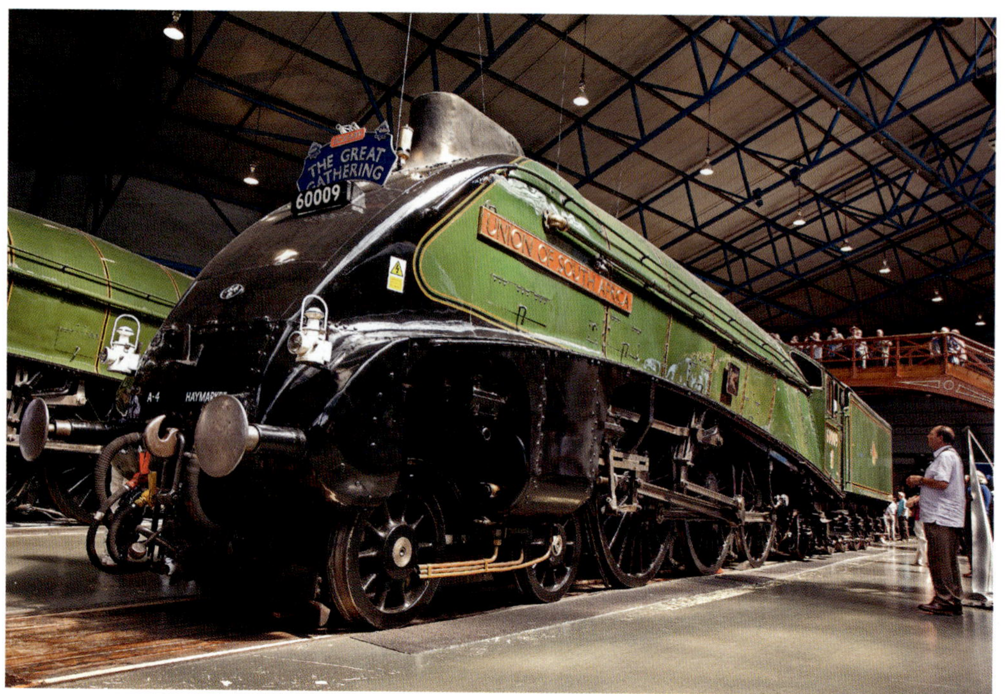

Gresley A4 6009 Union of South Africa at the National Railway Museum, York, during the Great Gathering of 2013. Canon 5D, 24-105mm lens, ISO 400, 1/50 at f5.

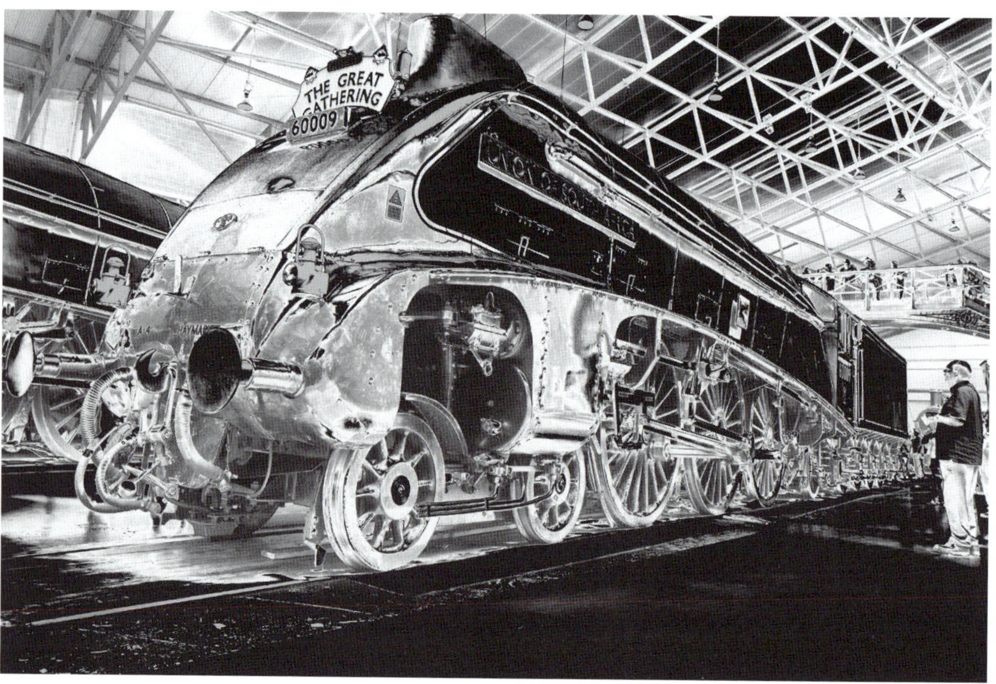

Digital imaging software allows for all sorts of unusual effects to be tried out—in this case the recreation of a solarisation technique. In Photoshop, a quick method is to use the **Filter**, **Styalize**, **Solarize** commands on the top menu, and then adjust the settings to suit.

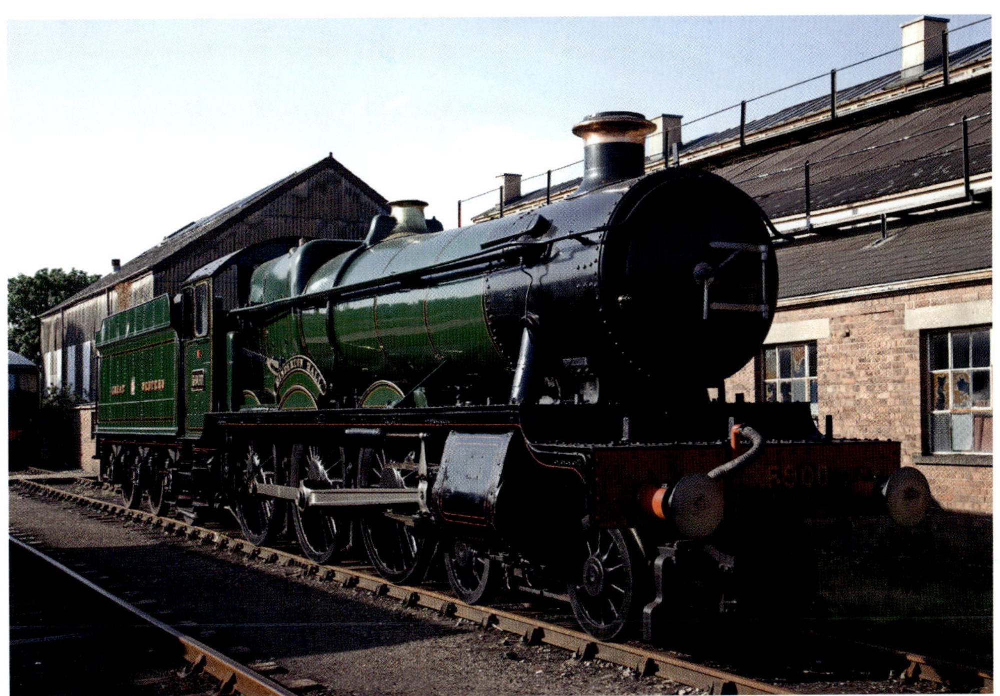

Great Western 6900 Hinderton Hall looks immaculate at Didcot Railway Centre. Canon 5D, 24-105mm lens, ISO 125, 1/100 at f7.1.

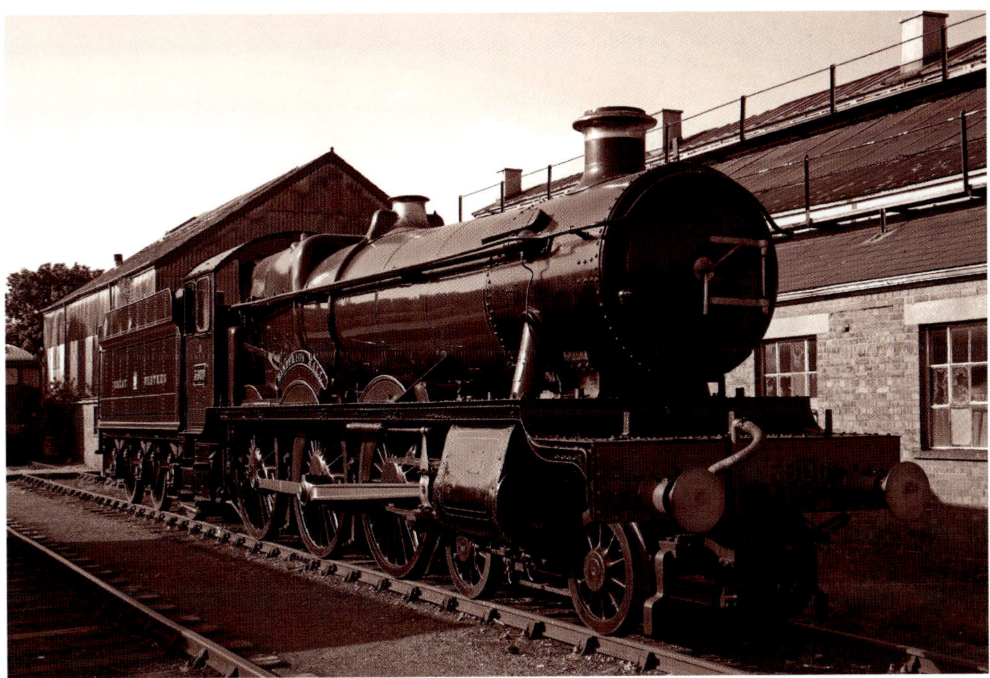

With just a few minutes work in Photoshop CS6, the application of sepia toning gives the image a distinctly historic feel. In Photoshop, having converted the image to black and white, choose **Image**, **Adjustments**, **Photo filter**, and then select **Sepia** from the list. Adjust the density to suit.

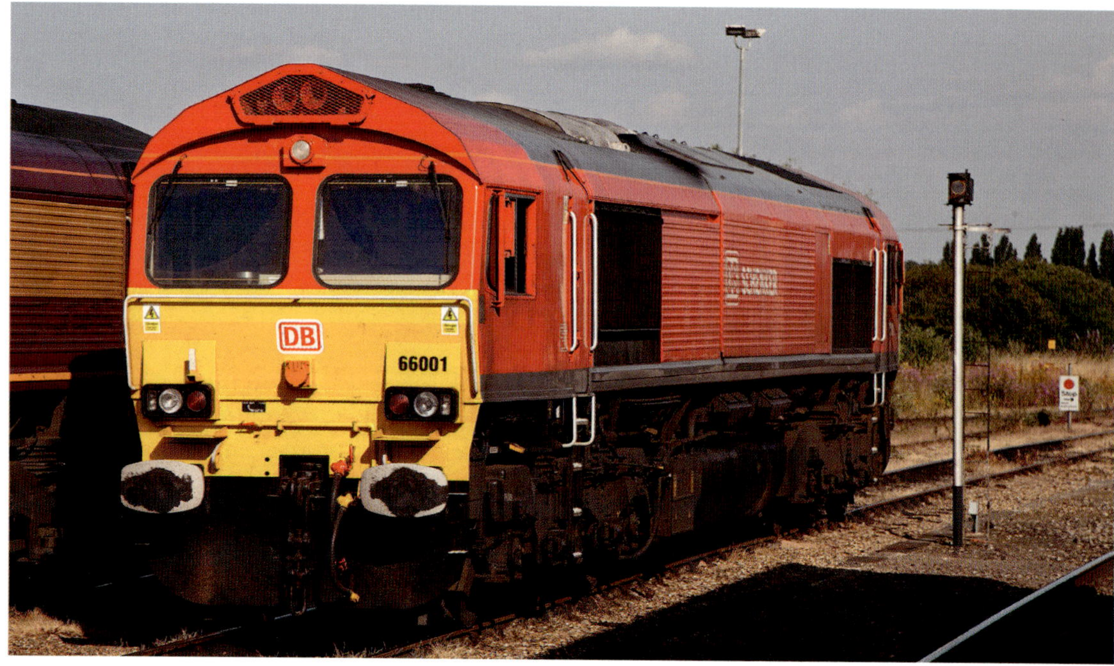

A distracting item is sometimes an unavoidable part of a railway photograph. Typically, lamps or branches visible above a train can spoil an otherwise memorable image. Although railway photographers may baulk at the idea of excessive digital manipulation, the removal of items is broadly acceptable, as long as the viewer is advised in a caption that some retouching work has taken place. Canon 5D, 24-105mm lens, ISO 125, 1/320 at f8. In Photoshop, use the clone tool on the side toolbar to remove the offending item. Beginners should use a fairly small radius setting to keep the amendment area small and unobtrusive.

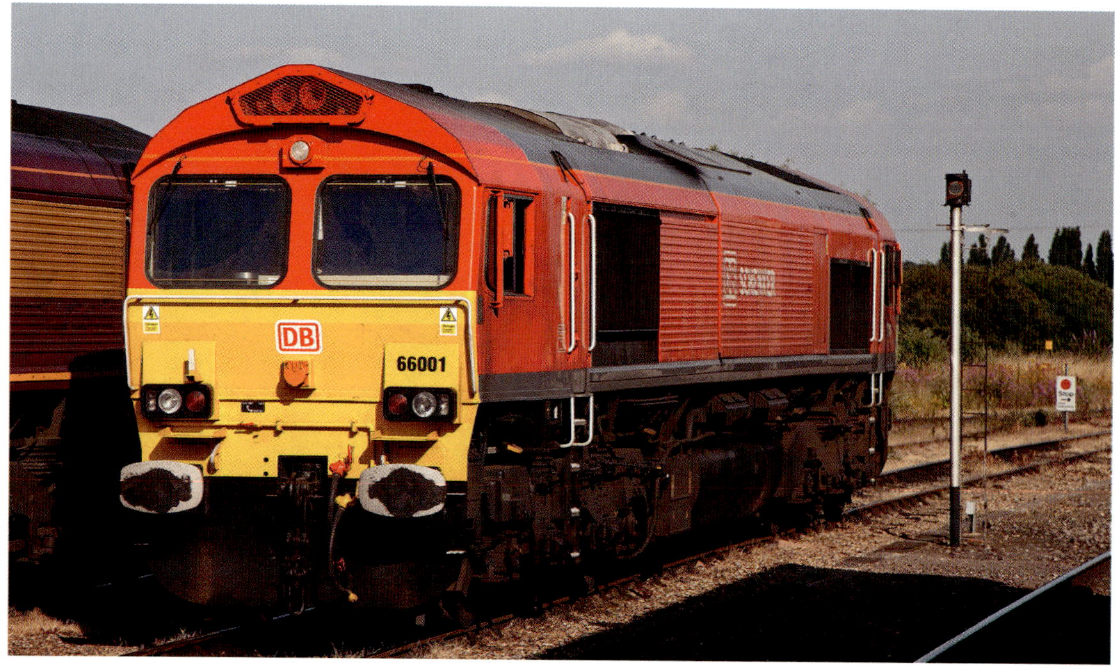

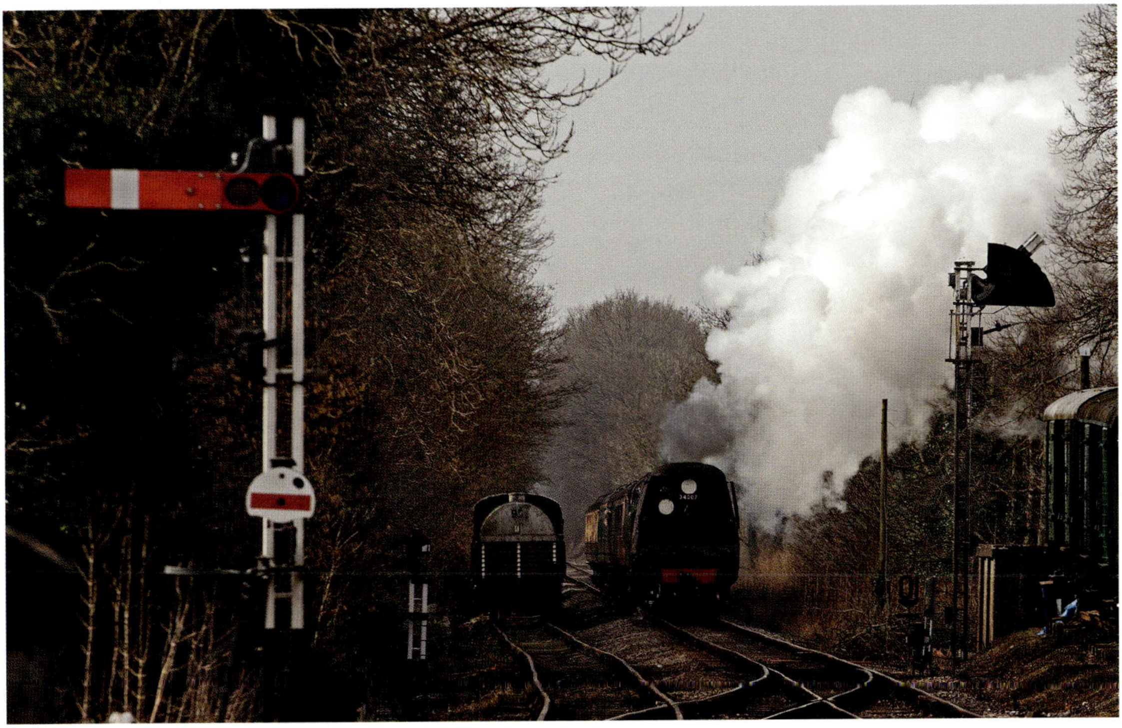

Both images are pleasing shots of 34007 as it approached Four Marks & Medstead, but conversion to black and white gives a much more historic feel to a typically Southern railway scene. Canon 5D, 70-200mm lens, ISO 160, 1/640 at f6.3.

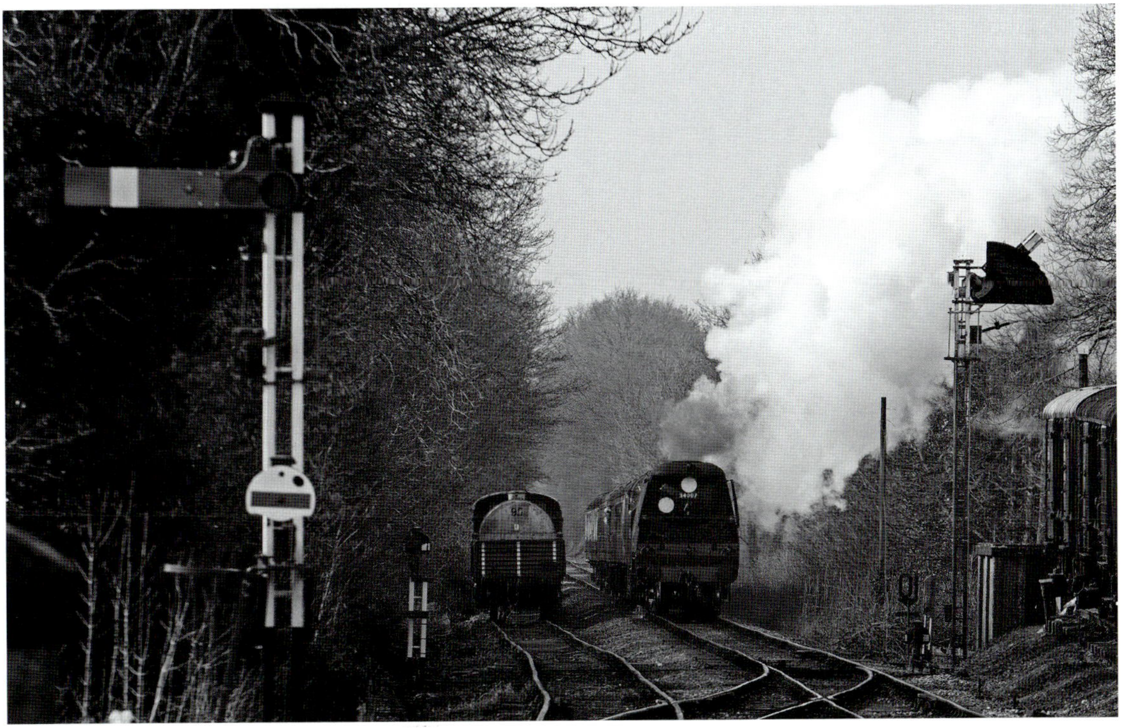

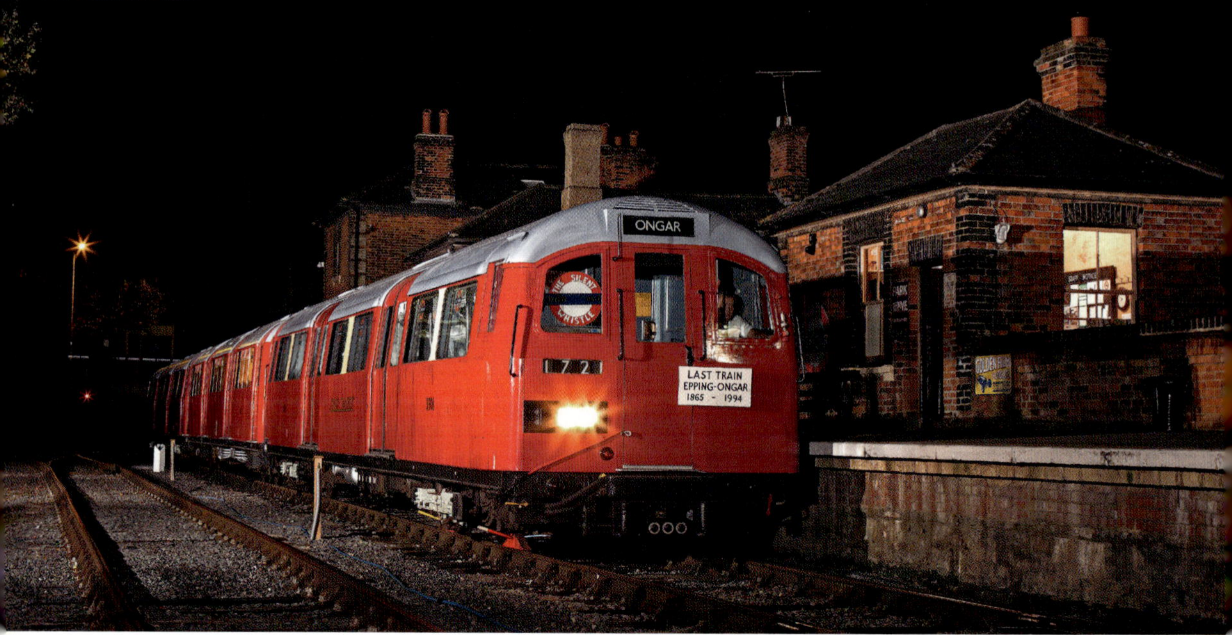

▲ In a 2014 charter recreation of the last train to operate on the Epping to Ongar line, the original Cravens 1960 tube train stands at Ongar as it did when it formed the last service departure in September 1994. Canon 5D Mark III, 50mm f1.4 lens, ISO 100, 10 seconds at f8.

▼ You never know where you will come across a train to photograph. During a family holiday to the USA, this ageing Baldwin oil-fired 2-8-0 locomotive was discovered near to the lowest place on earth, at Death Valley's Furnace Creek Ranch, California, over 200 feet below sea level. Canon 5D, 24-105mm lens, ISO 125, 1/160 at f9.

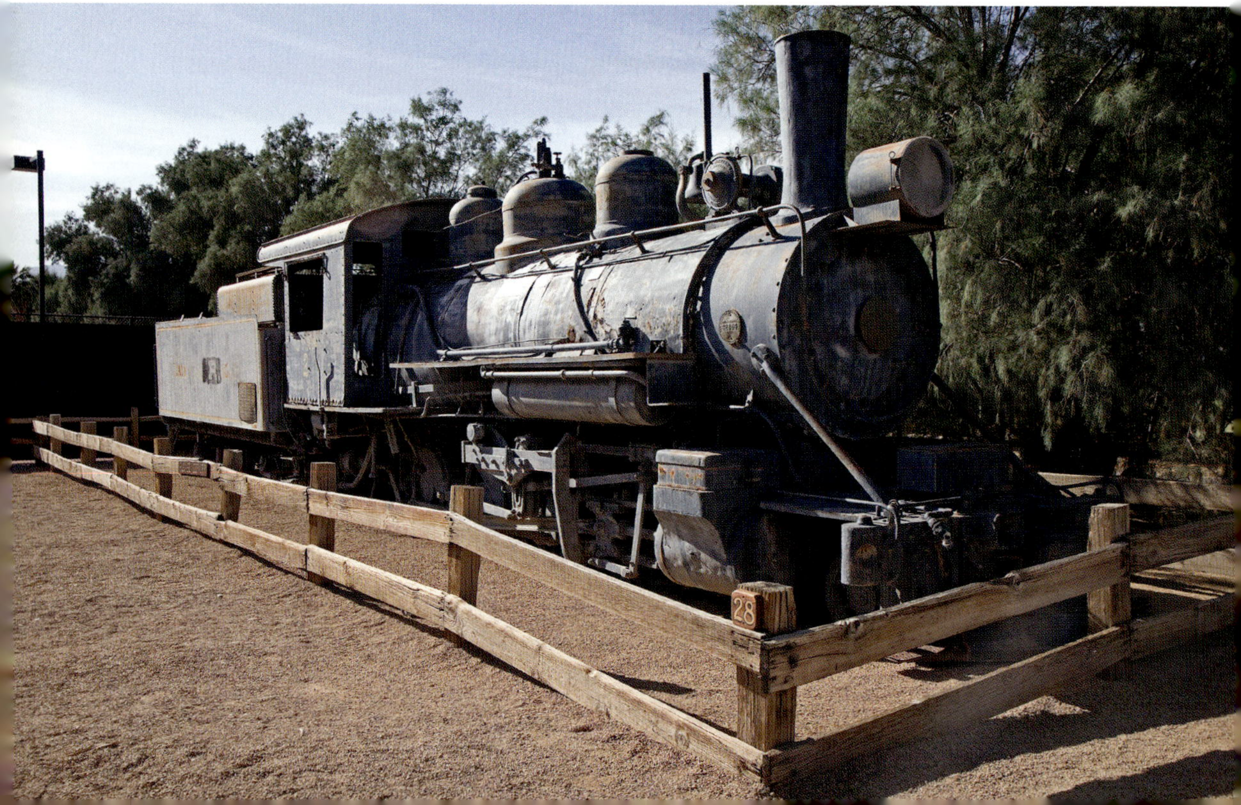

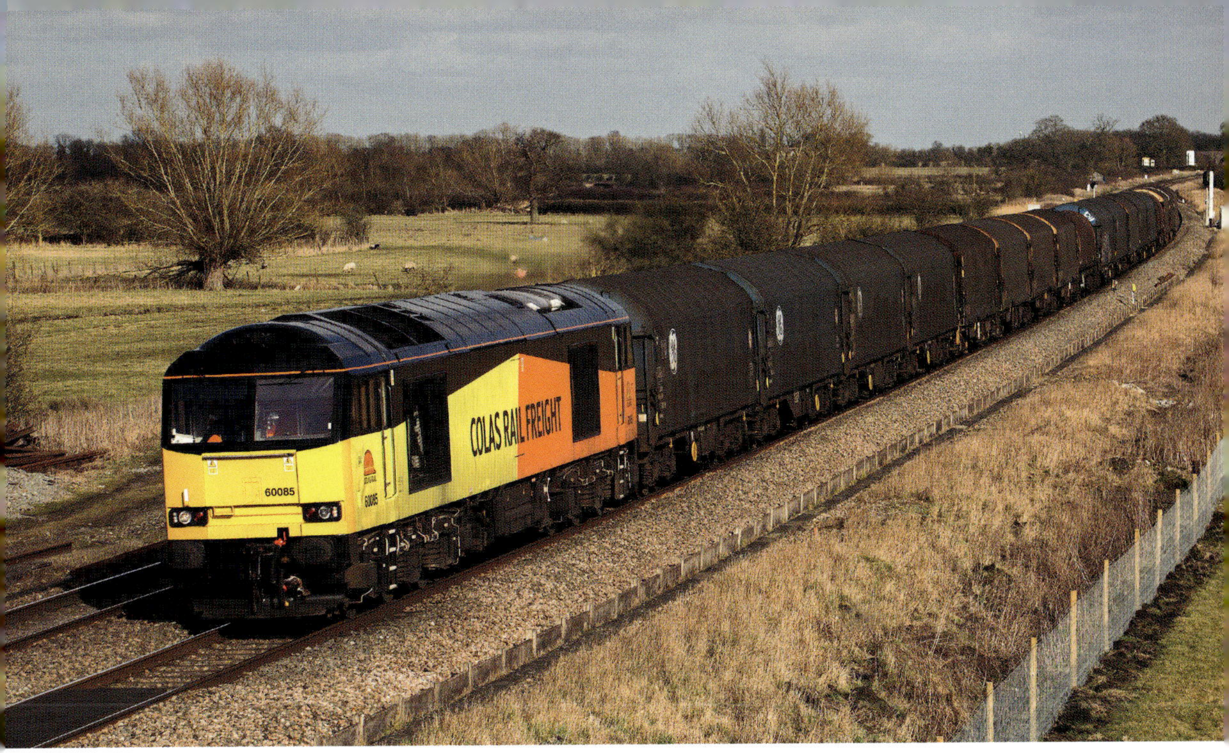

▲ On 27 February 2015, 60 085 speeds down the GW main line at Shrivenham with the Tilbury–Llanwern steel train. The high vantage point from a footbridge gives a good view of the complete train as it sweeps around the curve. Canon 5D Mark 3, 24-105mm, ISO 320, 1/1000 at f 6.3.

▼ After a lengthy delay at Leamington Spa, Class 52 D1015 Western Champion arrives at Banbury in winter sunshine with a Pathfinder charter train to Canterbury. The platform lamps are unavoidably prevalent but a medium telephoto lens setting helps to concentrate the eye on the loco front in the crisp winter sunshine. Canon 5D Mark 3, 24-105mm, ISO 200, 1/640 at f6.3. Photo taken 13 December 2014.

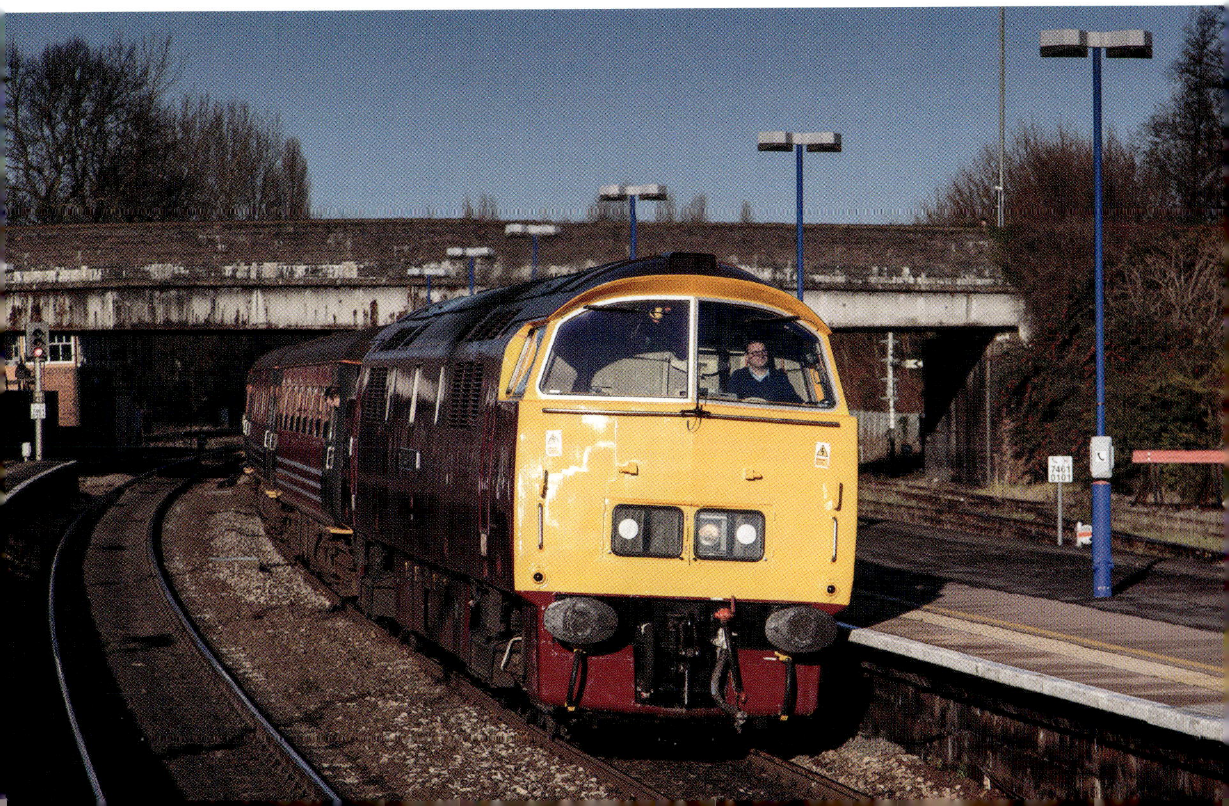

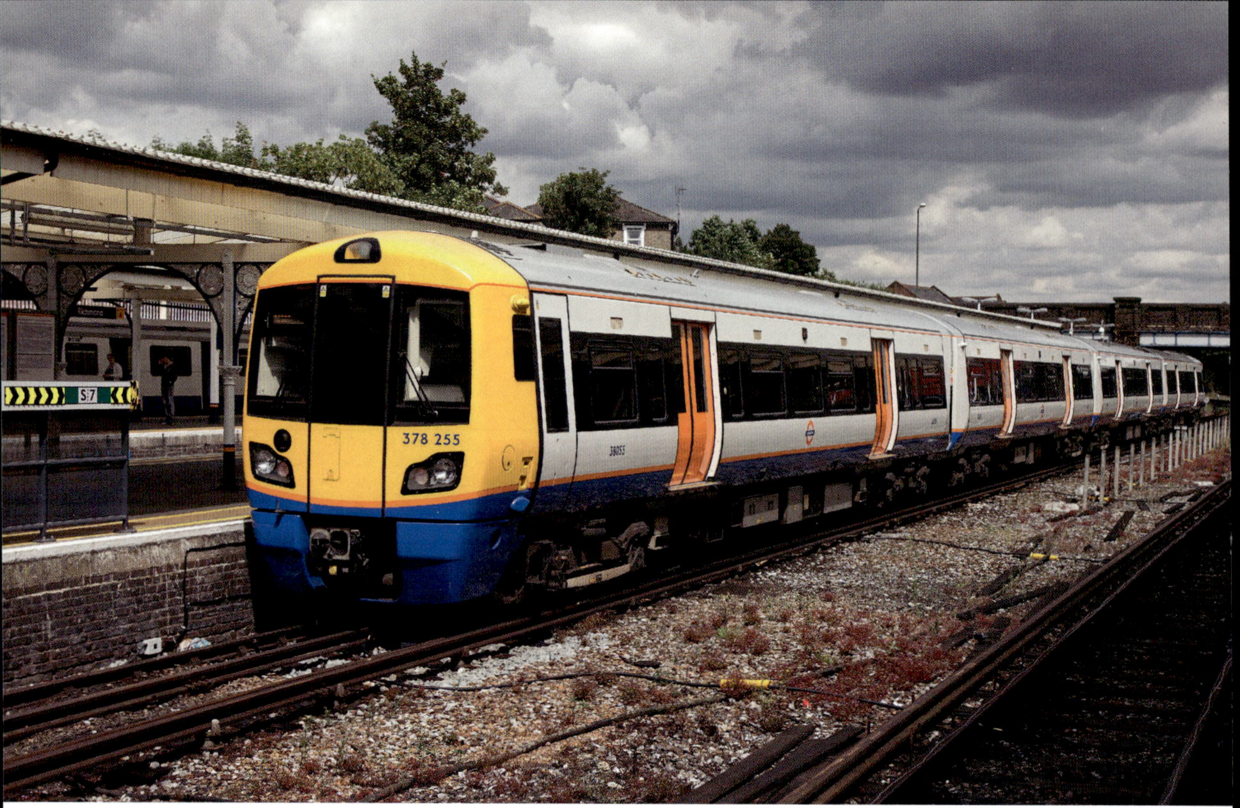

▲ EMU's seldom attract much attention, but 378 255 in the sun at Richmond in West London, with a dramatic sky for a background in July 2014, demanded a photo. Canon 5D Mark 3, 24-105mm, ISO 200, 1/320 at f11.

▼ The statue of Sir John Betjeman faces the Class 373 Eurostar units at London St Pancras station, almost paying homage to the grandeur of the impressive station. Canon G9 compact, ISO 80, 1/100 at f3.2.

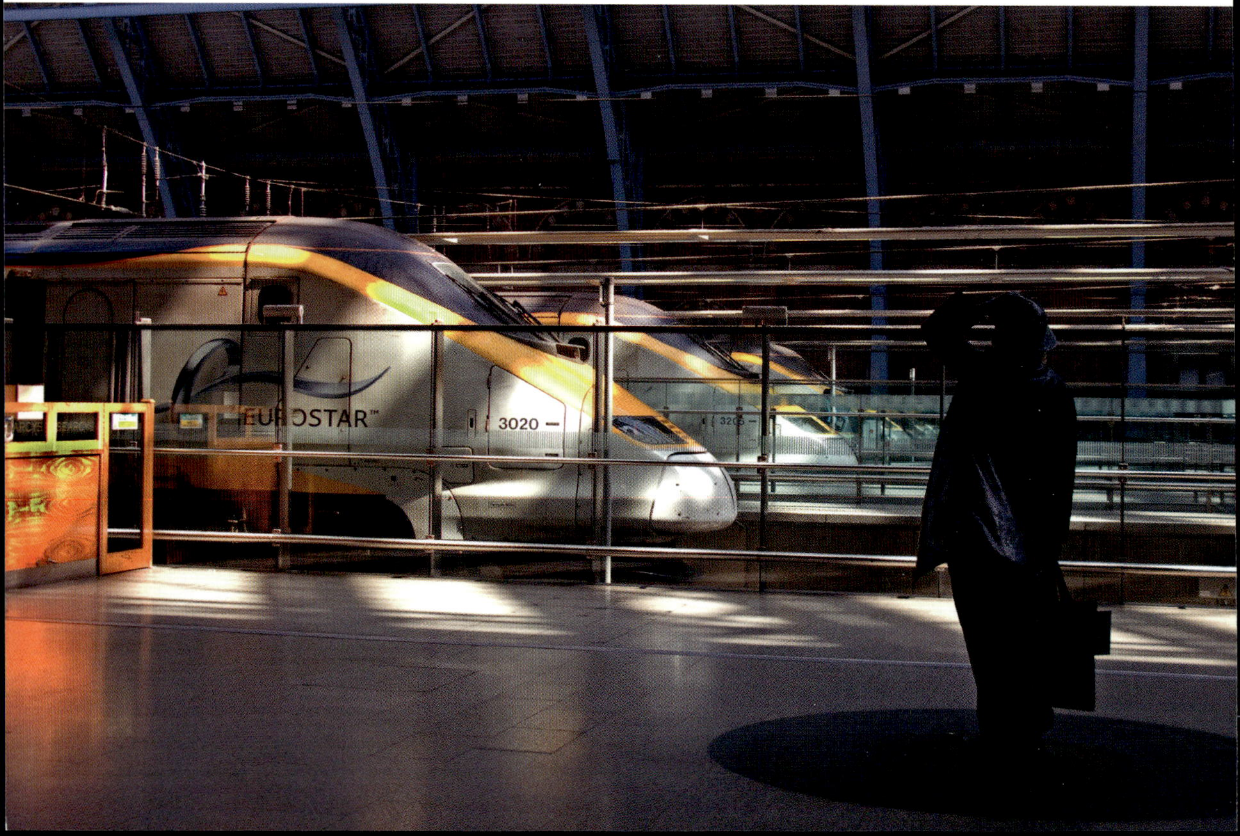

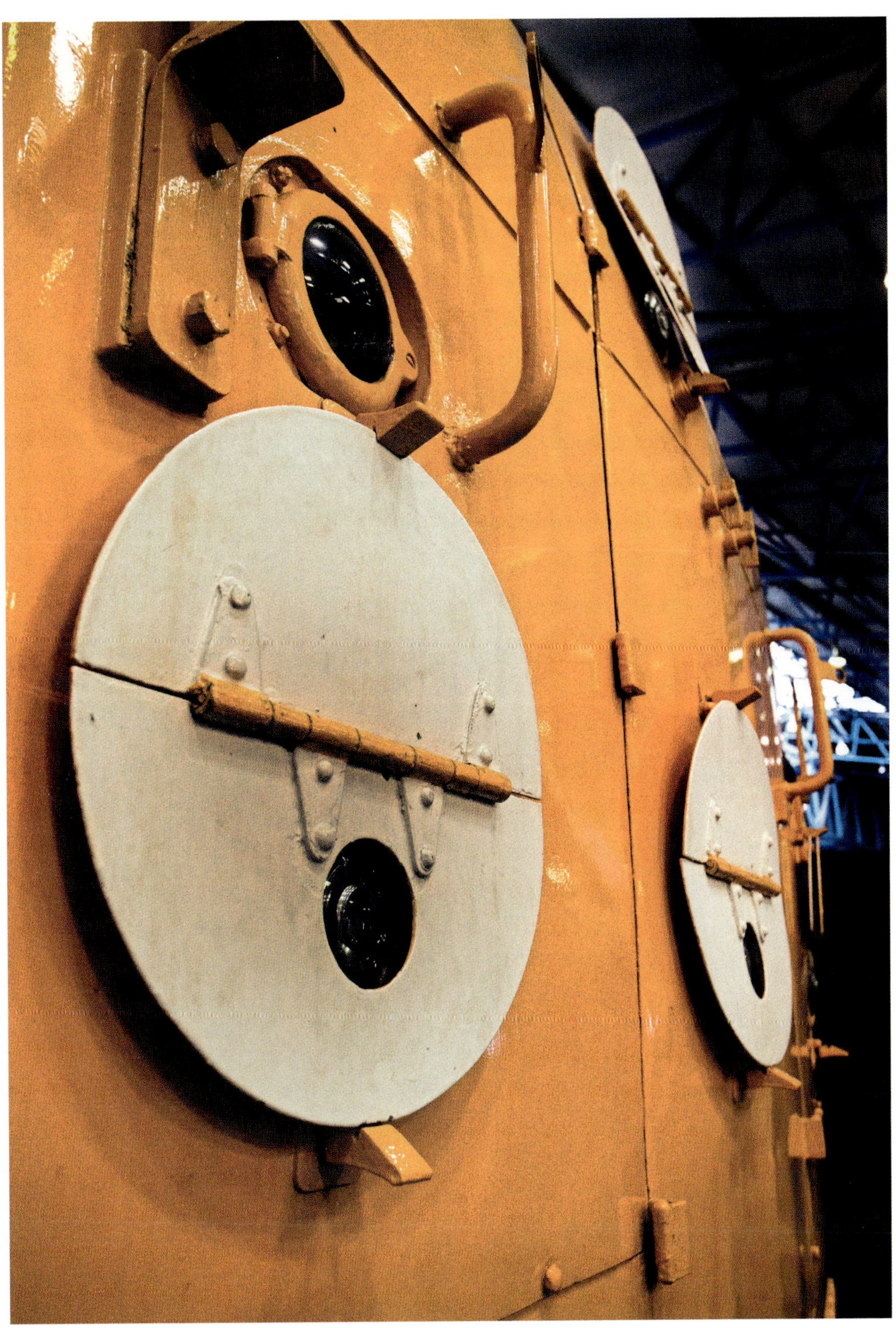

The headcode discs of 31 018 at the National Railway Museum in York make for an interesting composition when viewed close up. Due to poor light in the depths of the museum, a high ISO setting was required for this hand held shot. Canon 5D Mark 3, 24-105mm, ISO 2000, 1/40 at f7.1. Photo taken in March 2015.

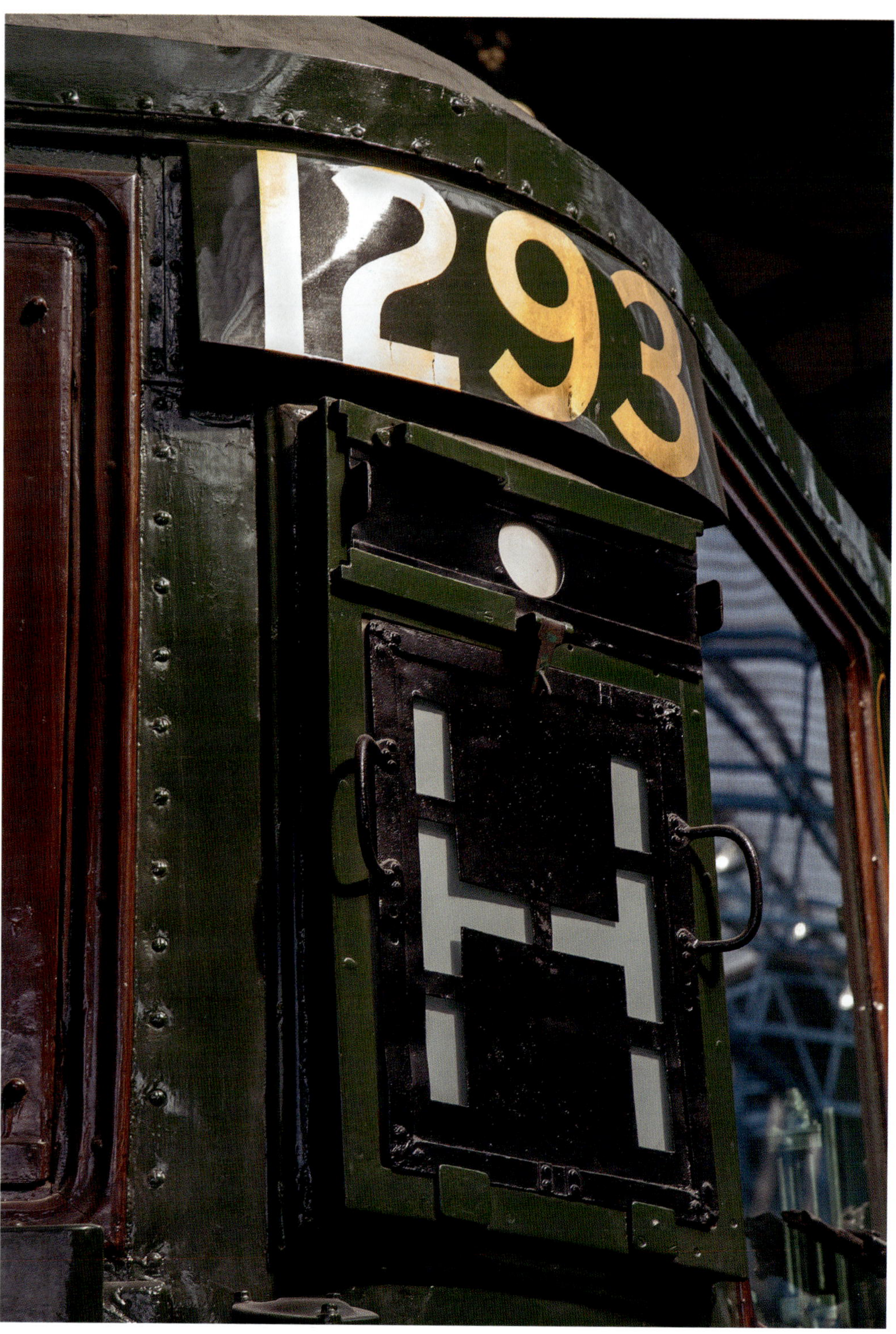

Similarly, the headcode of this historic EMU at the York museum makes for a wonderfully moody image. The unit is the driving motor coach of a 3 SUB, later rebuilt and converted into 4 SUB 4308. Canon 5D Mark 3, 24-105mm, ISO 400, 1/40 at f9. Photo taken in July 2013.

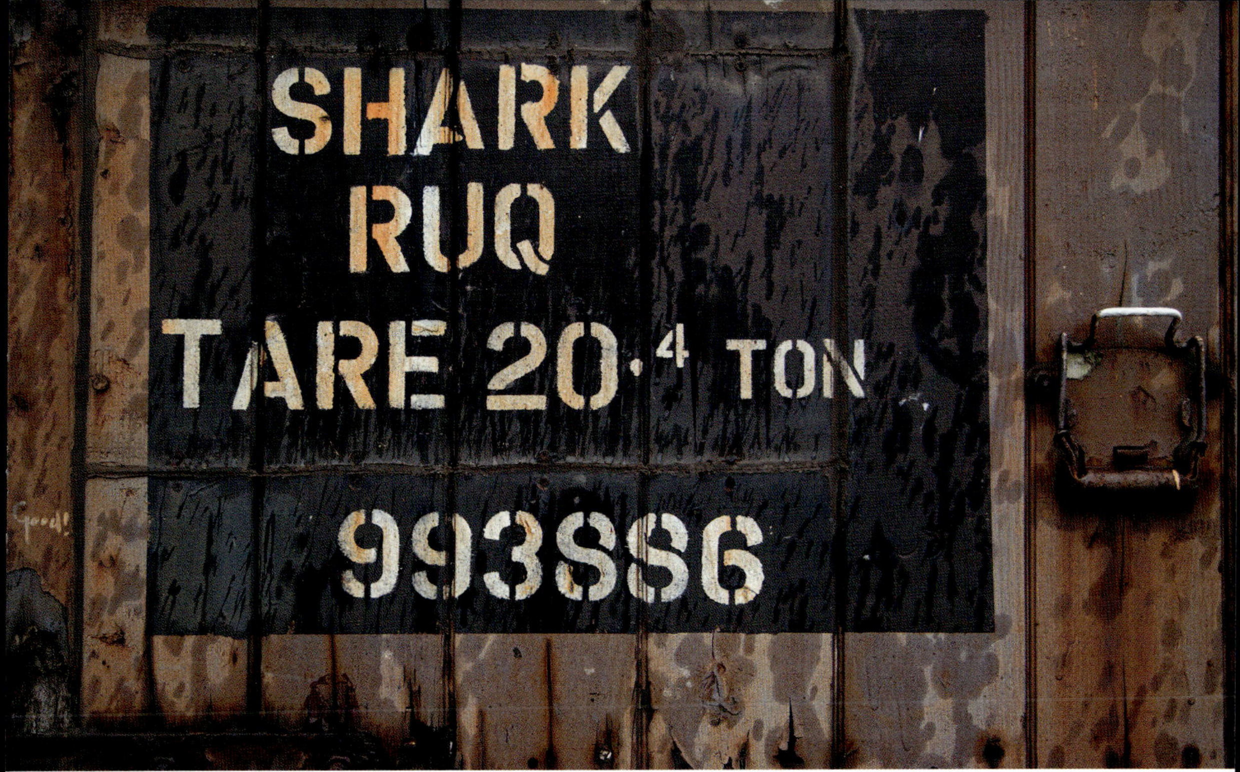

▲ One can almost smell the damp wood in this April 2014 close up of a wagon identification panel. The saturation was boosted slightly during computer processing to bring out the deep colour of the bodywork. Canon 5D Mark 3, 24-105mm, ISO 500, 1/250 at f4.

▼ This elderly couple spent a while chatting and watching the trains pass at Denchworth, near Didcot. It was only as one passed that I saw them watching the HST disappear westbound. One can only imagine the changes they have seen there over the years. Canon 5D Mark 3, 70-200mm, ISO 200, 1/1000 at f5. Taken 27 February 2015.

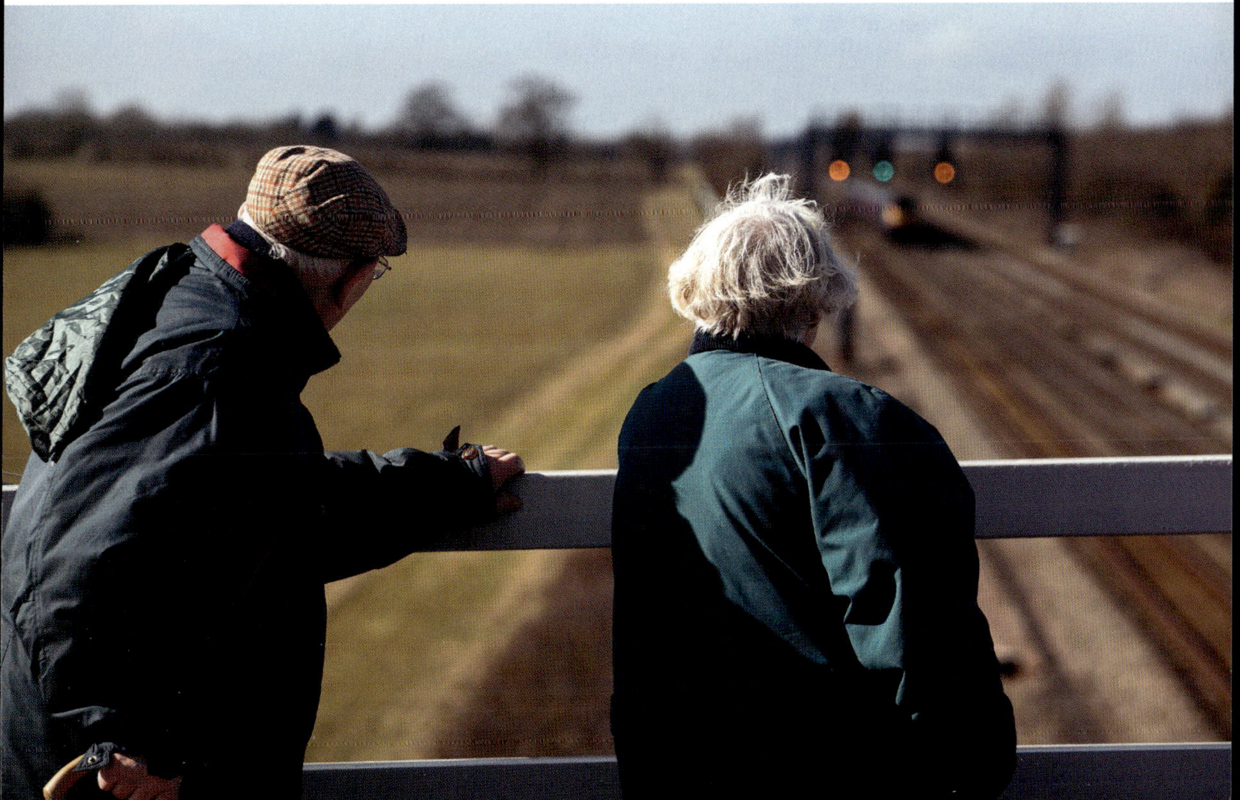

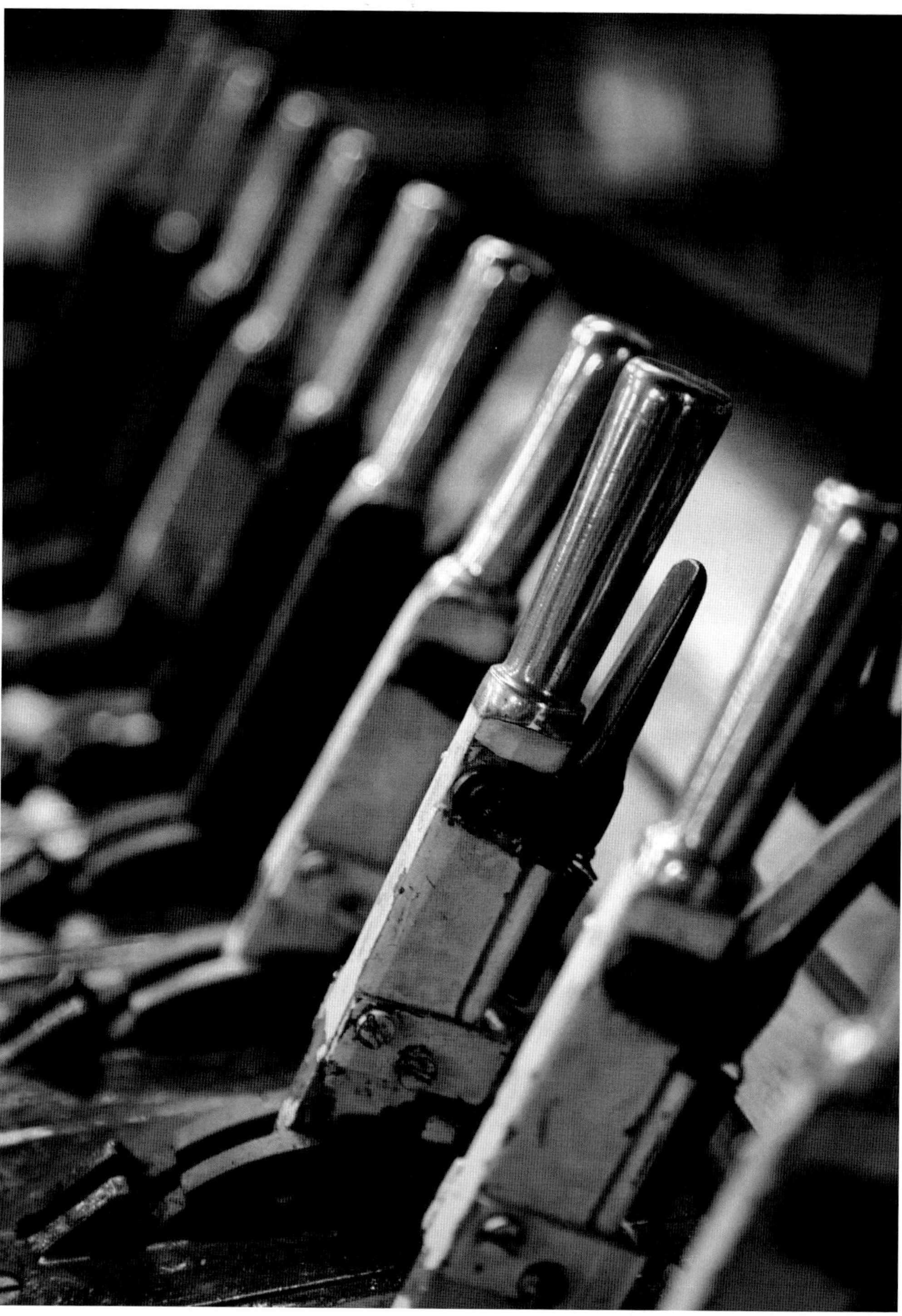

The LT Depot in Acton, West London, holds occasional open days during which one can see not only historic London tube stock, but much of the behind-the-scenes equipment saved over the years. This close up of a signaling panel was a little flat in colour, but converting to black & white has given the image of the levers a degree of added 'punch'. Canon 5D Mark 3, 24-105mm, ISO 1000, 1/20 at f4.

 Gallery

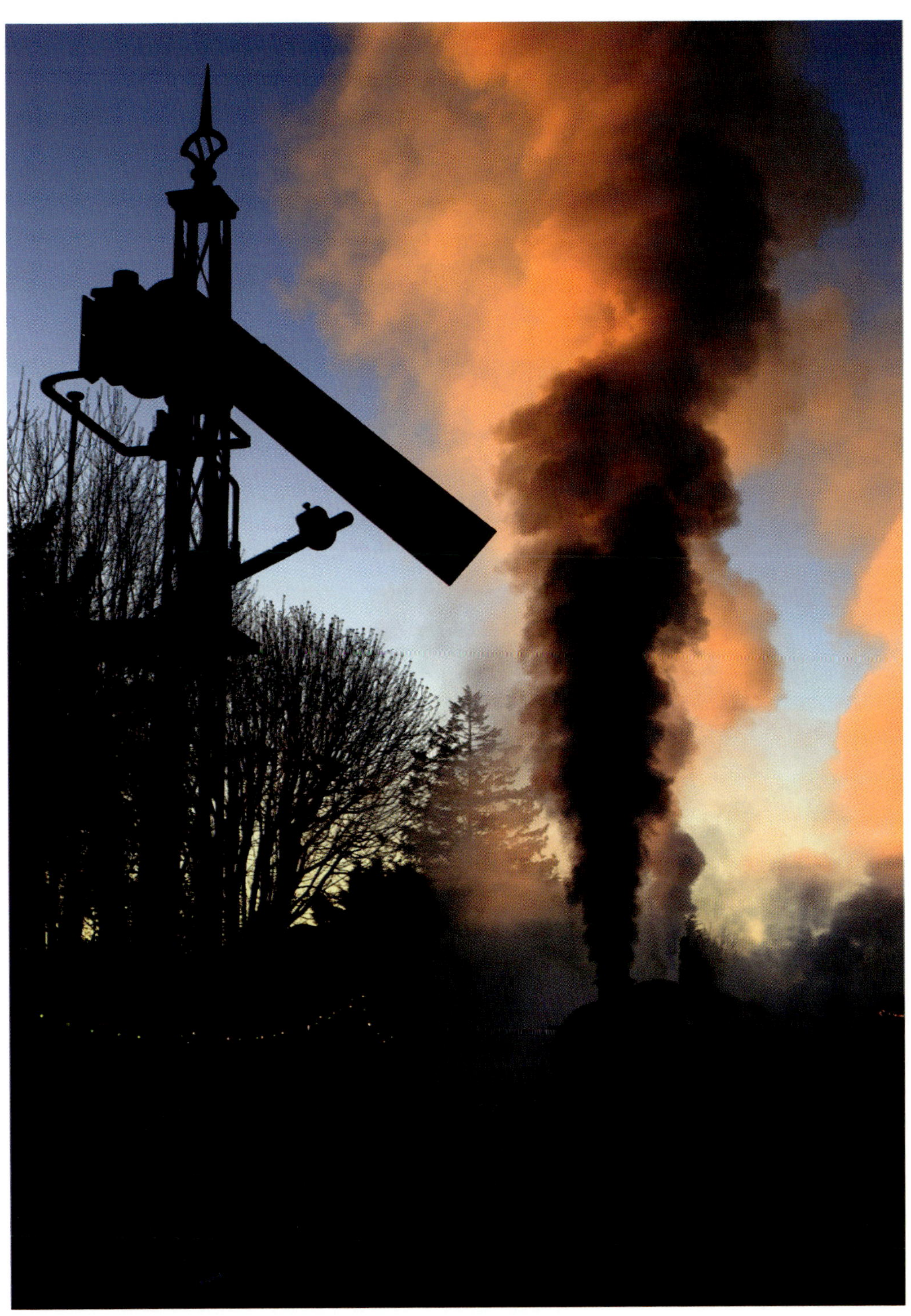

The setting December sun meant conventional photography was impossible, but the smoke from 45379 made for a superb silhouette at Arlesford on the penultimate day of 2014. The colours were boosted in Adobe Lightroom during processing. Canon 5D Mark 3, 50mm, ISO320, 1/160 at f10.

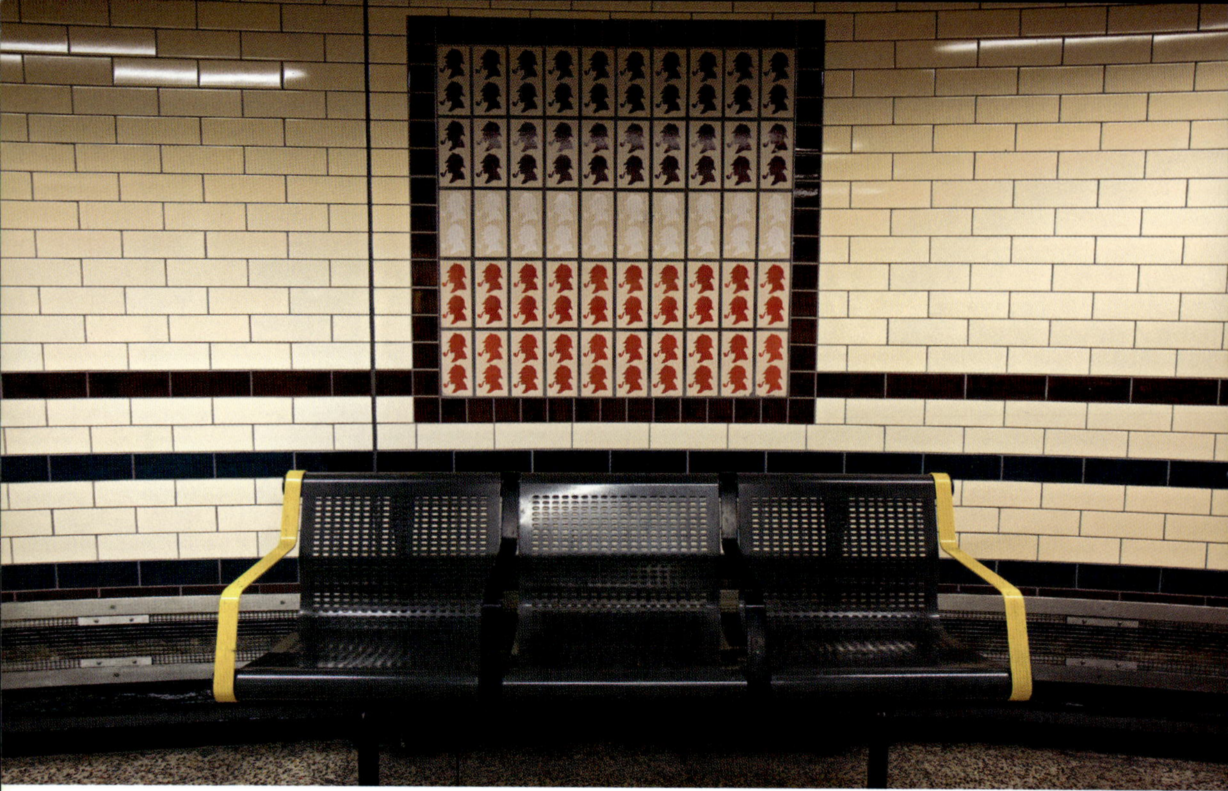

▲ Although at first glance a fairly anonymous bench, the mural behind give a huge clue as to the location. Canon 5D Mark 3, 50mm, ISO 1250, 1/50 at f4.5. Photo taken in June 2014 at Baker St Underground station in London.

▼ Sometime, the details in a scene can make captivating images in their own right. During a night time photo charter in Devon, I noticed this oil lamp glowing, with the milk tank wagons as a backdrop. The time exposure helps to diffuse the light, giving a 'warm' effect. Canon 5D Mark 3, 24-105mm, ISO 100, 13 secs at f4.

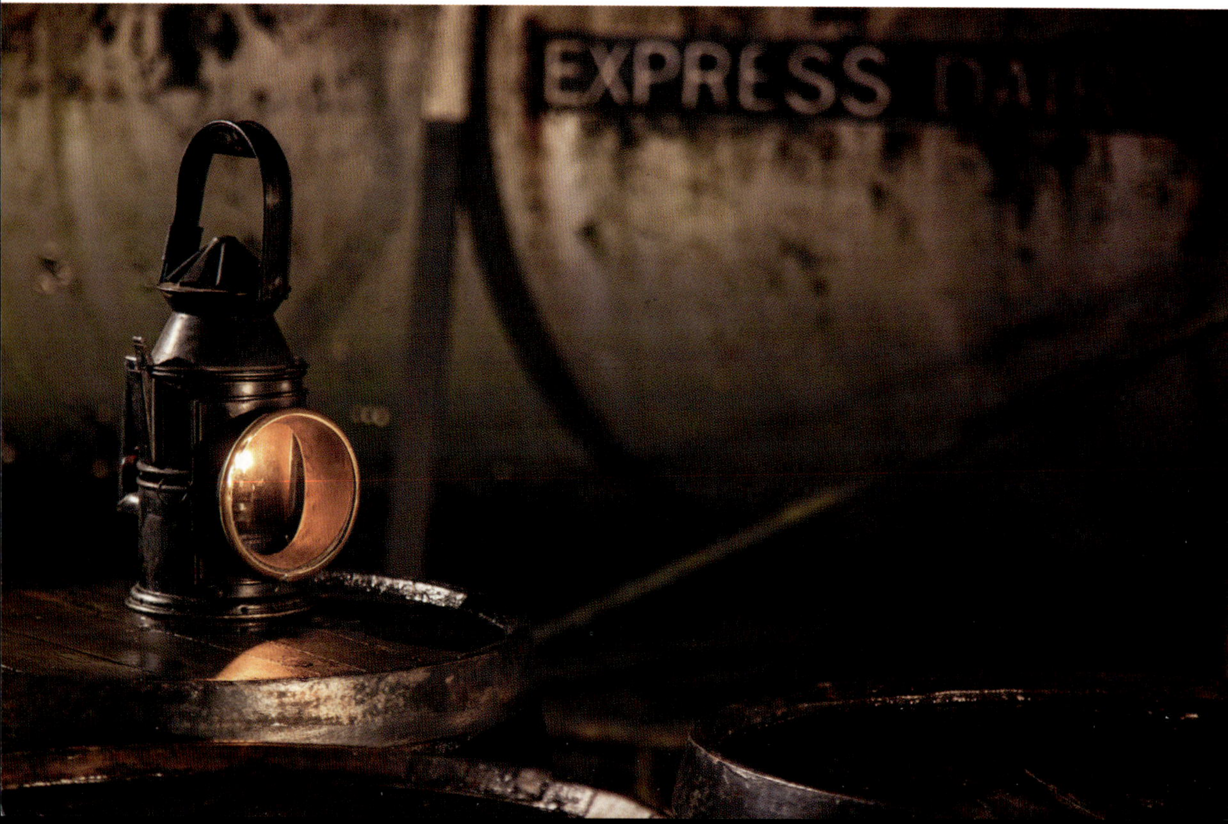

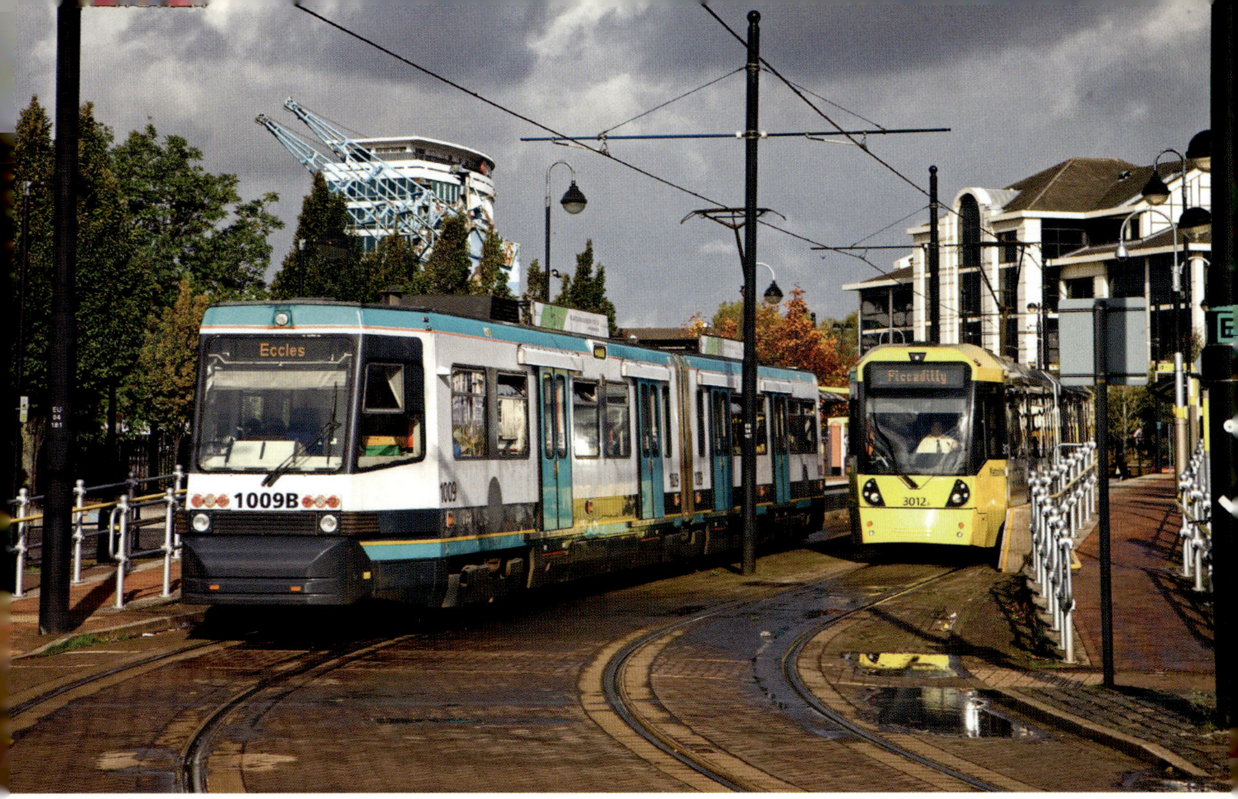

▲ Old and new Manchester trams passing at the Salford Quay stop in October 2013. The bright colours stand out against the dark sky, and the puddles from the recent shower complete the scene. Canon 5D, 24-105mm, ISO 400, 1/500 at f11.

▼ While attempting to get this image of two S stock Metropolitan line units passing, I managed to record myself in the platform mirror on the left hand side! Canon 5D, 24-105mm, ISO 400, 1/640 at f10.

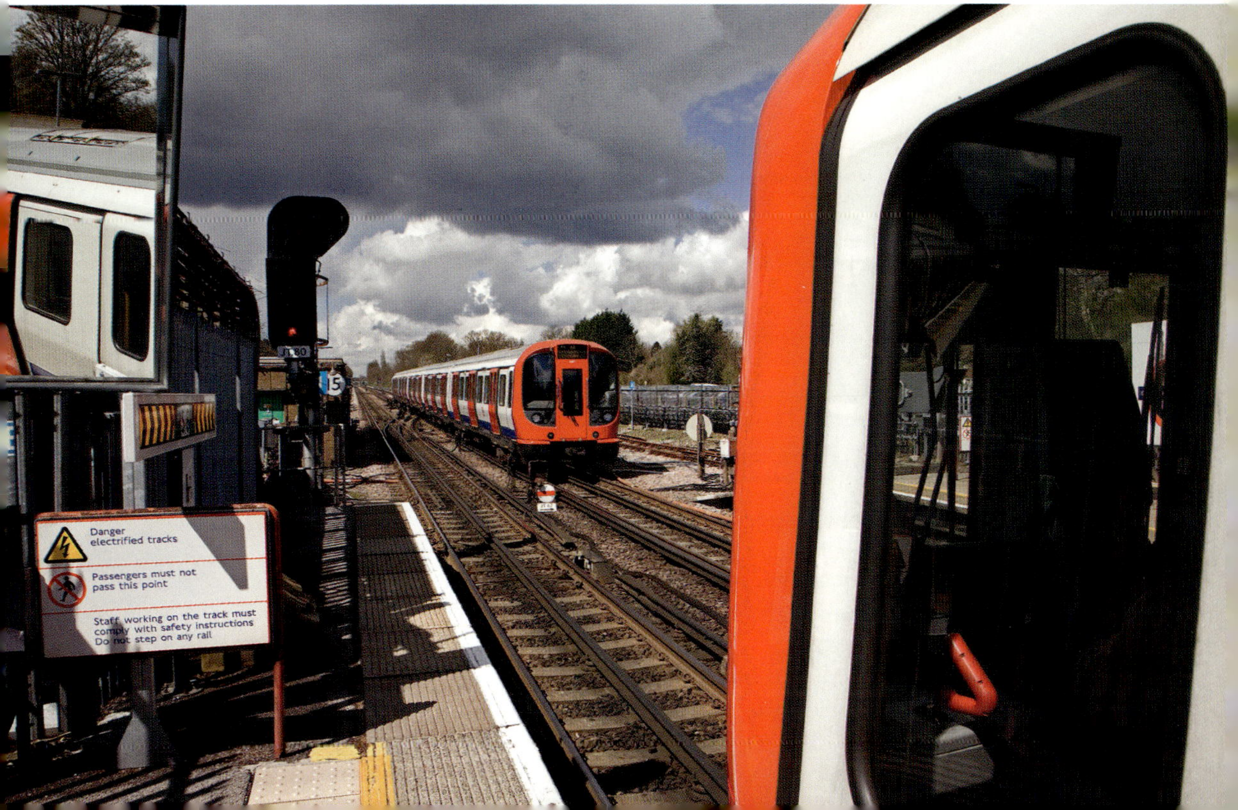

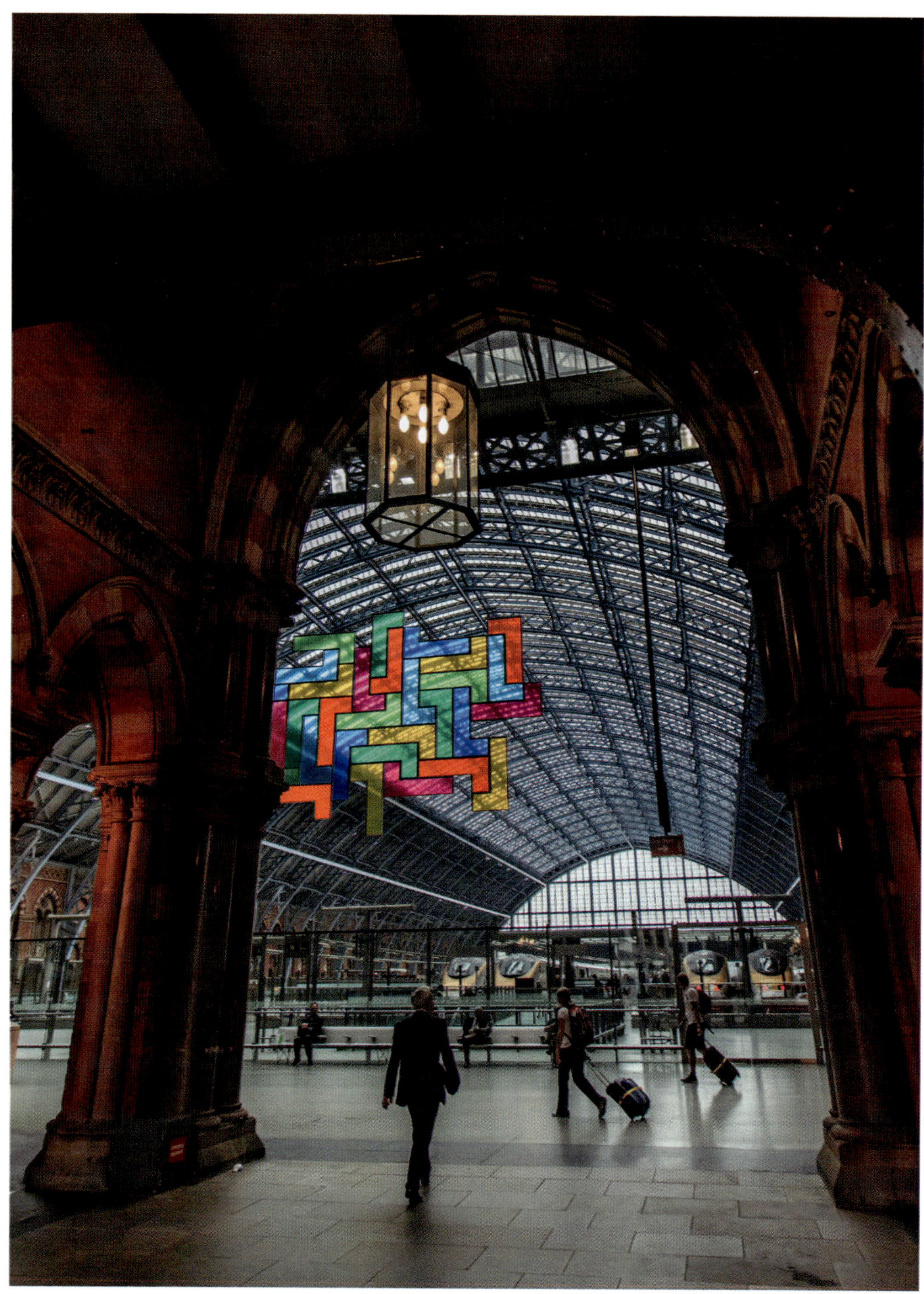

Although the wide angle lens distorts the image slightly, I wanted to show the contrast between the historic arch at St Pancras station and the modern hanging sculpture, and of course the Eurostar trains. The passing passengers complete the composition and help to give an impression of scale and purpose to the August 2014 photo. Canon 5D Mark 3, 24-105mm, ISO 400, 1/320 at f4.5.

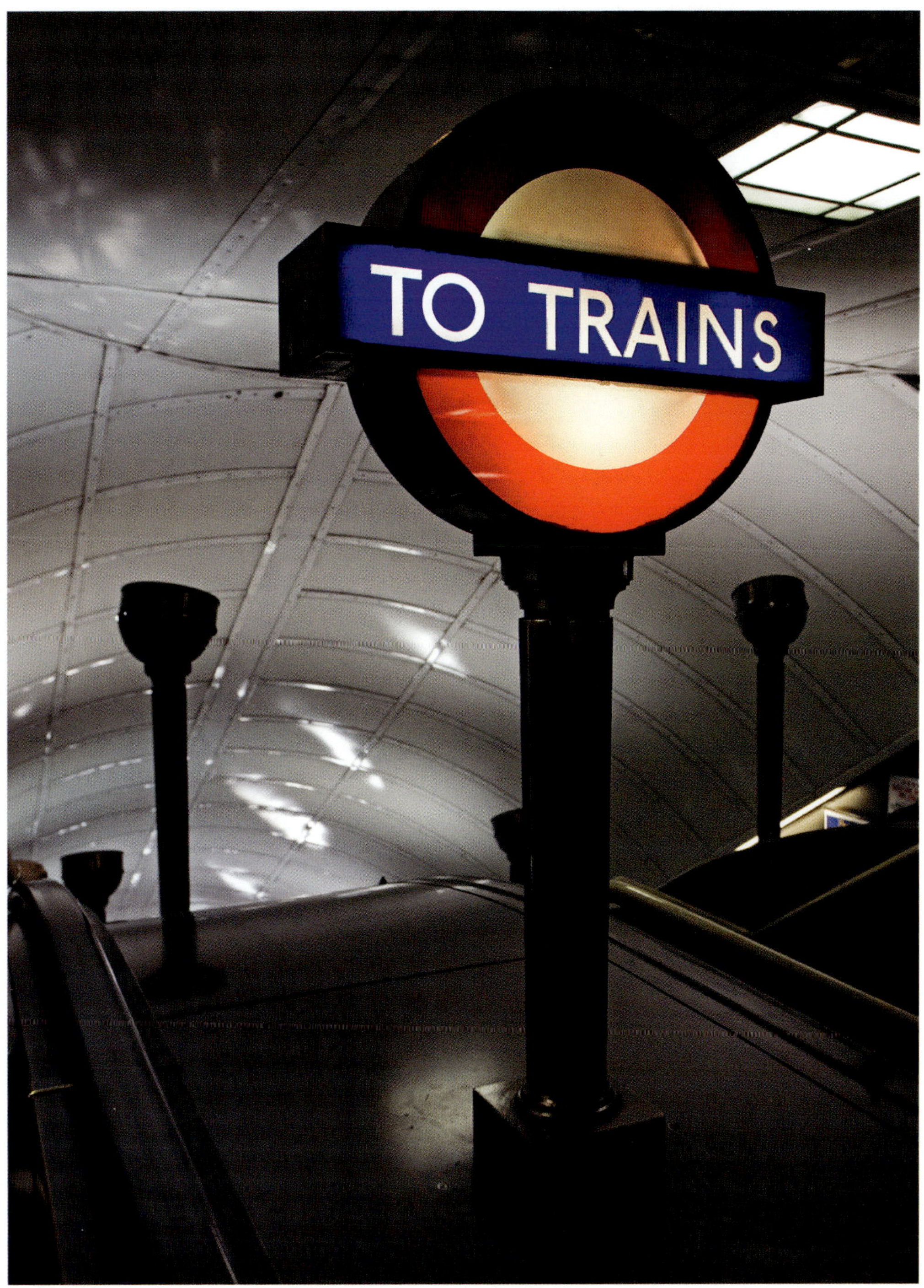

Many art deco signs and lamps still adorn several London Underground stations, such as these at Swiss Cottage. Ambient light is poor, and due to the throughput of passengers, photography needs to be hand held. Image captured in June 2014. Canon 5D Mark 3, 50mm, ISO 1250, 1/80 at f6.3.

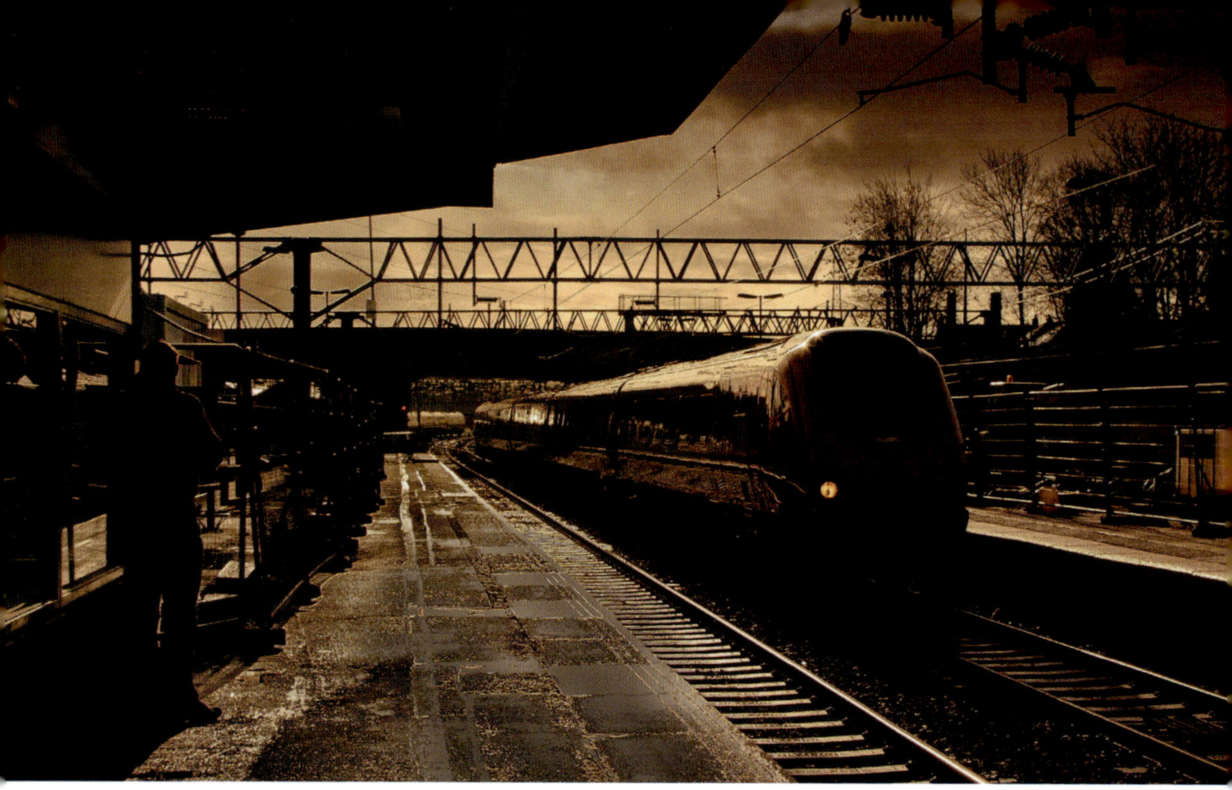

▲ In this February 2013 view, a Voyager Cross-Country unit is slowing for its stop at Stafford. The low angle of the sun makes for a semi-silhouette, with plenty of glints off the rain soaked platform. The image has been warmed up a little in post-processing by adjusting the colour saturation. Canon 40D, 24-105mm, ISO 400, 1/500 at f13.

▼ In this 2015 recreation of a steam era milk train collection at a country station, the human re-enactor was required to hold a rigid position while the assembled photographers took their time exposures. The location is Staverton, with GWR 4566 at the head of the train. Canon 5D Mark 3, 50mm, ISO 100, 30 secs at f6.3.

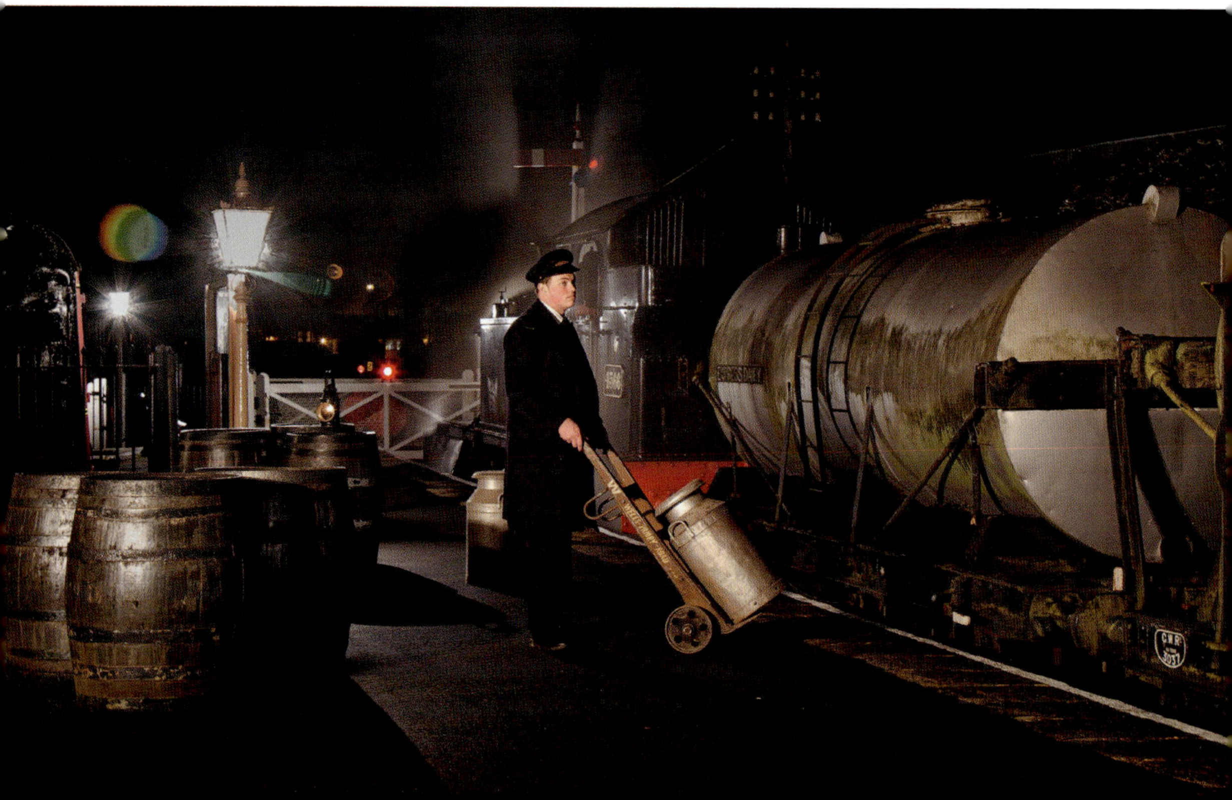

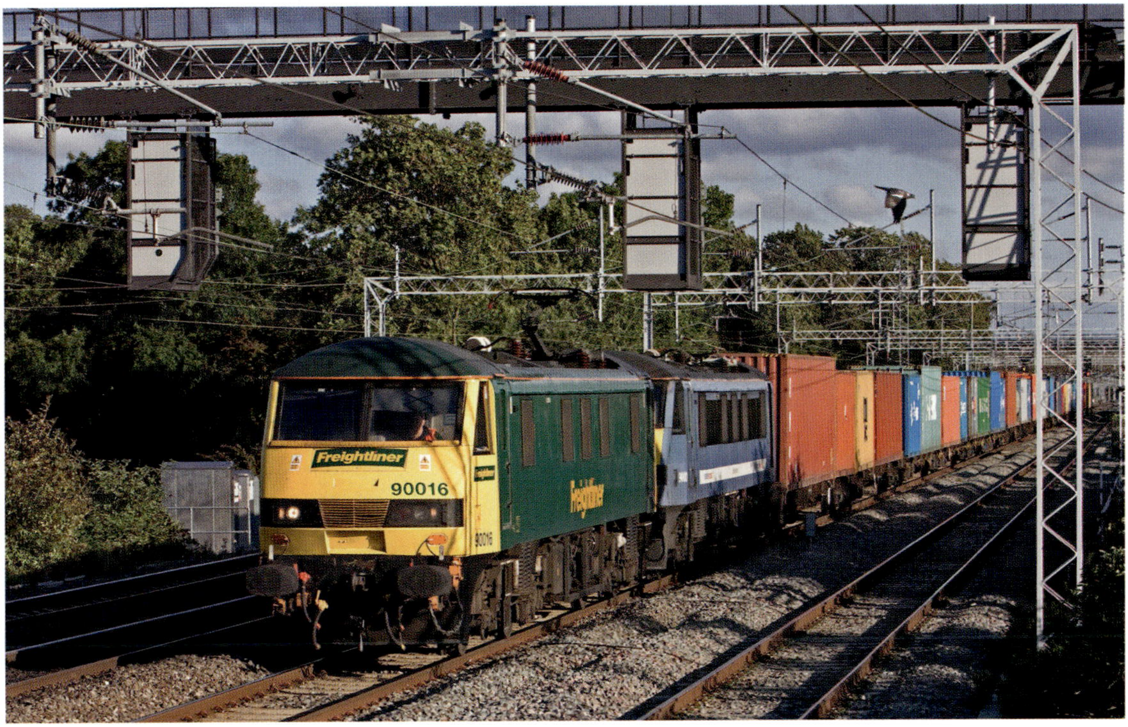

▲ 90 016 and 90 001 lead a colourful consist as they head a Freightliner container service north past Cathiron on 8 September 2009. The viewpoint at this particular location requires shooting through a palisade fence, restricting the angle available to the photographer. Canon 40D, 70-200mm, ISO 250, 1/500 at f8. Although this shutter speed has frozen the action, a faster setting is recommended and should have been used.

▼ A unidentified class 90 behind bars at York. By choosing a low f number setting, the fence is in focus while the loco and station sign are blurred, making for an artistic image. Canon 5D Mark 3, 24-105mm, ISO 250, 1/160 at f5.6.

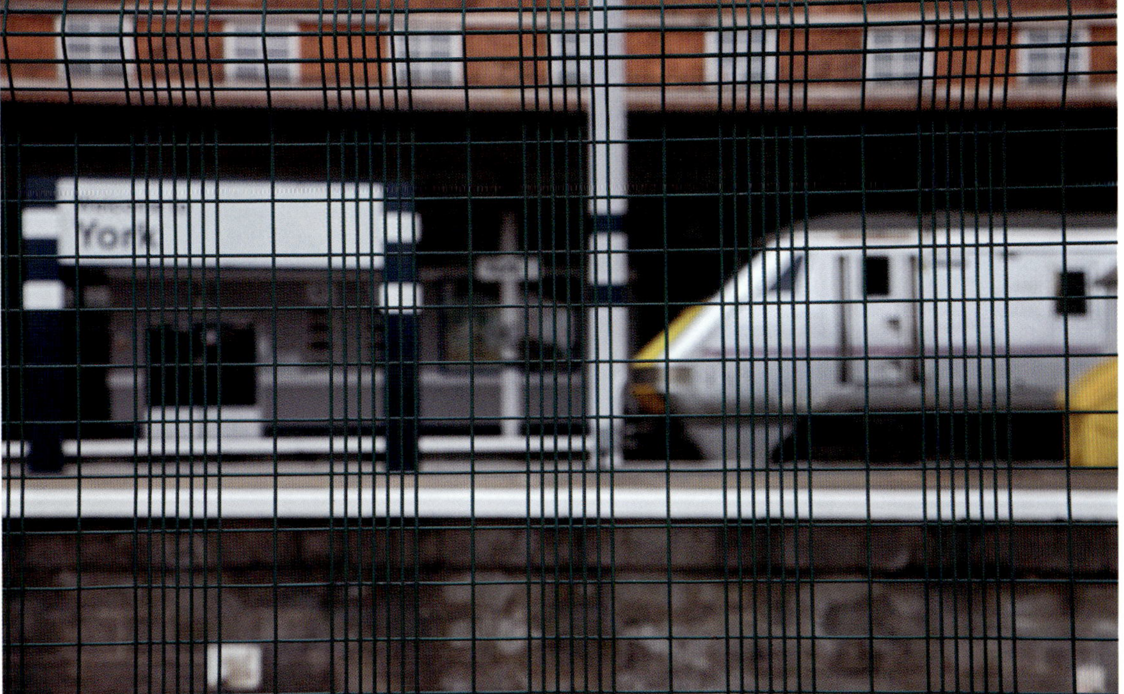

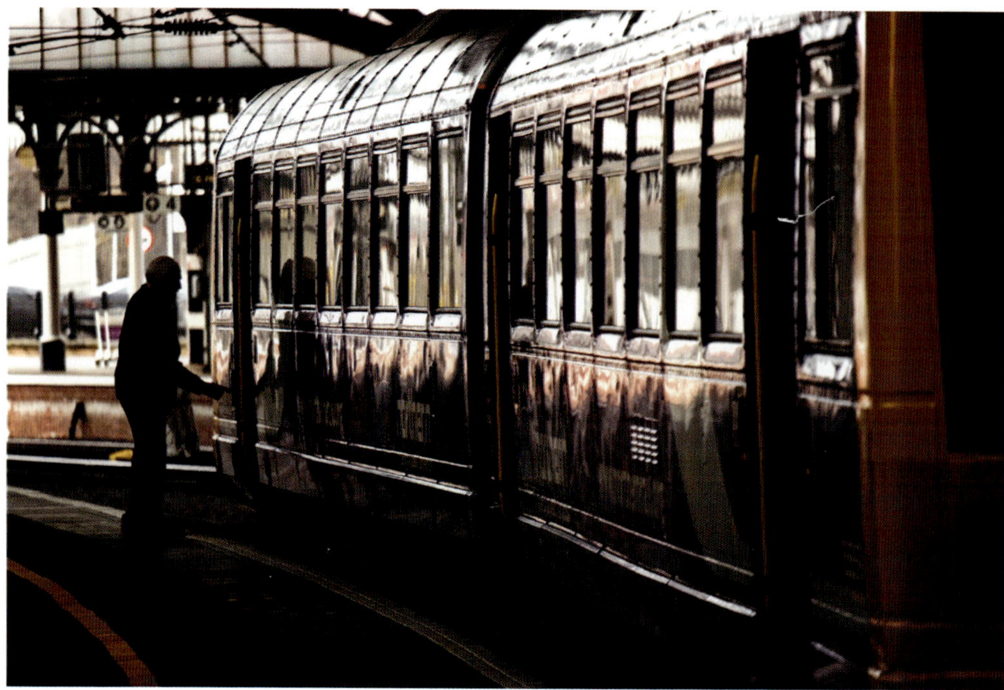

▲ Press to enter. A train cleaner at York gains access to a class 142 unit, ahead of its next working. Although the station interior was dark, light from the brighter northern end offered a monochromatic glint along the bodywork, accentuated by the choice of a telephoto lens to compress the image. Photo taken 19 March 2015.

▼ A slightly unusual image as the platform really is numbered zero. The location is London King's Cross in March 2015. The numbering oddity came about when a former postal dock was converted to provide additional platform capacity. A slow shutter speed was used to ensure the walking passengers would appear blurred. Canon 5D Mark 3, 24-105mm, ISO 400, 1/20 at f5.6.

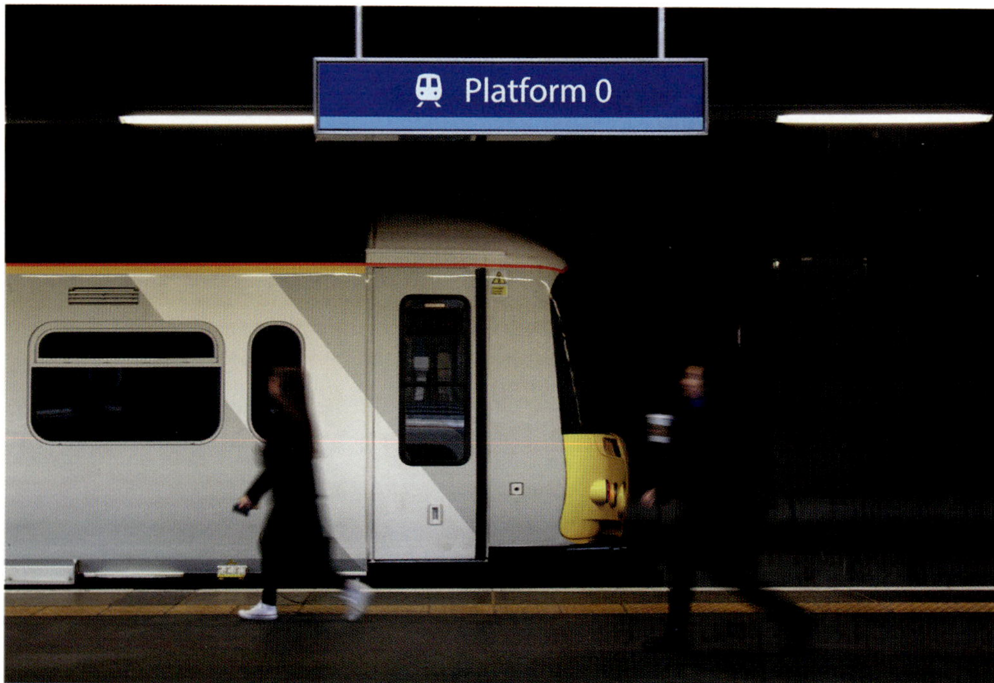

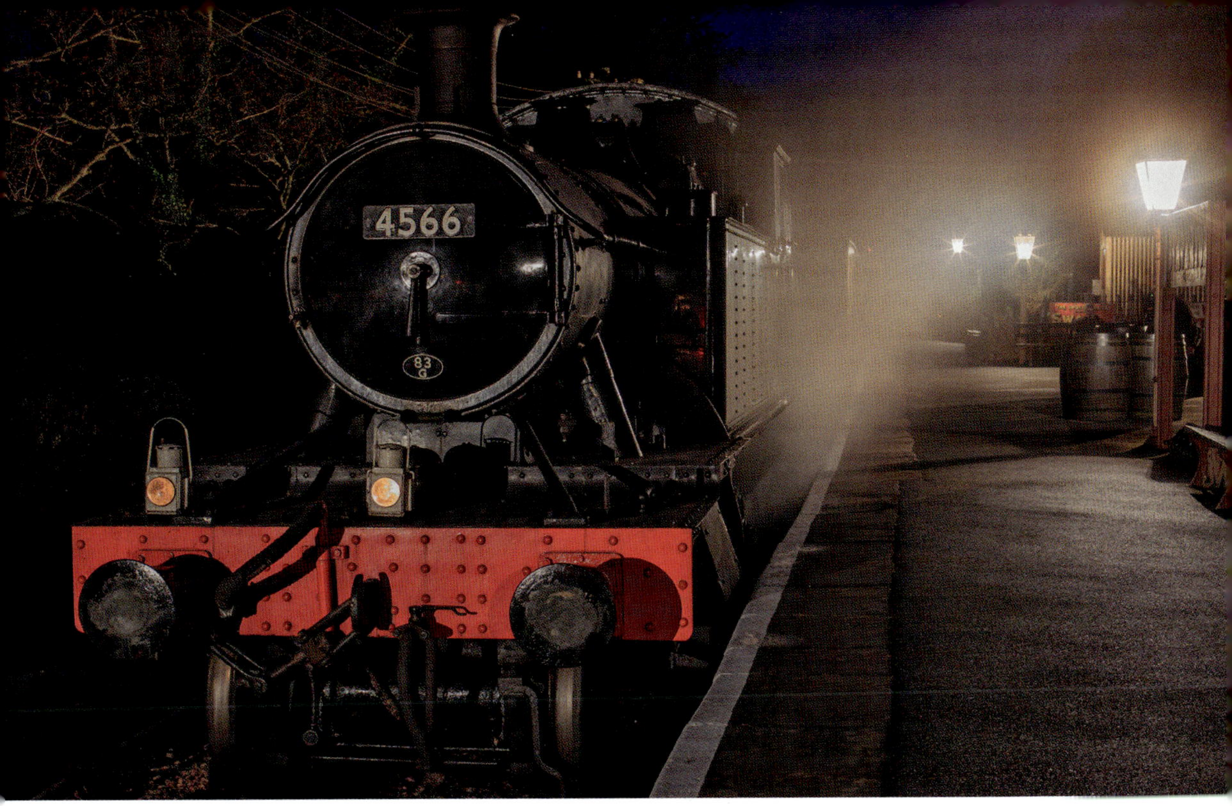

▲ A 'traditional' night scene recreation during a photo charter at Staverton in Devon. The long time exposure allows the slowly escaping steam to produce a wispy, almost ethereal effect. Canon 5D Mark 3. 50mm, ISO 100, 15 secs at f8.

▼ When tripods are impractical or just not allowed, the incredible low light capability of modern DSLRs can be a lifesaver. Taken handheld, this image simply would not have been possible even a few years ago. Celebrity 91 111 poses alongside a stablemate at King's Cross in March 2015. Canon 5D Mark 3, 24-105mm, ISO 5000, 1/25 at f4.

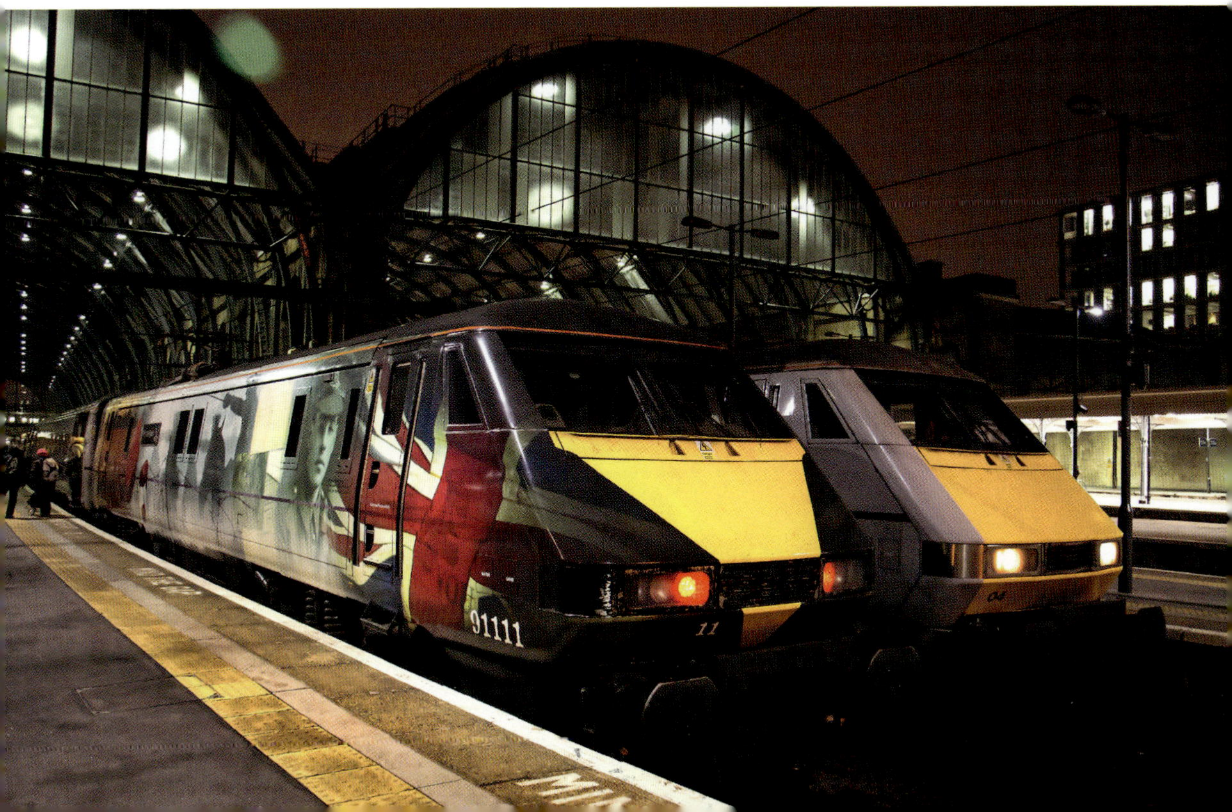

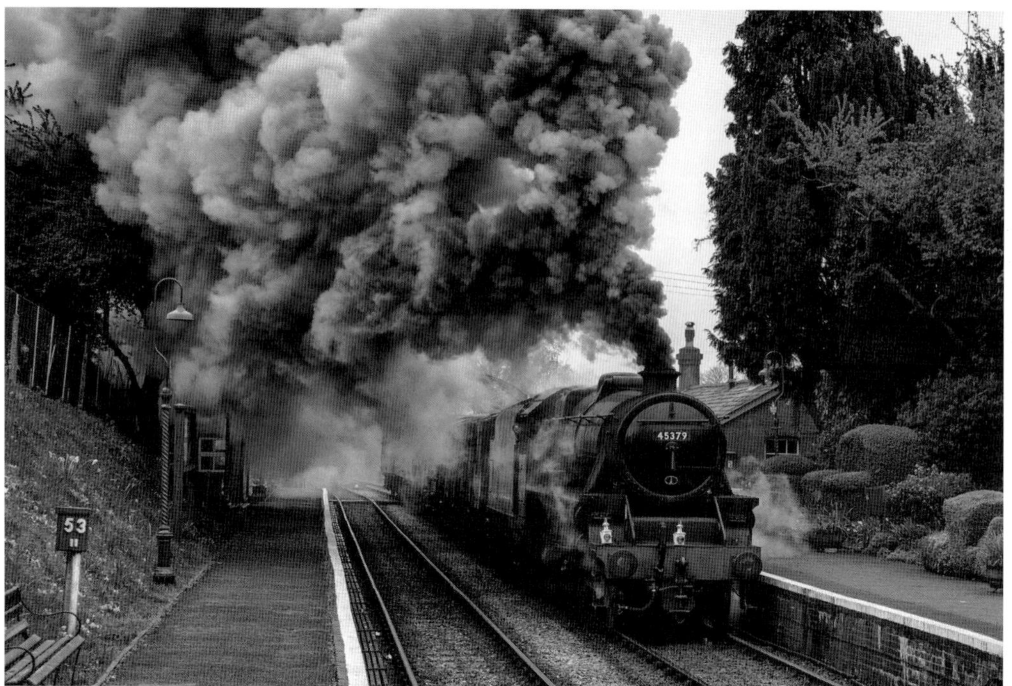

▲ One of the attractions of staged opportunities for railway photographers is the smoke effect often possible thanks to cooperative traincrews. Black 5 45379 makes a superb sight as it enters Four Marks in Hampshire, during March 2015. Canon 5D Mark 3, 24-105mm, ISO 1000, 1/400 at f5.6.

▼ After a staged photographic runpast, this angle was noticed as the train slowed to a stop. The signboard provides a handy frame for the coaches and billowing smoke. If the weather had been sunny, this angle would have been impossible due to the orientation of the line at this particular point. Mid Hants Railway, April 2015. Canon 5D Mark 3, 70-200mm, ISO 1000, 1/250 at f8.

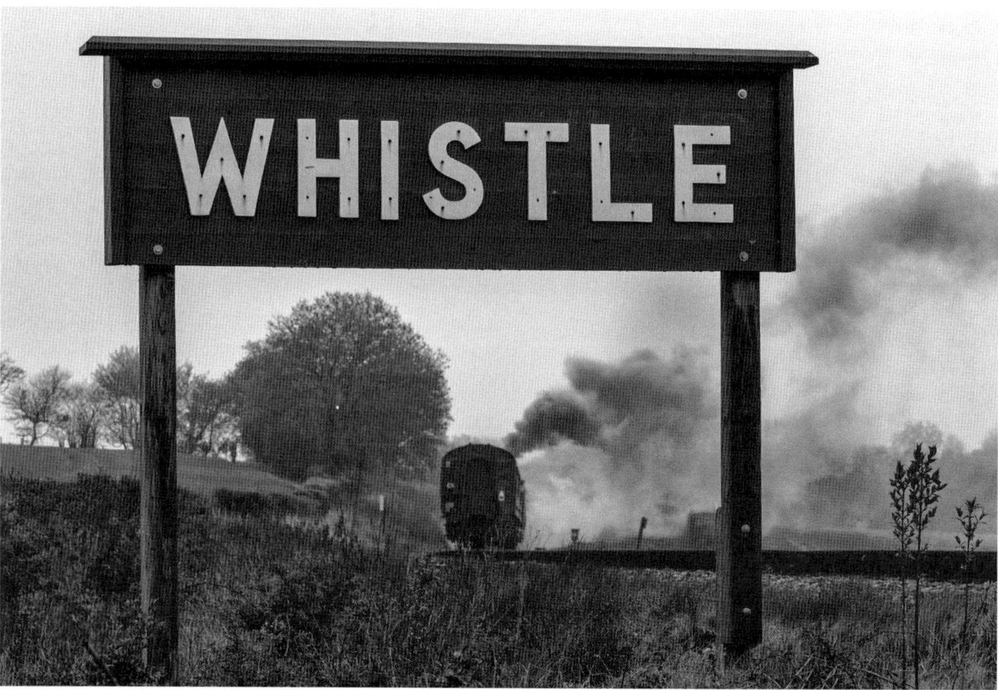

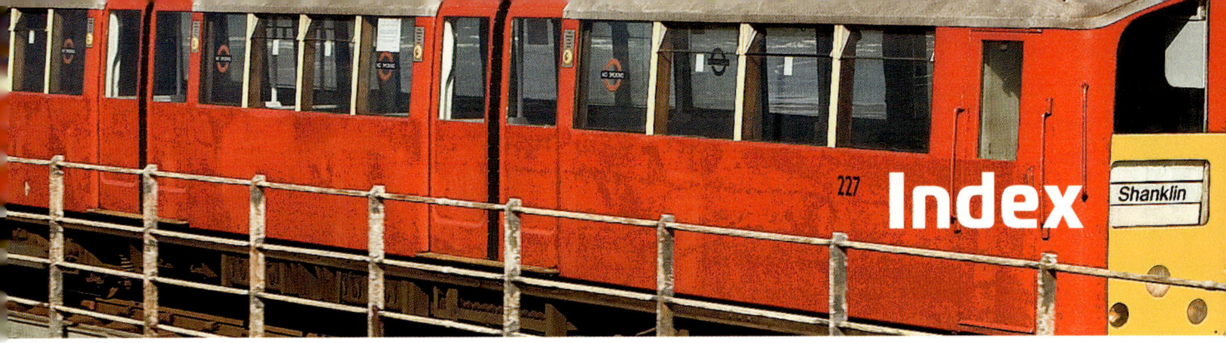

Index

ABOUT THE AUTHOR

Jeremy de Souza has been taking railway photographs for almost 40 years, and although too young to have witnessed the end of regular steam in the UK, he has recorded many of the dramatic changes in the British and European rail scene. Originally a committed film user, Jeremy migrated to digital photography in the early 1990s, amassing a fascinating collection of several thousand railway images. From his Hampshire home, he still travels regularly to pursue his hobby, searching for that ever elusive 'perfect' railway photograph.